WITHDRAWN

WEST FARGO PUBLIC LIBRARY
109 3rd Street East
West Fargo, ND 58078

D0206204

THE
HISTORY OF
SOMALIA

ADVISORY BOARD

John T. Alexander
Professor of History and Russian and European Studies,
University of Kansas

Robert A. Divine
George W. Littlefield Professor in American History Emeritus,
University of Texas at Austin

John V. Lombardi
Professor of History,
University of Florida

967,73
N659

THE HISTORY OF SOMALIA

Raphael Chijioke Njoku

The Greenwood Histories of the Modern Nations
Frank W. Thackeray and John E. Findling, Series Editors

 GREENWOOD

AN IMPRINT OF ABC-CLIO, LLC
Santa Barbara, California • Denver, Colorado • Oxford, England

Copyright 2013 by Raphael Chijioke Njoku

All rights reserved. No part of this publication may be reproduced, stored in a retrieval system, or transmitted, in any form or by any means, electronic, mechanical, photocopying, recording, or otherwise, except for the inclusion of brief quotations in a review, without prior permission in writing from the publisher.

Library of Congress Cataloging-in-Publication Data

Njoku, Raphael Chijioke.
    The history of Somalia / Raphael Chijioke Njoku.
        p. cm. — (Greenwood histories of the modern nations)
    Includes bibliographical references and index.
    ISBN 978–0–313–37857–7 (cloth : alk. paper) — ISBN 978–0–313–37858–4 (ebook)
1. Somalia—History. I. Title. II. Series: Greenwood histories of the modern nations.
DT403.N55   2013
967.73—dc23   2012040399

ISBN: 978–0–313–37857–7
EISBN: 978–0–313–37858–4

17 16 15 14 13   2 3 4 5

This book is also available on the World Wide Web as an eBook.
Visit www.abc-clio.com for details.

Greenwood
An Imprint of ABC-CLIO, LLC

ABC-CLIO, LLC
130 Cremona Drive, P.O. Box 1911
Santa Barbara, California 93116-1911

This book is printed on acid-free paper (∞)

Manufactured in the United States of America

FOR RAPHAEL CHIJIOKE JR.

Contents

Series Foreword

The *Greenwood Histories of the Modern Nations* series is intended to provide students and interested laypeople with up-to-date, concise, and analytical histories of many of the nations of the contemporary world. Not since the 1960s has there been a systematic attempt to publish a series of national histories, and as series editors, we believe that this series will prove to be a valuable contribution to our understanding of other countries in our increasingly interdependent world.

Some 40 years ago, at the end of the 1960s, the Cold War was an accepted reality of global politics. The process of decolonization was still in progress, the idea of a unified Europe with a single currency was unheard of, the United States was mired in a war in Vietnam, and the economic boom in Asia was still years in the future. Richard Nixon was president of the United States, Mao Tse-tung (not yet Mao Zedong) ruled China, Leonid Brezhnev guided the Soviet Union, and Harold Wilson was prime minister of the United Kingdom. Authoritarian dictators still controlled most of Latin America, the Middle East was reeling in the wake of the Six-Day War, and Shah Mohammad Reza Pahlavi was at the height of his power in Iran.

Since then, the Cold War has ended; the Soviet Union has vanished, leaving 15 independent republics in its wake; the advent of the computer age has radically transformed global communications; the rising demand for oil makes the Middle East still a dangerous flashpoint; and the rise of new economic powers like the People's Republic of China and India threatens to bring about a new world order. All of these developments have had a dramatic impact on the recent history of every nation of the world.

For this series, which was launched in 1998, we first selected nations whose political, economic, and socio-cultural affairs marked them as among the most important of our time. For each nation, we found an author who was recognized as a specialist in the history of that nation. These authors worked cooperatively with us and with Greenwood Press to produce volumes that reflected current research on their nations and that are interesting and informative to their readers. In the first decade of the series, more than 40 volumes were published, and as of 2008, some are moving into second editions.

The success of the series has encouraged us to broaden our scope to include additional nations, whose histories have had significant effects on their regions, if not on the entire world. In addition, geopolitical changes have elevated other nations into positions of greater importance in world affairs and, so, we have chosen to include them in this series as well. The importance of a series such as this cannot be underestimated. As a superpower whose influence is felt all over the world, the United States can claim a "special" relationship with almost every other nation. Yet many Americans know very little about the histories of nations with which the United States relates. How did they get to be the way they are? What kind of political systems have evolved there? What kind of influence do they have on their own regions? What are the dominant political, religious, and cultural forces that move their leaders? These and many other questions are answered in the volumes of this series.

The authors who contribute to this series write comprehensive histories of their nations, dating back, in some instances, to prehistoric times. Each of them, however, has devoted a significant portion of their book to events of the past 40 years because the modern era has contributed the most to contemporary issues that have an impact on U.S. policy. Authors make every effort to be as up-to-date as possible so that readers can benefit from discussion and analysis of recent events.

In addition to the historical narrative, each volume contains an introductory chapter giving an overview of that country's geography, political institutions, economic structure, and cultural attributes. This is meant to give readers a snapshot of the nation as it exists in the contemporary world. Each history also includes supplementary information following the narrative, which may include a timeline that represents a succinct chronology of the nation's historical evolution, biographical sketches of the nation's most important historical figures, and a glossary of important terms or concepts that are usually expressed in a foreign language. Finally, each author prepares a comprehensive bibliography for readers who wish to pursue the subject further.

Readers of these volumes will find them fascinating and well written. More importantly, they will come away with a better understanding of the contemporary world and the nations that comprise it. As series editors, we hope that this series will contribute to a heightened sense of global understanding as we move through the early years of the twenty-first century.

Frank W. Thackeray and John E. Findling
Indiana University Southeast

Preface and Acknowledgments

Drawing on a large repertoire of primary and secondary sources, my focus is to provide an account of Somali history, politics, and culture from the earliest times to the present. The major areas of coverage include all the major themes, notably precolonial and indigenous societies and state systems, migrations and settlements, and the expansion of international trade and penetration of Arab merchants and settlers into the Somali Peninsula. Other themes covered are the coming of the Europeans and the partition and colonial domination starting from the late nineteenth century, anticolonial struggles, the different colonial regimes, attainment of independence, and the enduring violent spasms that have rocked the project of nation building since 1960. The last chapter of the book, which offers some ideas on how to reconstitute and retool the shattered postcolonial nation-state, will be found of immense interest for politicians, mediators, scholars, and other interest groups.

As much as possible, I have tried to use the specific Somali historical crosscurrents to illuminate common themes of precolonial, colonial, and postcolonial history of the Horn Region in particular and African history in general. This approach has been followed in a tidy manner in order to avoid any distractions for the reader. If now and then

I sounded a bit more Somali-centric, it is because there is a need to underpin the African side of the story rather than privileging the outsider's perspective.

As the people continue to wrestle with war and peace in an effort to make meaning out of the enduring chaos, the weight of the problems tends to challenge, if not diminish, the brave and brilliant efforts of the empire builders and nationalist figures of yesteryear; the resilience and adaptability of the common Somali; the avalanche of poetic, literary, and revolutionary and counter-ideological ferments men and women of this great land have produced. The question no one can answer with certainty today is whether clan-based separatist tendencies (perhaps the greatest adversary in the history of Somalia) could be rescinded for the country not to die, to remain as one. Of course, it is only the future that holds the appropriate answer to this question.

Still, as Ngugi wa Thiong'o reminds us, a morsel of wheat must expire to bear abundant fruit. Indeed, under the hazy smoke of gunpowder and the ashes of life-altering, land-altering destructions and death, one can see a bright light at the end of the tunnel. This optimism is found in the fact that Somalis have survived diverse forms of adversities—both natural and man made. Like the prehistoric rocks that litter the arid landscape, the Somalis are built tough; they have endured and adapted over several millennia and will once again overcome the present chaos. To this end, it is essential to say that Somalis alone best understand their problems, and they alone know how to fix them.

It would have been absolutely difficult to undertake writing this book without the encouragement and goodwill of several people—not all of whose names I can include here. I must thank Professors Frank W. Thackeray and John E. Findling—the *Greenwood Histories of Modern Nations* series editors—and Professor Glenn Crothers for their kind invitation to this project.

I am greatly indebted to the African Studies program at Indiana University Bloomington (IUB) for offering me a summer Library Residency Fellowship in 2009 to conduct research at the prestigious Lilly, Herman B. Wells, and African Studies Department libraries. With funds from a U.S. Department of Education Title II-C grant, a preservation agreement was reached between IUB and institutions like the Somali Studies International Association to rescue and preserve hard-to-replace materials on Somali studies at the IUB libraries. I am particularly indebted to Drs. Samuel Obeng and Marion Frank-Wilson of IUB, who patiently and painstakingly guided me through volumes of primary and secondary collections on Somali history.

I owe special thanks to many friends and colleagues who either scouted for materials or read initial drafts of this monograph. For instance, the insider perspectives my Somali contacts and friends like Maryam and Amina Ahmed, and Adan Makina provided were totally invaluable. I must quickly add that all errors of statement and interpretations are mine alone.

More importantly, I must thank the Acquisitions Editor for Geography and World Cultures, ABC-Clio, Ms. Kaitlin Ciarmiello, who treated my delays with professional understanding. The brilliant comments and suggestions Kaitlin provided me with proved vital for improved standards and general conformity with style and contents.

I am eternally grateful to Professors John McLeod, Tracy K'Meyer, Tom Mackey, Ann Allen, Dean Joe Wert, Christine Ehrick, Blake Beattie, Jeanie Burnett, Stephanie Bower, Yuxin Ma, Yu Shin, Justin McCarthy, Mark Blum, Bruce Tyler, Robert Kebric, Ed McInnis, John Cumbler, Daniel Krebs, Matthew Church, Ms. Lee Keeling, Jon-Paul Moody, and others. Your immense goodwill helped bring this project to completion.

I must not forget to thank my dearly loved wife and kids for their usual cooperation and motivation. Whether it is on occasions when I returned home late from the library or when I left home on short notice for either research or conference trips, my family ably guarded the home front with the understanding that in this profession, a scholar is an ardent wanderer who frequently migrates to where the fountain of knowledge beckons.

Acronyms

AFIS	*Amministrazione Fiduciaria Italiana della Sommalia*/Administration on the Trust Territory of Somalia
ASF	Allied Somali Forces
AU	African Union
CISS	Commonwealth of Independent Somali States
DFSS	Democratic Front for the Salvation of Somalia
DRC	Democratic Republic of the Congo
GDP	Gross Domestic Product
ICG	International Crisis Group
ICU	Islamic Court Union
IGAD	Intergovernmental Authority on Development
ITG	Interim Transition Government
IUP	Islamic Union Party
JVA	Juba Valley Alliance
LAS	League of Arab States
NCRPS	National Commission for Reconciliation and Property Settlement
NEC	National Election Commission
NGO	Non-Governmental Organization
NSA	Northern Somali Alliance

NSS	National Security Service
OAU	Organization of African Unity
OIC	Organization of Islamic Conference
PINR	Power and Interests News Report
RAMB	*Regia Azienda Monopolio Banane*/Royal Banana Plantation Monopoly
RRA	Rahanweyn Resistance Army
SAIS	*Societa Agricola Italo-Somalia*/Italo-Somali Agricultural Society
SAMO	Somali African Muki Association
SDA	Somali Democratic Alliance
SDM	Somali Democratic Movement
SECF	Somali Eastern and Central Front
SIA	Somali Islamic Association
SNA	Somali National Alliance
SNAASL	Somali National Academy of Arts, Sciences and Literature
SNDU	Somali National Democratic Union
SNF	Somali National Front
SNM	Somali National Movement
SNU	Somali National Union
SPDU	Somali People's Democratic Union
SPM	Somali Patriotic Movement
SRC	Supreme Revolutionary Council
SRRC	Somali Reconciliation & Restoration Council
SRSP	Somali Revolutionary Socialist Party
SSA	Somali Salvation Alliance
SSDF	Somali Salvation Democratic Front
SSF	Somali Salvation Front
SSNM	Southern Somali National Movement
SYC	Somali Youth Club
SYL	Somali Youth League
TFG	Transition Federal government
TNA	Transition National Assembly
TNG	Transitional National Government
UDUB	Allied People's Democratic Party (UDUB)
UIS	University Institute of Somalia
UN	United Nations
UNESCO	United Nations Educational, Scientific and Cultural Organization
UNITAF	Unified Task Force
UNOSOM	United Nations Operation Somalia
UNTAP	United Nations Technical Assistance Program
USC	United Somali Congress

USC/PM	United Somali Congress/Peace Movement
USC/SNA	United Somali Congress/Somali National Alliance
USC/SSA	United Somali Congress/Somali Salvation Alliance
USF	United Somali Front
USP	United Somali Party
USSR	Union of Soviet Socialist Republic

Timeline of Historical Events

15,000–8,000 BCE	The Laas Geel, one of the earliest known rock cultures in Africa, exists on the Somali Peninsula.
4,000 BCE	Proto-Somali I—the Jiddu settlers arrive in the Horn (proto-Somali I).
4,000 BCE	The Jalelo, the oldest evidence of burial customs exists.
3,000 BCE	Proto-Somali II (also called pre-Rendille or Garre) emerges.
3,000–2,000 BCE	Domestication of the camel (dromedary) in Somalia.
2,500–2,475 BCE	Egypt's Fifth Dynasty under Pharaoh Sahure documents the earliest known Pharaonic trading expedition to the fabled Land of Punt (Somalia).
1,475 BCE	Queen Pharaoh Hatshepsut sends a trading voyage to Punt.
1,000 BCE	Omo-Tana (or Sam), the Proto Somali III speakers (including the Garre and the Tunni), break away from the original Cushitic family and occupy the Juba River region of Somalia.
150 BCE	Himyarite (South Yemen) presence in the coastal enclaves of East Africa including Somalia. As'ad al-Himyari rule Mogadishu and environs.

100 CE	The Sam frontiersmen complete occupation of the Ogaden plains.
100–700 CE	An anonymous Greek merchant and author of the *Periplus of the Erythraean Sea* (who resides in Egypt) gives a description of the coastal trading towns of East Africa including Zeila and Mogadishu in Somalia.
547 CE	Cosmas Indicopleustes writes *The Christian Topography of Cosmas, an Egyptian Monk* providing glimpses of the "Trade in Ethiopia."
615 CE	Prophet Muhammad and his entourage take refuge on the Horn.
1270–1285	Ifat rulers send a military expedition against Shoa kingdom.
1286	Ibn Sa'id al-Maghribi (1212–1286), a Muslim geographer, notes that Mogadishu is Madinat al-Islam, an Islamic center.
1300	Start of hostilities between Christians and Muslims in the Horn. The Abyssinian kingdom (Ethiopia) demands tributes from the sultanates of Bali, Hadya, Harar, Fatajar, Dawaro, and Ifat.
1331	Ibn Battuta (the Berber-Muslim), globe-trotter, visits East African port cities of Zeila and Mogadishu.
1386	Sa'd al-Din II succeeds Haq al-Din II as new Sultan of Ifat.
1415	By the courtesy of Emperor Yeshaq (r. 1414–1429) of Abyssinia, first written record of the word "Somali."
1415	Ethiopian emperor and patriarch of the Coptic church raids the Ifat sultanate, killing Sultan Sa'd al-Din II.
1434	The Ming ruler's expedition arrive in Mogadishu.
1445	Weary from relentless wars with Abyssinia, Muhammad ibn Badlay of Awdal (Adal) sultanate accepts to pay annual tribute to Abyssinia.
1450	The Persian Zuzni Dynasty comes to power in Mogadishu.
1485	Duarte Barbosa of Portugal visits Mogadishu.
1491	Vasco Da Gama visits East Africa.

1499	Jan. 3, Vasco Da Gama launches attack on Mogadishu.
1503	Portuguese expedition force destroys the city of Barawa.
1527	Imam Ahmed Gurey and his Somali armies defeat the Ethiopians. The Portuguese come to Ethiopia's aid.
1543	Feb. 28, Portuguese army commanded by Christopher Da Gama helped Ethiopia defeat the Muslims.
1555	Adal Sultanate breaks up into small states.
1560	The Ajuuraan state in south-central Somalia emerges.
1750	The Geledi Sultanate (later known as Afgoy) emerges in Ay Ulay in the southern Shabelle River valley.
1800	The Majerteen Sultanate rises in the Bandar Alula area.
1839	Britain establishes a garrison in Aden.
1854	Richard Burton of the British navy visits Zeila.
1856	Birth of Mohammad (aka "Mad Mullah") Abdille Hassan.
1869	The Suez Canal opens; prompts increased interests of European powers in the region.
1870s	Keenadicd founds the Hobyo (Obhia) Sultanate.
1875	Egypt occupies Somali coastal towns of Zeila, Berbera, and parts of the interior.
1884	Mahdist revolt in the Sudan forces Egyptian army to withdraw from Somali lands.
1885	Italy seizes control of Massawe in Eritrea.
1887	Great Britain officially proclaims protectorate over Somaliland.
1887	Menelik II, founder of modern Ethiopia, conquers the Harar area of western Somalia.
1888	An agreement between the British and the French determines each country's sphere of influence in Somalia.
1888–1889	Italy signs protectorate treaties with the Majerteen and Hobyo Sultanates.
1893	Italy hoists its flag in Merca.
1896	Menelik II defeats the Italian colonial forces at the historic battle of Adowa.

1898	The Benadir company replaces the Filonardi company as Italian imperial agents.
1899	Sheik Mohamed (the "Mad Mullah") Abdille Hassan and his Dervish fighters launch war of resistance against the European colonial presence.
1905	Mar. 5, Mohamed Abdille Hassan signs the Ilig Agreement with Italy.
1906	Anglo-Italian agreement signed by Cavalier Pestalozza of Italy and General Swayne of Britain formerly accepts Baran as part of the Majerteen sultanate.
1910	Italy forms the *Corpo di Polizia della* Somalia (Somali Police Force) comprising the Italian *Carabinieri* officers and Somali recruits.
1920	Dec., Sheik Mohammad Abdille Hassan dies from the worldwide influenza epidemic.
1935	Italian fascist government invades Ethiopia, creating the so-called Italian Province of East Africa: Eritrea, Somalia, and Ethiopia.
1941	Britain defeats Italy in the battle of the Horn and seizes control over Italian Somaliland.
1947	Creation of the Somali Youth League (SYL), the major nationalist party in the ex-Italian colonial territory.
1950	The United Nations takes over Somaliland as a trust territory under the Italian Trustee Administration.
1951	Somali National League (SNL) emerges as the major nationalist party; leads the quest for independence of British Somaliland.
1960	June 6, British Somaliland gains independence.
1960	Jul. 1, amalgamation of British and Italian-administered Trust Territory as the Somali Republic.
1964	Abd ar-Razak Hussein replaces Dr. Shirmarke as prime minister. The Ogaden question led to war with Ethiopia.
1967	June, Dr. Abdi Ali Shirmarke defeats Aden Abdullah Osman Daar in the presidential elections; appointment of Mohamed Ibrahim Egal as prime minister.
1969	Oct. 15, an aggrieved guard assassinates President Shirmarke.

1969	Oct. 21, Siad Barre executes a successful coup and establishes the Supreme Revolutionary Council (SRC).
1971	The writing of the Somali language in the Latin script.
1974	Somalia joins the League of Arab Nations (LAN).
1978	Mar., Soviet and Cuban forces help Ethiopia regain control of Ogaden.
1981	The DFSS (later SSDF) was formed by the Majerteen; launching of the SNM by the Isaaq group.
1988	Apr., Ethiopia momentarily stops its support for rebels after a peace accord with Somalia.
1988	May, the northwestern towns of Burao and Hargeisa seized by the SNM.
1988	June, Somali troops under General Morgan's command launched a punitive expedition against the SNM in northwest.
1991	May 16, SNM declares independence of "Republic of Somaliland," with its chairman, Abd ar-Rahman Ahmed Ali (aka "Tur"), as president.
1991	June, national reconciliation conference is held in Djibouti without the SNM; attendees include SPM, USC, SDM, SPM, and DFSS.
1991	Jul., second national reconciliation conference holds in Djibouti; Ali Mahdi confirmed as President for a two-year period.
1992	Jan., UN troops led by the United States enter Mogadishu; General Aideed opposes the peacekeepers.
1992	Apr., General Barre finally absconds from Somalia.
1992	Apr., the United Nations sets up UNOSOM I.
1992	June, 50 UNOSOM II observers deployed.
1993	Jan., 33,000 UNITAF forces enter Somalia.
1993	June, 24 members of the Pakistani UN soldiers killed by Aideed's forces.
1993	Oct. 3, the date of the *Maalinti Ranger*; 18 U.S. troops and over 300 Somalis die in clashes in Mogadishu.
1993	Oct. 15, captured U.S. pilot Michael Durant regains freedom.

1995	Jan., 2, General Barre dies in Nigeria.
1995	Mar., UNOSOM mission formally ends.
1996	Jan., Gen. Aideed shot dead. April 8, his son, Hussein, takes over as "president."
1998	Jul., self-governing "Puntland State of Somalia" declared in SSDF-controlled northeast Somalia.
1998	Sept., Puntland launches 69-member Parliament; Puntland charter released, advocating federal structure for Somalia.
2000	May, Arta, Djibouti peace summit begins; several leaders and clan elders attend.
2000	Dec., 10,000 recruited by the TNG to form new national army.
2001	May, Somalilanders approve new constitution and independence in a referendum.
2001	June, Yusuf Haji Nur appointed president of Puntland, becoming successor to Abdullahi Yusuf.
2001	Nov., Jama Ali Jama chosen as new president of Puntland.
2004	Aug., a new transitional parliament is installed at a ceremony in Kenya. The members elect Adbullahi Yusuf president in Oct.
2006	Feb., first sitting of the transitional parliament on Somali soil since establishment in Kenya in 2004.
2007	Nov., new prime minister, Nur Hassan (or Nur Adde), sworn in.
2008	Mar., the United States launches missile attacks on alleged al-Qaeda member suspected in the 2002 terror act on Israeli-owned hotel in Kenya.
2008	Jul., gunmen kill Osman Ali Ahmed, Head of UN Development Program in Somalia.
2008	Nov., Somali pirates ransom Saudi super oil vessel for $25 million.
2009	June, a brazen attack at a hotel in Beledweyne claims the lives of Somali security minister and 20 others.

2009	Sept., al-Shabaab declares allegiance with Osama bin Laden, the al-Qaeda kingpin.
2010	Jul., al-Shabab militants claim responsibility for a twin attack in Kampala, Uganda. The blast kills 74 World Cup soccer fans.
2011	June 17, al Shabaab vows allegiance to al-Qaeda's new emir al Zawahiri.
2011	July, UN estimates that over 750,000 Somali face starvation.
2011	Sept. 30, Shabaab fighters commence raids near Kenyan borders.

1

The Land and the People of Somalia: An Overview

LOCATION

Sitting between the equator and the Tropic of Cancer at 0° 0'N 41° 0'E, the Republic of Somalia, or *Jamhuuriyadda Soomaaliya* in the Somali language, was constituted on July 1, 1960, following a historic fusion of the former British Somaliland (the North) and the former Italian Somalia (the South). The country occupies an approximate landmass of 246,331 sq. miles (638,000 sq. km) that has the shape of the number seven. It is slightly bigger than the United Kingdom (242,900 sq. miles) and a little smaller than the state of Texas (268,601 sq. miles). With a projected population of 10.1 million people as of July 2010, the fragile component parts of modern Somalia sit on a strategic peninsula sprawling the coastal plains of northeastern corner of Africa.[1] The other countries that make up the unique projecting rhinoceros horn-like geopolitical region now commonly known as the "Horn of Africa" are Ethiopia, Djibouti, and Eritrea.

Somalia is bordered to the northwest by Djibouti; to the northeast, the Somali Peninsula projects into the Arabian Sea. The entire north is bordered by the Gulf of Aden with Yemen on the other side of the sea, and the entire eastern shores are prominently delimited by the Indian Ocean. The contiguous seas—the Gulf of Aden, the Arabian Sea, and the Indian Ocean—have provided a rich source of seafood, while since ancient times serving as a highway for a lucrative international commerce linking up the East African societies with the Middle East, India, China, Europe, and the wider world.

Somalia's entire coastlines, the longest in Africa, measure about 1,800 miles from the lava fields of the neighboring northwestern country of Djibouti to the southernmost parts bordering Kenya. To the west, Somalia shares unclearly determined and often violently contested boundaries with Ethiopia. As will be elaborated on in Chapter 3, the ambiguous border relationship with Ethiopia has been a source of persistent tension and often violent conflicts between the two neighbors. These conflicts that predate the colonial era have become more entrenched and were a topic of serious concern for the British on the eve of Somaliland's independence.[2]

GEOGRAPHY

History and geography are intricately connected. The case of Somalia once again demonstrates that geography holds the key to a better grasp of a people's history, culture, technology, economy, politics, and national characteristics, as well as its pace and challenges of development. Somalia's landscape, consisting mainly of highlands, plateaus, and both flat and undulating plains, contrasts at different points in accordance with the country's varying seasonal climates and vegetation zones. In this East African region are found some of the oldest rocks on the continent, dating back to the Mesozoic era (i.e., the so-called age of dinosaurs starting at c. 250 million years ago).[3] The timeless age of these prehistoric rocks stands today as a solid reminder that Africa is the oldest continent in the world. The rocks also preserve fossils that can be studied to appreciate how nature, humans, fauna, and environment have interacted across different millennia in the evolution of culture in this part of Africa.[4]

Entering the country from the northern shores of the Gulf of Aden, the sprawling terrain is dominated by the rugged and undulating Karkaar Mountains running from the northeast tip of the Horn of Africa to the northwest border regions with Djibouti. In general, the entire northern region is defined by three successive and contrasting terrains: the coastal *Guban* (scrub land), the mountainous *Golis*, and the central plateau *Haud*. Sandwiched in-between the coastal plains

SOMALIA

(ABC-CLIO)

of the Gulf of Aden and the imposing mountains is the Guban, a low-lying stretch of territory whose name is derived from its desert environment and translates to "burned from lack of water." The Guban's topography is characterized by a network of dry riverbeds (*tog*), ridges, and knolls. It is typically dry and drab, with searing heat and frequent sandstorms. The crisscrossing broad and shallow watercourses form beds of dry sand except in rainy seasons when they are filled with rainwaters. This makes the Guban seasonally useful during the short rainy season that runs from May to June when nomads flock to the area to cool off, farm, and graze their animals.

Farther south, a lesser range of highlands called the *Ogo* or *Oogs* leads to the Golis zone. In other words, this area of the north has two mountain ranges (the Golis and the Ogo). At its highest peak at Shimber Berris, the Golis Mountains reaches up to 9,000 ft. (2,743.2 m) high. The Ogo gradually slopes eastward toward the Indian Ocean. A prominent part of this northeastern section of the plateau is the long and broad Nugaal Valley, which is discernible with an extensive network of intermittent seasonal waterways. The Nugaal waters empty into the Indian Ocean at the village of Eyl (Eil) in the northeast. To the west, both the Golis and Ogo mountains merged with the highlands of Ethiopia at the historic eastern Ethiopian city of Harar (Harrar). In contrast to the northeastern region of Somalia, which is usually dry, annual rainfall in the western region of the Golis could be up to 20 inches (0.5 m). Further inland, the western plateau gradually slopes southward, merging into the Haud zone or the central plateau.

The Haud, extending from three corners—the city of Hargeisa (northwest), the Doollo plains (west), and the Nugaal valley (east)—is a broad, undulating terrain that provides some of the best arable and grazing lands. The attraction of the Haud for grazers is further enhanced by natural depressions that temporarily become lakes during the rainy season. The Haud actually cuts through the southern borders, stretching about 60 miles into Ethiopia. The two countries have often engaged in violent conflicts over the right to pasture around the borderlines. Prior to 1960 when British Somaliland regained its independence, Ethiopians had shared pastures with Somali herdsmen.[5] Since the 1960s, such acts of cooperation have diminished for reasons apparently connected with the arbitrary boundaries created under colonial rule, population increase, drought and desertification, and famine and crop failures, in addition to vested ideological, political, and economic interests of both countries.

In the southern region of the country are two strategic rivers, the Webi Shebelle (Shebeelle) and the Juba (Jubba), both of which originate in Ethiopia, running in the southeastward direction toward the Indian Ocean.[6] The stretch of lands in-between these two rivers is exceedingly fertile, and much of it is exclusively reserved for food production. The sections of the land that are not cultivated support an abundance of wildlife. One can say that the Shebelle River and the Juba River together constitute the soul of the country's heartland. The two rivers are crucial to the nurturing and sustenance of life in

Somalia. They provide the waters for the irrigation of crops; however, the amount of water depends greatly on the amount of rainfall brought by the two rainy seasons starting from around March/April.

Altogether, there are four seasons, comprising two wet seasons (*gu* and *dayr*) and two dry seasons (*jilaal and haggaa*). The seasons run intermittently in the following order: *gu* (April–June), *haggaa* or *xagaa* (July–September), *dayr* (October–November), and *jilaal* or *jiilaal* (December–March). In the midst of extreme variations, most parts of the lands get no more than 19.7 inches (500 ml) of rainfall per year. With the exceptions of the coastal areas, certain highlands in the north, and the southwest, some significant parts of the lowlands in the north receive as little as 1.97–5.91 inches (50–150 ml) of rainfall annually. The problem of sparse rainfalls in this part of the Horn is a result of the eastward direction of the winds of the tropical monsoons. While the monsoon winds bring seasonal rains to the Sahel and the Sudan, they tend to lose their moisture upon getting to Djibouti and Somalia.[7]

The first period of the rainy season, known as the *gu*, roughly begins in March/April, lasting through June/July. As inhabitants of the cold regions of North America and Europe yearn for the summer season, so do Somalis long for the *gu* or the "long rains," as it is often called. The *gu* season comes as a huge relief for people, animals, and plants after the four months of *jilaal* dryness that precede it. The initial round of rain, if it comes in abundance, momentarily transforms the desert environment into a blossoming garden, which produces a fresh supply of fodder. In the central grazing plateau, the lush grass grows very tall, before the subsequent heavy downpours starting from May through June.

During this period, there is plenty of water, milk, meat, and food. The land, reprieved from four months of harsh dryness, usually comes alive with celebrations, ritual and social functions, and recreational activities, including music, drama, poetry, and other forms of intellectual and artistic creations.[8] Somalia is a country of a million and one poets. Writing as an eyewitness in 1856, British soldier and colonial administrator Sir Richard F. Burton observed about the place of oral poetry in the indigenous society. "The country teems with poets, poetasters, poetitos, and poetaccios: every man has his recognised position in literature as accurately defined as though he had been reviewed in a century of magazines."[9] Similarly, Somali historian Said Samatar adds, "Poetry is the vehicle by which Somalis ask the three eternal questions: Where do I come from? Who am I? And where do I go from here? Somali poetry is not art for art's sake. . . . Somali poetry is didactic, not purely aesthetic."[10]

Other cultural activities like marriage and religious festivals are also celebrated at this time: there are peace offerings and blessings, and old and new alliances/disputes are either rekindled or settled in this happiest period of the year for the pastoral/rural communities. In his masterful autobiography *A Mouth Sweeter Than Salt*, Toyin Falola reminds us that his indigenous Yoruba people of modern Nigeria recorded dates of birth not by the Western calendar year but by events and seasons.[11] This is also true for the Somalis, who at this period celebrated birthdays by the number of *gu* seasons a person has witnessed. For instance, a person born in July 1983 will not necessarily mark her thirtieth birthday in 2013, but would rather calculate the number of *gu* seasons she has celebrated with her people.

The second seasonal rainfalls, the *dayr*, come with light rains from October through November—i.e., after the *haggaa* dryness (July–September). Over this shorter period, the showers are erratic but all the same useful especially coming in-between the *haggaa* drought and even harsher *jilaal* season, which is generally the most miserable season for pastoralists. For the nomads and planters, the timing and amount of annual rainfalls are critical determinants of the sufficiency of grazing and the prospects of a successful harvest.

Like the climate, the temperature exhibits variations that in some places contrast extremely with the overall average records. Somalia's climate combines elements of arid, semiarid, and tropical nature across different zones. Overall, the mean daily temperature is somewhere between 86 and 104°F (30–40°C), except for the higher elevations along the coastal shores of the Indian Ocean where it alternates between 68 and 86°F (20–30°C). Nonetheless, northern Somalia has the greatest variations in temperature. This could range from below freezing point on clear nights in the highlands in the month of December to more than 113°F (45°C) along the coastal plains next to the Gulf of Aden in July. While the annual monsoon wind heavily determines the daily temperature and amount of seasonal rainfalls, the temperature and the rains in turn determine the variety of plants and shrubs found in Somalia.

It is probable that about 5,000 genuses of vascular plants with lignified (i.e., converted into wood) tissues for conducting water are found in the entire Horn region. Out of this variety, at least 2,500, or 55 percent, are native to the region. In Somalia, most of these plants are concentrated in the "garden" area around the Juba and Shebelle Rivers. Some of the popular indigenous plants include the acacia trees, aloe plants (valued for its medicinal properties), and other vegetation such as juniper trees. The most popular, however, remain the boswellia tree, from which frankincense is tapped, and the commiphora tree, which produces myrrh resin. The ancient Egyptians processed myrrh from the region for high-grade incense used in religious festivals and rites. The common understanding today is that the Egyptians referred to the area known today as Somalia as the famed Land of Punt from which they received their steady supplies of myrrh and frankincense.

Historians note that Queen-King Hatshepsut's (reigned c. 1492–1469 BCE) greatest success as the ruler of ancient Egypt is closely associated with an expedition sent to the ancient kingdom of Punt.[12] As the paintings on reliefs, tombs, and temples of the era show, the Egyptian ships returned from trading expeditions loaded with ebony, ivory, leopard skins, spices, and live monkeys for private zoos. The sailors also brought back huge quantities of incense, medicines, and myrrh, much valued for its perfume. Hatshepsut had the fragrant trees planted near her temple.

What most parts of Somalia lacked in diversity in plants was made up for with a more diverse fauna. A wary visitor to the country today might not see enough evidence of the rich variety of fauna that has been hunted to near extinction due to increasing aridity and human activities. Much of the degradations happened during the colonial period as privileged European officers hunted out the wildlife.[13] Originally the central regions of the country were natural habitats for lions, cheetahs, leopards, elephants, buffalo, zebras, giraffes, and hippopotamuses; while donkeys, sheep, gazelles, giraffes, and antelope inhabit the semiarid regions of the country. There were also the Warsangli linnet (*Carduelis johannis*) found only in northern Somalia, flamingoes, golden-winged grosbeak, and the mythical hoopoes.[14] The oral tradition claims that the hoopoe used to have a golden crest, but to avoid being hunted to extinction, the species' family implored King Solomon (c. 970–931 BCE), the ancient ruler of Israel, "to change their crests to a chestnut shade—because too many people were killing them for their gold."[15] What is not quite clear in the tradition is how King Solomon came into the picture, but it is not difficult to imagine that the ancient Somali obviously knew a lot about the Biblical Israeli monarch, renowned for his wisdom, affluence, and power.

ECONOMY

One of the major surprises of Somalia's lack of a functional central government since 1991 is the people's ability to maintain a vigorous informal economy. The limited but notable success of private enterprise since the anarchy of the 1990s is perhaps an indictment of the failures of former state control of the economy beginning in 1969, with the rise of Gen. Said Barre to power and his inclination toward a socialist economy. In the late 1980s, the Western credit and aid agencies compelled Somalia to implement the Structural Adjustment Program (SAP), recommended by the International Monetary Fund (IMF). This measure was put in practice until 1991 with no positive results, especially with hindrances posed by the country's civil conflicts and wars.[16]

In general, the economy is mainly sustained by agriculture and livestock production, forestry, fisheries, money transfers, and telecommunications. To this list may be added high sea piracy and other forms of organized crime. Agriculture, livestock, forestry, and fisheries account for the bulk of the gross domestic product (GDP). Rural farmers producing sorghum, maize, cotton, corn, sugarcane, and bananas generate sufficient surpluses to sustain domestic informal markets. The bulk of the bananas, sugarcane, cotton, and frankincense are exported to complement the much-needed foreign earnings that come mostly from livestock export.[17] In the early 1980s, over 1 million cattle, mostly goats and sheep, were exported annually as surplus. Over the past two decades, this additional source of foreign earnings has been lost to persistent problems of wars, droughts, and famines. Small forestry (primarily production of frankincense and myrrh) and fisheries (which have shown a modest growth in the past three decades) bring additional foreign earnings.

The agricultural sector of the economy sustains the manufacturing sector, which prior to 1990 contributed just 5 percent of the GDP. The fledgling manufacturing industry is organized above all on processing agricultural products. The most developed aspect of the manufacturing sector are the operations concerned with the processing of sugar, milk, and hides and skins. The manufacturing industry has not performed as expected, and since the 1990s has virtually ceased to play any significant role in the economy.

The land is blessed with mineral resources, although these are not in extraordinary reserves, to help Somalia make a huge break from poverty. Some of the minerals include copper, uranium, iron ore, tin, bauxite, gypsum-anhydrite, quartz and piezoquartz, salt, meerschaum, unconfirmed quantities of gold, oil, and natural gas deposits. A study in 2000 shows that Somalia's mining industry, which contributed a mere 0.3 percent of the GDP in 1988, remains marginal and substantially unexploited except for the informal and unlawful activities of private entrepreneurs.[18] While there are deposits of oil and natural gas, it is yet to be ascertained whether these actually exist in profitable commercial quantities—hence Somalis tend to rely on trade to augment the shortfalls of the predominantly pastoral economy.

Overseas trade occupies an important part of the Somali economy. The livestock and cash crops like banana, myrrh, and frankincense, in addition to its strategic location on a major international crossroads, made Somalia a popular market for East Africans, Arabs, Europeans, Indians, and Chinese businessmen. The major export partners are Saudi Arabia, United Arab Emirates, Yemen, and Italy. In 2009, the UAE and Yemen accounted for 58 percent and 20 percent of the trade, respectively. Products like ebony, ivory, wild animals, skins, spices, gold, resins, gums, woods, charcoal, and cosmetics are also bought from the Somali ports for foreign products like food, machinery, electronics, and transportation equipment by Italy, Britain, Norway, Djibouti, Kenya, Belarus, and Bahrain.[19]

No discussion on the economy would be complete without mention of the contributions of the Somali diasporas to the homeland's economy through an informal remittance system. It is difficult to determine how many Somalis are in the diasporas, but a conservative estimate by the UNDP in 2001 put the figure somewhere around a million.[20] Many Somalis had been moving out of the country to work in different parts of the world prior to 1988 when the civil war broke out; however, the war has caused large population movements, thereby setting in motion a new pattern of migrations to African countries, Asia, European Union countries, and North America. A significant number of these refugees have been granted asylum in the United States, and their favorite destination seem to be Minneapolis-St. Paul, Minnesota.[21]

Whether in Europe, the Americas, and Asia or in neighboring African countries, the Somali diasporas have maintained a strong link with their kith and kin in the homeland through constant telecommunication contacts. Several studies have discovered that remittances from overseas to family members and for business investments add up to between US$500 million and US$1 billion per annum.[22] For a country with a $2.37 billion GDP in 2010, the remittances from overseas constitute a significant source of revenue.[23]

The frequency of this source of foreign earnings has kept the telecommunication sector of the Somali economy flourishing. Somalia, in the 1990s, established a number of partnerships with foreign companies like the Norwegian Telenor and the American Starlight Communications. Also the indigenous company Al-Barakaat allied itself with the U.S. telecommunication company giant AT&T. In 2002, Telecom Somalia was added to the list that has been growing rapidly since 1997. Somalia is served by mobile networks with subscribers estimated at 100,000. Additionally, there are about 83,759 (or 1.2 percent of the population) Internet users according to a study by the European company NovaTech in 2005. The country's Internet Café is growing at the rate of 15.6 percent per annum. The subscribers to these services are mainly residents in the big cities like Mogadishu, Hargeisa, Berbera, and Puntland where the services are easily accessible.[24]

As dangerous as it sounds, piracy has become a flourishing industry in Somalia. Broadly speaking, three categories of people are involved in the pirate gangs. The first group is constituted by ex-fishermen (estimated at 1,500), who are crucial in the planning and execution of the operation given their mastery of the high sea. The second group are bands of veterans of the Somali wars or ex-militiamen. This group undertakes the decisive risks involved in approaching and attacking ships that ply the high seas. The third are the individuals who have the advanced knowledge of modern gadgets and technology such as global positioning systems (GPS), cell phones, and other advanced equipment like military weapons. Most of those who make up this group are young people recruited for their skill with electronic gadgets needed to run a high seas pirate operation.[25]

Pirates depart for the Somalian coast from the Ukrainian cargo ship MV *Faina* on October 8, 2008. (Jason R. Zalasky/U.S. Navy)

The pirates carry out their operations off the long sea channel running from the Red Sea to the Gulf of Aden to the Indian Ocean. In 2009, for instance, around 114 attacks were recorded, and this has continued to escalate as ordinary Somalis are wooed by pirate gangs to "invest in one of the 72 'maritime companies' and hope that their favorite pirate band strikes it rich with the successful ransoming of a captured ship and crew."[26] The Puntland region has become a kind of corporate business run in similar fashion as the stock exchange markets where investors are wooed by companies to bet on a company's stocks. Overall, it is estimated that victims of the pirates have paid out more than $100 million in ransoms to the pirates since 1992.[27] A good portion of the ransom payments have been invested in real estate, telecommunications, transport, and businesses in Somalia; in neighboring Kenya and Djibouti; and in the lucrative Dubai real estate economy.[28]

The word "pirate" in the Somali language is equivalent to *burcad badeed*, which literarily means "ocean robber." Ironically, individuals engaged in the crime such as the one who identifies himself simply as Boyah strongly disagree that he and his partners in crime are "ocean robbers." According to Jay Bahadur of *The Times* of London who interviewed some of the pirates of Puntland in April 2009, the pirates self-identify as *Badaadinta badah*, or "saviors of the sea." This is more or less an equivalent of the U.S. or British "coast guard."[29]

This self-identification raises implications and concerns over the problem of illegal fishing and other criminal acts that have been perpetrated by foreigners off Somali territorial waters. For instance, a 2006 report noted that with the collapse of the central government in the 1990s, Somali waters became a "free-for-all" destination for foreign trolleys and fleets illegally carting away an estimated $300 million worth of seafood each year.[30] It is disturbing that sometimes illegal acts like the dumping of toxic wastes in Somalia were perpetrated with the full knowledge and active participation of European governments. The United Nations Environmental Program (UNEP) corroborates these allegations with a report that radioactive uranium and other hazardous deposits have been found in the Somalia mainland. These materials were carried onto the mainland by the December 2004 tsunami that originated off the coasts of Indonesia.[31]

Thus, when Boyah, a native of Eyl, jokes that he is the chief of the coast guard and that his activities on the high seas are a "legitimate form of taxation levied on behalf of a non-operational government that he represents in spirit, if not law," he makes a valid point that cannot be totally ignored.[32] In whatever way the world will judge the Somali pirates, it is important to consider their own point of view. As several pirates of the Eyle insist, piracy will end when the problem of illegal fishing is fixed and proper compensations paid for toxic wastes. "We are waiting for action."[33]

THE SOMALI PEOPLE

Modern Somalia is made up of 85 percent ethnic Somalis, and the rest are small-minority Bantu, Bravenese, Bajuni, Rerhamar, Eyle, Galgala, Tumal, Yibir, Gaboye, Pizu, Rehanweyn, Reer, Harar, Ogadenis, and Asharaf.[34] The major languages of the people include Somali, the primary language; and Arabic, the language of Islam, which is also one of the four languages in official use. The other official languages are Italian and English, which are widely spoken as a medium of communication to the wider non-Islamic world.[35] In a sense, Somali society was formed as a nation of migrants, but because of the preponderance of the Somali language as both a unifying factor and a marker of ethnicity, it is assumed by outsiders that the nation had a greater degree of national homogeneity than most other African countries. It should not, however, be overlooked that although the ancestors of the Somali came from the Ethiopian Highlands, they were, over time, joined by diverse elements from the Cushitic race, Bantus, Arabs, and a sprinkling of Indians, Italians, and Lebanese.

As elaborated on in Chapter 2, it is difficult to piece together the earliest history of Somalia due to an acute lack of written sources. This makes it a difficult task to accurately pinpoint when the ancestors of present-day Somalia first settled in the area. What historians are doing today is using a variety of sources—including ancient texts; travelogues; personal diaries or journals; oral evidence passed down the generations; and archaeological, linguistic, and anthropological sources—to reconstruct the past as much as practicable.

These sources have revealed that the present inhabitants of the country have an ancient history. This understanding is contrary to previous postulations that have tried to place the Somali homeland in the area surrounding the Red Sea's western coast or even in southern Arabia. For instance, writing in 1912, Ralph E. Drake-Brockman, a British colonial scholar, had speculated that the Somali are a "Hamito-Semitic race" and that their birth could be traced to 696 CE, when one obscure Arab visitor named Darod was shipwrecked on the Majerteen coast.[36] Such speculations are common in the old colonial historiography as the Europeans attempted to ascribe every element of cultural achievement found in Africa to outside migrants.

The new light shed on African history by vital archaeological materials indicates that the modern ancestors of Somalia known to medieval Arab visitors as "Berbere" had settled on the Horn of Africa by 100 CE. The oral tradition claims that the early Somali settlers were part of the Cushitic race, and that they originally came from the Ethiopian Highlands and its surrounding areas. The Somalis are most closely related to the Oromo of Ethiopia and the Afars (Danakili) of Djibouti.[37] If we rely on the linguistic evidence, it suggests a migration from southern Ethiopia no later than the fifth century CE.

However, this hypothesis cannot be taken uncritically because cave paintings, dating back to 9,000 BCE, found in northern Somalia, as well as studies of ancient pyramids, ruined cities, and stone walls confirm that an ancient civilization thrived here at least from the late Paleolithic or Stone Age. This, along with the fact that the ancient Kingdom of Punt once flourished within Somali borders, leads to the conclusion that Nilo-Cushitic migrants had established themselves in the area much earlier than the Bantu migration began off the borders of modern-day eastern Nigeria and western Cameroon c. 2,500–2,000 BCE.[38] It is believed that the Somali people prevented the Bantu and Galla peoples from penetrating Somalia. It is not clear when the Bantu movements reached the upper side of East Africa, but this could probably be somewhere between 1000 and 500 CE. Given the proximity of the Kikuyu of modern Kenya, who are part of the Bantu stock, it may be reasonable to speculate that some elements of Bantu culture may have infiltrated the Somali culture through nomadic movements and through agriculture, religion, and other cultural relationships. The ancestral language of Somalia is Afro-Asiatic, spoken widely from North Africa to the Horn Region.

The Arab population of modern Somalia were latter migrants, some of whom, through their participation in the seaborne trade across the Red Sea, via the Aden Sea, and the Indian Ocean, began to establish permanent settlements in Somalia. By the eighth century, the population of traders from Arabia and Persia had grown remarkably in the coastal cities of Somalia. A good number of the traders were Muslim merchants who had well-established trading connections on the Indian Ocean and the Red Sea. Particularly, cities like Zeila (Zeyla), Mogadishu, and their immediate neighborhoods were swollen by Arab Muslims. Over time, the settlers made Islam the dominant faith in the region. Zeila, once a walled commercial city called Seylac, was popular for its coffee and slave markets; hence it was a favorite destination for foreign merchants and visitors.

POLITICAL STRUCTURE

Somalia is perhaps best identified today as a country without a viable central government. It has been under an endless Interim Transition Government (ITG) with little or no legitimacy in the eyes of the various competing groups in the country. The current order of government must be considered within the historical circumstances under which the African postcolonial state was configured. As fully discussed in Chapter 3, the Somali nation-state was designed by foreign powers without moral consideration for the people; these powers' actions would alter every aspect of the Somali people's lives, including politics.[39]

The indigenous people were traditionally organized in highly decentralized clans, despite the fact that they have developed to widely adopt Somali or *Samaal* as an ethnolinguistic group. There are originally six main family clans: Isaaq, Dir, Hawiye, Darod, Digil, and Rahanwein, based on common ancestry. Each of these is further divided into subclans and lineages or families tied together by blood and loose alliances (Table 1.1).[40]

The size of the clans can range anywhere from 100,000 to 1 million people. The Digil and the Rahanwein, which are agricultural groups, are found mainly in the southern areas between the Juba and Shebelle rivers. The two groups together constitute about 20 percent of the country's population. The more pastoralist clans—Dir, Darod, Isaaq, and Hawiye—represent about 70 percent of the population, while 10 percent of Somalis live in urban centers like Mogadishu, Hargeisa, Berbera, Bossasso, Merca, Kismayo, and Brava. The urban dwellers

Table 1.1. Clan Structure: Major Family Clans

Main Family Clans	Subclans
Dir	Issa, Gadabursi, Bimal
Isaaq	Saad Muse, Issa Muse, Ayub, Habr Yunis, Aidagalla, Arab, Mohamed Abokor, Ibrahim, Muse Abokor, Ahmad (Toljaalo)
Darod	Marehan, Ogaden, Majerteen, Dulbanhante, Warsangeli
Hawiye	Hawadle, Waadan, Habr Gedir, Abgal, Murosade, Gaalgale
Digil	Dabarre, Jiddu, Tunni, Geledi, Garre
Rahanwein	Thirty-three clans in two loose alliances: Maalinweyna, Harien, Helleda, Elai, and others; Gassa Gudda, Hadama, Luwai, Geledi, and others.

are found mostly in Mogadishu, with a population estimated at 2 million in 2002.[41] Nonetheless, constant fighting and population movements have displaced traditional clan territories as more young people cross clan divides in numbers never seen before.

In an indigenous society that was not used to political centralization, the clan constituted the largest unit of political organization for precolonial Somalis. This system of government was supported by the family and lineage organizations renowned for their fierce independence. Membership in a clan usually evokes a deep sense of pride and loyalty in the individual, and this tends to take precedence over country. The system has proved resilient despite centuries of alien influences, as its recent reinventions in both Somaliland and Puntland grow stronger.

The Somali Peninsula and the entire East African coast running from Brava (Baraawe) in southern Somalia to Kilwa in Tanzania were frequented by merchants and businessmen from different continents. Over time, different parts of this commercial emporium came under different rulers, including the shah of Persia, the vassalage of Brava under Portuguese control in the sixteenth century, the Omanis of Zanzibar, the sheriffs of Mocha (Yemen), and the Ottoman Turks. Muslim systems of authority expanded and peaked from the eighteenth century, enduring until the late nineteenth century, but never actually encompassed all parts of the territory at any given time. It was at one point interrupted by the Portuguese, for instance with the vassalage of Brava, which came under Portuguese influence in the sixteenth century.

By 1900, the Somali Peninsula had been divided into four different zones of foreign control made up of three European powers and one African power. The British seized the north central area; the French claimed the northeast (i.e., present-day Djibouti); the Italians appropriated the southern region; and the Ethiopians made claims to Ogaden in the west. Also, the southwest region known as the "Northern Frontier District" was partitioned into British East Africa—now part of modern Kenya.[42]

While the various colonial powers implemented different policies of colonial administration, anticolonial movements grew virulent in Somalia under a radical Muslim cleric, Mahammad Abdille Hassan, who the British identified as "Mad Mullah."[43] Rallying the Somalis to fight against what he branded "Christian infidels," the group soon occupied themselves with the total liberation of Somalia from colonial domination.

Although unsuccessful, Hassan's Pan-Somalia/Pan-Islam ideological movement sowed the seeds of later nationalist consciousness championed by the emergent Somali urban petty bourgeoisie in the post–World War II period. To this end, the first nationalist party, the Somali Youth Club (SYC), was launched in 1943 by the newly educated elite. The club soon metamorphosed into the Somali Youth League (SYL) in 1947, the same year Italy was compelled by the victorious Allies to denounce its right to rule its former colony of Italian Somaliland.[44] Three years later, in 1950, the United Nations granted Italy the right to administer Somalia as a trustee territory for 10 years leading to independence in 1960.[45] From this point onward, the road to independence became a struggle among the interests of the colonial powers, individuals, and local and regional considerations.

When British Somaliland was granted freedom on June 26, 1960, nationalist figures in the country quickly approved of its merger with the UN Trustee Territory, the former Italian Somaliland as advocated by the SYL. The union materialized with the formation of the independent Somali Republic with Dr. Aden Abdullah Osman elected as the republic's first president. Soon after, the optimism that greeted the newly won independence was replaced by disillusionment as several challenges of building a united and strong nation-state confronted the new leaders. Among them were poverty and interclan rivalry. Somalia struggled with this problem until 1969 when Gen. Siad Barre seized power in a military coup. He ushered in a socialist model of leadership that was primarily geared toward creating a new Somali patriotism.

On January 27, 1991, Barre's military dictatorship was overthrown by a rainbow coalition of opposition groups. The groups did not make any solid plans to reconstitute a new government of national unity, and consequently, Somalia exploded into a fratricidal conflict.[46] The United Nations authorized a humanitarian mission coded "Operation Restore Hope" to reestablish hope to a desperate people. Despite the UN efforts, Somalia sank deeper into a ruinous dance of destiny. Chapter 7 offers a detailed examination of the dynamics in which the humanitarian intervention turned into a nightmare for all involved. At this point, it is difficult to predict the likely end result of the dozens of irredentist and secessionist movements currently in operation within and outside Somalia's borders, but some theories will be offered in the last chapter. The discussions to come can only make sense with a greater knowledge of the Somali national character.

NATIONAL CHARACTER

"National character" is a subjective term denoting some observed cultural behaviors in a society without consideration of individual differences. As an analytical tool, it is used to describe certain lasting behavior patterns and unique lifestyles found among the populations of a particular ethnic or national group. The location, geography, history, religion, economy and mode of production, immigration and emigration, experience of conflicts and wars, culture, colonial rule, politics, and so on have all contributed to shaping what could be described today as the Somali national character. In a sense, discourses of national characters are concerned with national identity. Identities are invented, reconstructed, and are therefore fluid, dynamic, and complex. Benedict Anderson and others have often argued that identity is an imagined construct.[47] Yet identity or national character is real because what a people think they are, and how outsiders perceive them—whether this perception held by the outsider is real or not—go a long way in shaping the nature of interactions between the outsider and the insider. In regard to Somalis, this is very much the case.

Given their predominantly nomadic lifestyle, the Somalis could be described as a people with a high capacity for endurance and adaptation. Drake-Brockman observed over a century ago that the life of the Somali in the interior prepares them for "enduring great hardships, and recovering from severe wounds in a truly wonderful manner."[48] British colonial officer Capt. Malcolm McNeill, who commanded a Somali garrison in pursuit of the "Mad Mullah" in the early 1900s, admitted the never-die spirit of the Somali: "As a soldier he is a splendid marcher, requiring but little transport and capable of enduring great fatigue."[49]

As the Igbo often say, "migrant people harbor no grudge."[50] With this philosophy in mind, the Somali, who are always on the move by nature of their environment and mode of production, are typically humble and respectful to others. At the same time, individuals who exhibit deep respect for others can also be volatile. Being on the go all the time means being ready to face challenges, as threats may unfold along the way.

This brings up the need to train the child as a warrior. Nomads are expected to confront any type of danger with bravery. The cultural expectation on the male not to shy away from confrontation has been one of the tests of manhood in the indigenous society. This way of life has loomed large in the recent conflicts and wars since the 1990s, manifesting in the form of warlordism, sectarianism, Islamic militancy, piracy, armed robberies, and violent reactions to political currents in the country.

Another crucial national characteristic of the Somali is his independent spirit. Writing in 1912, Drake-Brockman also noted that: "The

Somali's great independence is hereditary, and can be traced from early times, but it is also largely due to his environment."[51] This sense of independence could be linked to attachment of individuals to the clan system, which is also revealed in the common avoidance of Western-style centralization of authority. Constant population movements and an unsettled lifestyle reinforce loyalty to the clan at the cost of strong patriotism. In other words, identity articulated in the context of the clan has endured despite a common heritage of Somali language, which would ordinarily bring about a strong Pan-Somali consciousness.

In light of this, Somalia's current state of political factionalism and lack of common unity offer a unique study in ethnonationalistic identity. This is more fascinating because Somalia is the one country in Africa that comes closest to having a common linguistic heritage, which often serves as the glue that holds a people together as a homogenous society. But the society is too steeped in "clan familism"—that is, a persistent orientation to the economic interests of the nuclear family.[52] As this phenomenon continues to manifest in the form of clan and subclan rivalries, it demands that scholars take a closer look at the concept of ethnicity, hence the argument made elsewhere contra the ethnonationalist paradigm that posits that ethnicity is the root of nationalism and that true nations are ethnic nations.[53] The example of Somalia reveals that ethnic conflict is not solely a problem of multiethnic states; it is also a problem of homogenous groups where political practices fail to take into account the people's inherited culture and sensibilities, especially where poverty is common.

Given that Somalia has had long-running contacts with peoples of diverse ethnicities and races, including Africans, Asians, and Europeans, it has blended diverse cultural practices. Cultural diffusions or rather exchanges on the Somali Peninsula have been ongoing for several millennia. Among others, Ethiopians, Kenyans, Serbians, Arabs, Yemenis, Indians, and Persians have greatly influenced everyday life in Somalia. For instance, the Islamic ideology brought by Arab merchants and clerics has been crucial in the molding of what we know as Somali people today. Although they retain some pre-Islamic traditions, the modern Somalis, who are now predominantly Muslims, claim noble ancestry from the Banu Hashim family of the Prophet Muhammad. The mainstream believers follow a sect in Sunni Islam known as the Sufi school of belief.

The Qadiriyya, Salihiyya, and Ahmadiyya sects in Islam have significantly contributed to determining the contemporary Somali character. In accordance with Islamic practices, for example, adherents try to refrain from such dietary habits as the consumption of alcohol, pork, or any meat prepared by non-Muslims. While Western culture has infiltrated several aspects of Somali society, there is still a strong respect for the indigenous values now dominated by Islamic traditions. For example, women are expected to dress modestly and wear headdresses while in public. As in most Muslim societies, Somali men usually wear turbans and long white garments.

Somalis are also naturally gifted with scholastic intellect.[54] They are intuitive and can easily discern one's inner minds within a short time of engaging them in a discussion. Perhaps the latter was the trait that Richard Burton observed among the nomads in 1856 when he wrote that the Somalis often speak in ways "so idiomatic that Arabs settled for years amongst the Somal cannot understand them, although perfectly acquainted with the conversational style."[55]

It is important to reiterate that the perception one may hold about the national character of a people is often subjective and hardly represents the individual differences found among the group. Also, whether the perceptions are positive or negative, they do not necessarily mean anything unique that is not found in any human society. Therefore, the Somali national character is nothing unique. It is produced by peculiar circumstances of history, memory, and environment. As they maintain contacts with their African neighbors as well as non-Africans through diplomatic relations, refugee movements, commercial, tourist, economic, technological, and military exchanges, the Somalis' culture, identity, and national characters will continue to unfold in response to the strength and exertions of both indigenous and alien practices.

NOTES

1. It is important to note that an accurate population count in the past three decades has been difficult given the problems of forced migrations and refugee movements caused by endless civil conflicts and wars, famine, and drought.

2. For a detailed read on this, see National Archives Kew (hereafter NAK), CAB/120/64 Somaliland Protectorate: Exchange of Territory with Ethiopia, December 22, 1953. See also NAK, CAB/24/256, Italo-Ethiopian Dispute, 17–18.

3. See R. R. Vargas and M. Alim, "Soil Survey of a Selected Study Area in Somaliland," FAO-SWALIM Project Report L-05, Nairobi, Kenya: February 2007, 3; and Thomas Schlüter, *Geological Atlas of Africa with Notes on Stratigraphy, Tectonics, Economic Geology, Geohazards, and Geosites of Each Country*, with contributions by Martin H. Trauth (Berlin and New York: Springer, 2006), 226–29.

4. See Glynn Llywelyn Isaac and Elizabeth R. McCown, eds., *Human Origins: Louis Leakey and the East African Evidence* (Menlo Park, CA: W. A. Benjamin, 1976), 568.

5. NAK, CAB 129/85, Somaliland Protectorate and the Horn of Africa, July 25, 1956, 1–19.

6. Mohammed Farah Aidid and Satya Pal Ruhela, *Somalia from the Dawn of Civilization to the Modern Times* (Jangpura, New Dehli: Vikas Publishing House, 1994), 5.

7. Vargas and Alim, "Soil Survey," 3.

8. See B. W. Andrezjewski, "Notes on Inshā' Al-Mukātibat 'Asrīyna Fī Al-Lughah Al-Sūmāliya by Muhammad 'Abdi Makāhil (Somali in Arabic Script)," in Andrezjewski Mss., Manuscript Department, the Lilly Library, Indiana University, Bloomington.

9. Richard Francis Burton, *First Footsteps in East Africa, or an Exploration of Harar* (London: Longman, Brown, Green, and Longmans, 1856), 115. See also Said S. Samatar, "Somalia Is a Nation of Poets," interview with Gloria Teal, Public Broadcasting Service (PBS) (Arlington, VA), May 18, 2010.

10. Samatar, Interview with PBS, May 18, 2010.

11. Toyin Falola, *A Mouth Sweeter Than Salt* (Ann Arbor: University of Michigan, 2004), 3–9.

12. See, for instance, F. D. P. Wicker, "The Road to Punt," *Geographical Journal* 164, no. 2 (July 1998): 155–67.

13. See Captain Malcolm McNeill, *In Pursuit of the "Mad Mullah" (Mohamed Abdullah): Services and Sport in the Somali Protectorate . . . with a Chapter by Lieutenant A. C. H. Dixon* (London: C. Arthur Pearson, 1902). McNeill's book is all about his insatiable appetite for game hunting of wildlife for pleasure.

14. Robert B. Payne, "Birds of the Horn of Africa: Ethiopia, Eritrea, Djibouti, Somalia, and Socotra," *Wilson Journal of Ornithology* 121, no. 4 (December 2009): 853–55.

15. S. M. Hassig, *Somalia* (Singapore: Times Edition, 1997), 13.

16. See, for instance, Ismail Abdi Samatar, "Structural Adjustment as Development Strategy? Bananas, Boom, and Poverty in Somalia," *Economic Geography* 69, no.1 (1993): 25.

17. F. Jeffress Ramsay, *Global Studies: Africa*, 9th ed. (Guilford, CT: McGraw-Hill/Dushkin Company, 2001), 71.

18. Ramsay, *Africa*, 70–71.

19. Ibid.

20. UNDP (United Nations Development Program), *Human Development Report 2001 Somalia* (Nairobi: UNDP, 2001), 132.

21. University of Minnesota Academic HealthCare Center, Minnesota's Somali Community (Minneapolis, 2001), 6.

22. Anna Lindley, *Somali Country Study: A Part of the Report on Informal Remittance System in Africa, Caribbean and Pacific (ACP) Countries (Re. RO2CS008)* (Oxford: ESRC Center on Migration, Policy and Society [COMPAS], University of Oxford, 2005), 6; Economist Intelligence Unit (EIU), *Country Report: Ethiopia, Eritrea, Somalia and Djibouti* (London: The Economist Intelligent Unit, 2002).

23. See United Nations, *Statistics Pocket Book: Somalia* (New York: United Nations Statistics Division, May 2010).

24. NovaTech, "The ICT Africa Marketplace: Information & Communication Technologies, East Africa and the Indian Ocean—Country Profile: Somalia" (Brussels: Proeinvest, 2005), 5.

25. See Tristan McConnell, "Foreigners Are the Real Pirates, Says Former Somali Fisherman," *The Times* (London), June 12, 2009.

26. Jeremy Hsu, "Somali Pirate Exchange Lets Investors Bet on Hitting a Ransom Jackpot," *Popular Science*, Dec. 2, 2009: 1.

27. Jeffrey Gentleman, "Somali Pirates Tell Their Side: They Want Only Money," *New York Times*, Sept. 30, 2008.

28. Joshua Keating, "Somali Pirates Driving up Kenya Real Estate Prices," *Foreign Policy* (Washington, DC), January 4, 2010.

29. Jay Bahadur, "'I'm Not a Pirate, I'm the Saviour of the Sea': Who Are the Pirate Bands Menacing Commercial and Toruist Shipping off Somalia?" *The Times* (London), April 16, 2009.

30. Ishaan Tharoor, "How Somalia's Fishermen Became Pirates," *Time*, April 19, 2009.

31. *United Nations Environmental Program (UNEP)*, "National Rapid Environmental Desk Assessment—Somalia" (Hafun), January 8, 2005.

32. Bahadur, "'I'm Not a Pirate."

33. Ibid.

34. See Danish Immigration Service, "Report on Minority Groups in Somalia September 17–24, 2000" (Copenhagen: September 24, 2000), 7.

35. NAK, Records created or inherited by the Home Office, Ministry of Home Security, and Related Bodies (hereafter HO), 421/2 1986–2000, 1.

36. Ralph E. Drake-Brockman, *British Somaliland* (London: Hurst & Blackett Ltd, 1912), 68.

37. Even Drake-Brockman admitted this similarity in philology but then erred by concluding that the Gallas of Abyssinia along with the Somali were of Semitic origin. See *British Somaliland*, 68–69.

38. Malcolm Guthrie, "Some Speculations in the Prehistory of the Bantu Languages," *Journal of African History* 3, no. 2 (1962): 273–82; Roland Oliver and Brian M. Fage, "The Emergence of Bantu Africa," in J. D. Fage and Roland Oliver (eds.), *The Cambridge History of Africa* vol. 2 (Cambridge and New York: Cambridge University Press, 1975–1986), 342–409.

39. For a disturbing read of this thoughtlessness, see NAK CAB/24/256, file marked "Secret C. P. 161 (35)," 1–9. Here, a committee appointed by the British Secretary of State for European Affairs categorically submitted in their report that "The Committee restricted itself to a study [of Ethiopia's conflict with Italy] from the narrow standpoint of the British material interests in and near Ethiopia." Such narrow interests guided the colonial powers' engagement in Africa.

40. NAK, HO 421/2, Annex B, 20.

41. NAK, HO 421/2, 1; United Kingdom Home Office, UK Home Office, Immigration and Nationality Directorate: Country Assessment—Somalia, October, 2002, 4.

42. NAK, CAB/24/256, 6–14.

43. McNeill, *In Pursuit*, 1–4.

44. NAK, CAB 129/8, Policy towards Ethiopia: Future of the Somali Territory, March 9, 1946, 1–3.

45. NAK, HO 421/2, 2.

46. Ibid., 4.

47. Benedict Richard O'Gorman Anderson, *Imagined Community: Reflections on the Origin and Spread of Nationalism* (London and New York: Verso, 1991), esp. 33, 145.

48. Drake-Brockman, *British Somaliland*, 97.

49. McNeill, *In Pursuit*, 267.

50. I got this common saying from the elders of my Achi (Igbo) village of southeastern Nigeria.

51. Drake-Brockman, *British Somaliland,* 102.

52. Edward C. Banfield, *The Moral Basis of a Backward Society* (New York: Free Press, 1967).

53. See Jack Forbes, "Do Tribes Have Rights? The Question of Self-Determination for Small Nations," *Journal of Human Relations* 18 no. 1 (1970): 670–79.

54. I wish to state that this is based on my personal observation and association with them.

55. Burton, *First Footsteps in East Africa,* 115.

2

Precolonial States and Societies

Three correlated ideas are central to an understanding of Somali precolonial history. These are Somalia's African origins, its location at a strategic gateway to the outside world, and the people's relationships with the environment. First, the Somali share a common history of origin, culture, and language borrowings with neighboring African groups, while systematically integrating alien cultures brought by visitors from outside, particularly those from across the Red Sea and the Aden Sea. Second, and closely related, is the country's location at a major international crossroads, which created a complex pattern of interrelationships and cultural exchanges among the various groups. This multicultural amalgam imposed a premium on the Somali identity. Third, the nature of the people's interaction with the environment explains the rise of culture and the trajectories its sociopolitical institutions have assumed today.

Given these considerations, Somalia's precolonial states and societies cannot be studied in isolation; they must be considered along with those of the various non-Somali societies that make up the Horn of Africa. This chapter focuses on the origins, migrations, and the precolonial states and societies of the geopolitics stretching from the coastal shores of the Red Sea and Gulf of Aden in the north and moving southward through the western borders with Ethiopia down to the fringes of Lake Victoria bordered by Ethiopia, Uganda, Kenya, and Tanzania. This approach will allow for a deeper appreciation of the relationship between Somalia and its African neighbors, including the well-known East African coastal societies that sprouted up as centers of international trade in ancient times and continued to rise in number and strength from Mogadishu in Somalia, to Sofola in Mozambique until the early twentieth century when the European colonial presence led to their decline.

One purpose of this chapter is to examine the relationship between the Somalis and the neighboring societies of this region and how this impacted the rise of the Somali as a distinct group, their movement into the present homeland, and the rise of cultures that over time saw the emergence of the famous coastal city-states. The most notable of these city-states like Mogadishu and Opone were contemporaries of the other cosmopolitan towns like Barawa, Mombasa, Gedi, Pate, Malindi (Kenya), Zanzibar Island, Kilwa (Tanzania), and Sofala (Mozambique). Their inhabitants exchanged items of trade and material cultures, and competed for prominence and survival during the flowering of the Afro-Arabo Swahili civilization.

ORIGINS

The old historiography originating from the colonial period has attempted to explain Somalia's past as the result of cultural diffusions from the Arabian Peninsula, and that particularly started to take shape from the arrival of the Arab Muslims on the Horn of Africa in the late sixth and early seventh centuries.[1] Historians now know that the people's rich history and culture dates back to several millennia, although details of that past have remained blurred as a result of the pervasive nomadic mode of production, which hardly supports solid and stable state institutions and the cosmopolitan lifestyle that comes with continuity and adaptation. Nomadic lifestyle was engendered and sustained by both the arid nature of the environment and the characteristic inclement climate. This makes Somalia a rare but fascinating paradox of nature. Although flanked from the north through south by the longest stretch of coastline on the continent, and with two major rivers cutting through the southern parts of the country, most of Somalia is arid land with scorching temperatures year round.

This condition, more than anything else, has made a pastoral lifestyle both endemic and systemic.

At present, no indigenous form of writing has been associated with the pastoralists beyond ordinary speculations about the existence of such culture in the ancient past. The Somalis do have a rich culture of oral traditions such as poetry and literature, which makes deciphering the details of their historical past no easier. Much of the existing accounts, sometimes encountered in forms of songs, poems, proverbs, legends, and fables—and that speak to genealogies of people, life and living, religion and wonders of this world—have been adapted over time, as they are handed down from one generation to the next. This is especially with the strong influence of alien cultures, particularly Islam, which have substantially colored the people's memory. While the oraltures are significant as they provide some narratives on the origins and movement of the people and their material cultures, historians must exercise discretion in relying on these accounts. When used along with more credible archaeological, linguistic, and anthropological sources, oral literature provides significant insights into the dark past.

In other words, historical memory, with its obvious shortcomings, has been critical in preserving elements of Somalia's history and cultural identity. For instance, where earlier speculations, in the familiar but now rejected Hamitic idiom, had tried to put Somali origins outside the continent, the people's tradition claims that their ancestors were an offshoot of the Cushitic people now believed to be indigenous to the Ethiopian Highlands. The Cushitic race comprises the Oromo, Afar (or Danakil), and Somali. Corroborating this assertion in 1957, a report by colonial officials on future policy in Somaliland and the Horn of Africa accurately described Ethiopia as "a polyglot kingdom containing peoples some of whom have affinities of race, religion and social habits with the Somalis."[2] All of the ethnolinguistic groups in the Cushitic family have been identified as part of the Afro-Asiatic language family in Africa.[3] Other members of the language family are Hausa (spoken in West Africa, especially in northern Nigeria), Berber (the Maghrib), Amharic (Ethiopia), Arabic, and Hebrew (Middle East).

Closely considered, the linguistic evidence reveals that a people's genealogy could be difficult to retrace because migrations and distance crossings within and across ethnic and racial lines have been a constant part of human society. It is also essential to note that migrations are not usually a one-directional movement but multidirectional. Across time and space, migrants have lent elements of their inherited culture to their host societies while adopting from or being assimilated into the local culture. Thus, any historical speculation premised on language alone could be misleading, especially when poorly construed. By a process of cleave and compare, new languages have emerged as offshoots of parent tongues—meaning that hybridization, cultural inventions, and other forms of inventiveness are as old as mankind.

In terms of the Somali genesis, linguistic and cultural studies have linked them to a sublanguage group, the Omo-Tana. This tongue is spoken today in Djibouti, Ethiopia, Somalia, and Kenya.[4] It is speculated that the Omo-Tana, who are also called Sam (after their mythical ancestor Samaale), broke away from the original Cushitic family in the first millennium BCE—that is, the period encompassing 1000–1 BCE. The original homeland of the Sam, or rather their known point of dispersal, has been traced back to the confluence between the Omo and Tana rivers, from which the name Omo-Tana derives. This is the territory running from Lake Turkana in northern Kenya and stretching eastward to the Indian Ocean. It is believed that the ancestors of the Somalis followed the trail of the Tana River to the Indian Ocean coastal shores prior to the first century CE. On the coast, the group, sometimes referred to as the proto-Sam, further broke into two; one of the splinter groups moved farther north, settling in southern Somalia, while the other half (the Boni) remained on the island areas of Kiunga and Lamu Archipelago, close to the northern coasts of Kenya near the border with Somalia.

The frontier group that first entered southern Somalia from northern Kenya lived a more settled life as exemplified in their development of a mixed economy based on agricultural cultivation and animal grazing. This rural economy still prevails in the region. From here, another group moved even further north, taking up settlements on the contiguous parts of the peninsula extending into the Arabian Sea. This group has been designated Samaale, or Samaal, in recognition of the legendary forebear of the main Somali clan families from whose name "Somalia" was coined in 1415 by the Ethiopian emperor Yeshaq in a gloating song of thanksgiving for his resounding victory over the Ifat kingdom.

Subsequent movements in search of pastureland took the Samaale further to different directions in the north. According to the German linguist Bernd Heine, the migrants had successfully occupied the vast Ogaden (Ogaadeen) plains to the west, as well as traversing the southern shore of the Red Sea by the first century (100) CE.[5]

This reconstructed account of Somali origins and population movements leaves much to be desired. First, the account says nothing about whether the areas the early Somali migrants moved into were uninhabited before their arrival. One is curious to know because the history of human origins and subsequent out-of-Africa migrations across the Red Sea's Babel-Mandeb straits (and other exit channels along the northern coastal plains) about 50,000 years ago suggests a long history of movements predating the Somali population migrations. Therefore, in any attempt to reconstruct the Somali genesis, it would be helpful to understand who the Somali frontier group may have met along the migration routes and the results of such encounters. The questions arise as to what circumstances welcomed the Somali frontier people on arrival? Who did they displace, conquer, or assimilate? Or who assimilated them? More puzzling is that the timing of the Somali population arrival in their present homeland, as propounded by scholars in light of the 1970s studies (predicated on linguistic) evidence, is clearly not supported by a 2002 archaeological discovery in northern Somalia.

Rather, results of the 2002 study by a team of French archaeologists reveal that one of the earliest evidences of human society and culture in the region was preserved in the cave paintings at Laas Gaal complex. Within the complex located in a nomadic village on the Naso-Hablod hills, outside the city of Hargeisa (Hargaysa), are found ruined houses, caves, and rock shelters.

Scientists date the site and the drawings holding one of the earliest known rock cultures in Africa to somewhere between 15,000 and 8,000 BCE—indicating the presence of the late Paleolithic Age and early Neolithic culture in the region. This finding is consistent with the oldest evidence of burial customs in the entire Horn of Africa region. The age of these tombs has been put at around the fourth millennium BCE. Additionally, the stone tools unearthed at the Jalelo site in northern Somalia remain the most important proof of the widespread rise of the Paleolithic cultures in both the Eastern and Western Hemispheres.

As the archaeologist Peter Robertshaw explains, the Doian culture and the Hargeisan culture flourished at these two Stone Age sites with their relevant industries.[6] Underneath each of the rock paintings were found ancient inscriptions that archaeologists have not been able to decipher. The paintings depict a giraffe, antelopes, a dog, and stocky humans who appear to be raising their hands before humpless cows with lyre-shaped horns. The cows appear to be dressed in ceremonial attire. Studies have revealed that this breed of cows with long horns were perhaps first bred in North Africa around 5,000 BCE but are today only found in West Africa.[7]

The rock paintings offer rare insights into the late Paleolithic or Neolithic Age in Somalia, while at the same time raising more questions about Somali origins, migrations, and settlements. First, they tell something about the high quality of the arts produced by the specialized craftsmen who lived in this period. This fact is corroborated by the condition of the drawings and paintings, which have retained their clear outlines and strong colors in spite of the corrosions of weather, age, wars, and other forms of human activities and natural conditions. Secondly, some scholars have interpreted positions represented on the rock paintings to mean that the people were worshippers of the cattle. Of course, it is easy to mistake actions and intentions in a picture of this nature; the truth is that in every generation in human societies, the people of that epoch are moved to represent themselves in paintings, murals, pictures, along with those things that held meanings in their immediate environment.

For the Laas Geel Neolithic society, some of those things that were highly valued obviously included domestication of animals and livestock grazing, including cows, dogs, antelopes, giraffes, camels, and so on. It is telling that the value placed on cattle has endured today among the Somali nomad communities in particular, and among the other ethnic groups found today in the Greater Horn of Africa and the Great Lakes regions—embracing Tanzania, Malawi, Zambia, Democratic Republic of the Congo (DRC), Rwanda, Burundi, and Uganda. Indeed, as a team of archaeologists led by X. Gutherz has noted, the rock drawings are among the oldest in Africa and demonstrate that even though ideologies have changed over thousands of years, the pastoralist way of life continues.[8]

Third, from the drawings it could also be deciphered that the physique of the inhabitants of this area was originally stocky—that is, they had a solid and heavy build. This is in sharp contrast with the leaner and taller Somalis of today. In connection with population movements and settlements, could this mean that the stocky men depicted in the rock painting had already settled here before the arrival of the Samaale frontier group? Or were they the same? If the former is the case, the previous inhabitants must have been either displaced or assimilated by the Somali upon their arrival. If the second is the case, then the Somali presence in the area must have happened long before the first millennium CE as projected by the German linguist Heine in the 1970s. It is reasonable to speculate that the Somali migrants had met an autochthonous people and either assimilated them, or were assimilated by them, or they succeeded in wiping out their hosts through acts of violence or by some kind of mysterious disease such an epidemic. Alternatively, but a more likely possibility, is that the leaner body type we see among the Somali today is a result of a crossbreeding with the autochthonous people. If the alternative hypothesis is accepted, it would mean that there was a primordial group, the Laas Geel who at least occupied the northern Somalia areas prior to movement of the frontier Somali elements into the region.

Fourth, the ceremonial garb the people adorned their cows with as represented in the paintings indicates an advanced, sophisticated, and affluent culture consistent with a more settled society. Even the necks of the cows were embellished with an ornament that has the look of plastron, a metal usually fashioned from the flat part of a turtle or tortoise.

Altogether, the material culture assembled indicates that the early Neolithic people of this region had enjoyed a more settled life than the present inhabitants, whose lives have been ravaged by drought and unending wars. While the details of the Laas Geel inhabitants' past may remain obscure for now, what is clearer is that approximately in the ancient era, the coastal areas of the Somali Peninsula were a prominent part of a prosperous early trading emporium that linked up inhabitants of several coastal enclaves with the visitors from Eurasia. One of these societies was recorded in ancient Egyptian sources as the Land of Punt.

ANCIENT LAND OF PUNT

Archaeological studies of ancient architectures excavated in Somalia in the form of ruined cities, pyramids, mausoleums, stonewalls, and unglazed shards of pottery, along with the ruined wall construction at Wargaade, Somalia, are some of the strong evidence of an early sophisticated culture that at one time thrived on the Somali peninsula.[9] The studies have also revealed that the ancient Puntites developed a system of writing that is yet to be decoded by scientists. Further, the results of the various studies have revealed that Punt was one among the other ancient trading city-states that were engaged in commercial relations with the ancient Egyptians, Mycenaeans, and Greeks since the second millennium BCE. The identification of the coastal cities, among them Punt, is one of the first substantiations of settled towns in the region. These city-states prospered not only because of their central locations, but because the fertile land around them allowed for the growth of plants such as the boswellia tree from which frankincense is tapped, and the commiphora tree, which produces myrrh resin from which the exotic ointment myrrh is extracted.[10]

The location and descriptions of these cities have led some scholars to variously believe that the mysterious kingdom of Punt was located in "either modern Mozambique or Somalia; or Sinai Peninsula, or Yemen, or somewhere in western Asia where Israel, Lebanon and Syria now lie."[11] Reporting in May 2010 on the conclusions of a more recent archaeological study, David Perlman declared that Punt "must have existed in eastern North Africa—either in the land where Ethiopia and Eritrea confront each other, or east of the Upper Nile in the low land area of eastern Sudan."[12] Among the leading Egyptologists of the American Research Center in Egypt who met in Oakland, California, in 2010 and endorsed the results of this research was Kathryn A. Bard. A well-respected Boston University Egyptologist, Bard has been focusing her research efforts for over a decade solely on the Red Sea harbor of Wadi Gawassi, from where it is believed the royal sailing expeditions were dispatched to Punt and returned with precious cargo.

If this more recent idea is upheld, it will stand on their heads all of what previous studies and speculations have believed about the ancient kingdom of Punt. But further studies are needed to conclusively affirm this new finding on Punt's location. Until then, the previous inconclusive but strong evidence is still relevant and worthy of consideration. These studies tend to support the assumption that somewhere in modern Somalia or the contiguous lands bordering it was Punt. Most of the descriptions have placed the location of the Punt kingdom somewhere south of Egypt, near the Red Sea, which modern Somalia and Djibouti would closely fit. Originally, the bordering country of Djibouti was an outpost of Somalia, and its proximity to both Sudan to the north and Eritrea to the south do not completely rule it out from the new area under study. Additionally, the coastal city-states produced and traded significant amounts of the precious goods that were associated with the people of Punt.

A question that has lingered for a long time is what has made the story of Punt a classic mythical tale?[13] A probable reason might be connected with its lack of a writing culture or rather the failure of modern scholars to interpret the ancient people's signs and scripts. Another possibility is that Punt was a small kingdom, perhaps only a trading enclave in the manner of Carthage, whose rulers did not have any need to acquire territories or expand its own in the mode of either the ancient Egyptians or Ethiopians.

As scholars continue to search for details about the actual site of Punt and its cultural achievements, what appears to be less in contention is that the Puntites traded spices, gold, ebony, myrrh, short-horned cattle, ivory, frankincense, and other valuable goods with the Egyptians, Phoenicians, Romans, Babylonians, Chinese, Indians, and other merchants that frequented the ancient coastal towns of East Africa.[14] The Egyptians left a description of Punt, which they also called Poun, Pwenet, or Pwene—that is, the "Kingdom of the Gods" due to the amount of precious goods it produced, particularly those crucial for Egypt's religious rituals.

Evidence of paintings found in Egypt indicates that Punt's first contacts with Egypt dates back to 2,500 BCE during the Fifth Dynasty when Pharaoh Sahure (r. 2,487–2,475) of the Old Kingdom sent a large fleet on a trading mission to Nubia and Punt to procure some of the important products and materials needed for religious and ceremonial functions.[15] The trading relations continued over the centuries until about a millennium later, when Queen Hatshepsut of the Eighteenth Dynasty began her reign of Egypt and desired to create a garden temple. In order to accomplish this, she sent a large fleet to Punt, at a time when the Puntites were ruled by King Parahu and Queen Ati. The successful expedition returned to Egypt with a tremendous amount of goods, including myrrh, malachite, and electrum. The expedition was recorded in reliefs and hieroglyphics at Deir el Bahari, which depicted the land of Punt and some of its products. It was also recorded that the kingdom was under the rule of a king and queen, whom Amelia Edwards described in an 1891 study as the "Queen Elizabeth of Egyptian history."[16] These reliefs are some of the very few remaining records of Punt available to historians today.[17]

Another major contribution of the ancient Somali was their domestication of the one-humped camel (*dromedary*), which revolutionized the land-borne trade in Africa (particularly the Trans-Saharan commerce between West and North Africa), somewhere around the third and second millennia BCE. Prior to the introduction of the camel, which some sources claim reached Egypt in 1,600 BCE and subsequently spread to Libya, the Maghrib, and the Western Sahara; pack animals like the horse, oxen, donkey, and other beasts of burden were employed in the trade with varied but limited results. This corroborates ancient sources, such as Herodotus's account that the camel was domesticated in southern Arabia and was first brought to the continent through Somalia from where it traveled north to Egypt. Herodotus recorded the use of 10,000 camels by the Persian ruler Xerxes I (r. 519–465 BCE) and his army in the Greco-Persian war of 480 BCE.[18] Although Herodotus may have overstated the figure, Xerxes' army most likely had brought some of these animals along when they previously intruded into Egypt in 484 BCE.

Members of a Somali family transport their goods on camels. (Corel)

Meanwhile, what is not disputed by any strong evidence is that the camel diffused into the Maghrib from the northeast. Whether the camel was brought straight from the Maghrib to the Western Sahara or, as some sources suggest, was brought by the Tuareg nomads direct from the northeast (Libya or Somalia) to the Lake Chad area is still in dispute.[19] Perhaps the critical utility of the camel in arid terrains and their acquaintance with this animal for centuries made the Somali gave it special prestige in their culture. Writing in 1901, Captain Malcolm McNeill of the British army noted that the Somalis believe in "camel worship." According to McNeill, "camels are, in fact, his fetish and his god, and their acquisition seems to be his main object in life."[20]

CLASSICAL AND MEDIEVAL PERIODS

Other sources of important information on the East African coastal peoples and the seaborne trade in the ancient and premodern era were left by an anonymous ancient Greek sailor, who wrote his *Periplus of the Erythraean Sea* in the first century CE, and Cosmas Indicopleustes ("who sailed to India"), whose book was entitled *The Christian Topography of Cosmas an Egyptian Monk* (547 CE).[21] Both books are rare resource documents depicting eyewitness accounts of the East African coastal city-states, including those located in the territories of modern Somalia. Apart from the well-known enclaves like Mombassa, some of the ancient city-states like Opone, Mundus, Malao, Mosylon, Sarapion, and Tabae, and others were integrated in a profitable trading network drawing merchants from Greece, Egypt, Phoenicia, Persia, Saba, Nabataea, and the Roman Empire. Therefore, one can assert that both the *Periplus* and *The Christian Topography*, which contains a chapter on "Trade in Ethiopia," in 547 CE were the very few books that first documented the importance of Somali coastal trading cities. Both sources agree that a good number of the cities were located in the northern region of Somalia, and this has been supported by contemporary archaeological research.[22]

In one interpretation, an anonymous Greek author (then a resident of Alexandria, Egypt) stated in a reported speech that "the city of Opone is said to have traded spices and slaves with Egypt." Although recorded as a third-party account, the evidence contributes a strong voice to the speculation that Punt was actually located within the territories of modern Somalia or thereabout.[23]

The available sources further reveal that the ancient Somali traders employed a locally made ship called the *beden* to transport their cargo from one port to the other. After the Roman conquest of the kingdom of Nabata in 25 BCE and their subsequent naval deployment to Aden to curb piracy, Arab merchants, upset by the Roman military presence in the region, resolved to censor Indian traders from trading in the free port cities of the Arabian Peninsula. The embargo was intended also as a punishment for Somali merchants who reaped huge profits from cinnamon brought by Indian merchants. As one of the best-guarded secrets of the Red Sea trade, the Romans and the Greeks had long been misled by Somali traders to believe that the Somali Peninsula was the source of cinnamon. The reality is that the Somali merchants imported cinnamon from India and China and then repackaged it for export to markets in North Africa, Europe, and the Near East. Following the Arab embargo, trade on the Somali end of the Peninsula, which was free from Roman control, continued as usual, with the Somali enjoying some advantages.

Another significant contribution of both the *Periplus* and *The Christian Topography* is what historians know today about the Somali past as well as the wider economic history of the East African coast, which is the mention of the Barbaria (Berbera), the term used for the modern northern city of Berbera. Cosmas particularly referred to "the city of Barbaria [Berbera], lying along the Ocean ... [as] the frankincense country."[24] The Greek sailor's account also noted that the East African coastal trading enclaves lacked a central government and functioned as city-states. This information resonates with our understanding of the precolonial African politics in general and that of modern Somali in particular having an independent-minded, clan/kinship basis of authority resistant to the organized/centralized authority system of a modern society.[25]

Precolonial government was primarily organized at the level of the clan. There was never a single, centralized government that ran the entire region designated today as the Somali country. Each clan was governed by its own set of rules and regulations. Clans consisted mainly of family members and were often democratic. As I. M. Lewis points out, all adult males partook in the decision-making process as councilors and politicians.[26] Chiefly figures were elected by either the people or a selected council of elders. In turn, often elders were elected or selected from among the highly respected in the community because of their assumed wisdom. The common practice in precolonial Africa was that by virtue of their superior chronological age, the elders of the clan had more wisdom and knowledge than the younger aspiring leaders. Another key element of the clan's self-government was intraclan and interclan alliances. These friendships were forged through marriage or other, more subtle ways like blood oaths or filial loyalty. In times of emergency, the people's volunteer army was created to tackle the common enemy. The army disbanded once the issue was taken care of. In other words, most matters were resolved from within. However, effective conflict resolution was contingent on the nature of the conflict or the terms and strength of existing associations a clan may have generated.

MEDIEVAL COASTAL CITIES

One of the major episodes that dominated the course of history on the coastal areas of East Africa in the medieval era was the presence of Arabs and their new religion of Islam. Islam was founded by the Prophet Muhammad in 610 CE, in the month of Ramadan (the ninth or holy month of fasting) when the Prophet of Allah first received a series of revelations that led to the rise of the new creed. Its vintage position on the Horn of Africa with access to the contiguous seas placed the Somali people in constant interactions with Arab and Persian traders and immigrants. Some of the migrants began to take up permanent residence in the coastal cities as the international commercial exchanges expanded and became more profitable. By the ninth century CE, these Arabs and Persians had either created or contributed to the development of new trading enclaves, which continued to flourish even as they were caught up with the Age of Islamic expansion when the new ideas and belief systems infiltrated into the area and gradually became a definitive ideological force.

In reality, the history of Islam on the Horn of Africa goes back to the early days of the new religion. According to Ethiopian sources, the first Muslims to enter the African continent in 615 CE were the Prophet Muhammad's immediate family, and other companions comprising a total of 83 families. The flight (*hijra*) from the Arabian Peninsula was prompted by an eruption of persecution against followers of the new religion whose ideology seriously threatened the preexisting belief system and its elite class. Islam's five "pillars," which comprise its core precepts and were in opposition to the status quo, included: (1) *shahadah*, profession of the belief that Allah is the one and only God, and Muhammad was his last messenger; (2) *salat*, praying five times a day; (3) *zaqat*, almsgiving; (4) *sawm*, abstinence from sex, food, and water from sunrise to sunset during the month of Ramadan, which comes in the ninth month in the lunar calendar year; and (5) the *hajj*, making a pilgrimage to the Holy Land in Mecca (located in Saudi Arabia) at least once in one's lifetime. However, the injunction on pilgrimage is conditional to the physical and financial ability of the believer to make the journey, which is usually observed in the twelfth month of the lunar calendar.[27]

Landing safely on the African side of the Red Sea, the Arab Muslims sought protection in the Christian kingdom of Aksum or Axum (modern Ethiopia). One of the cities (then under the jurisdiction of King Ashama ibn Abjar, the powerful Axumite ruler) the refugees settled was Zeila (Zeyla), which is now part of modern Somalia.[28] Aksum's rulers provided the Muslims shelter and hospitality as long as it took for the situation in Arabia to improve, thus enabling Prophet Muhammad and his party to make the return trip back to Arabia in 628 CE. Between this period and the death of the Great Prophet of Allah in 632 CE, other individual Muslims crossed the Red Sea into Africa for personal reasons other than evangelism. They perhaps preached about the new faith but never tried to force it on the Africans. Seven years after the death of Muhammad, however, the age of militant Islam commenced when armed Muslim Arabs marched across the Red Sea from the area where Aksum was located into the African continent in 639 CE. A strong passion to expand and consolidate the tenets of the new faith to all corners of the globe informed the Muslims' program of violence. The invaders' philosophy was apparently to first "win the political kingdom and the religious would be added." Within a decade, the Muslims not only seized total political control of the Arabian Peninsula but also extended the political borders of Islam across the Red Sea from Nubian lands into the Byzantine territory of Egypt.

Indeed, the period from 1150 to 1250 represents a milestone in Islam's role in reshaping the evolution of Somali history. Much of the history of this period was described by Yaqut al-Hamawi, the twelfth-century, Syrian-born historian who visited the region. According to Hamawi, Berbers, described as "dark-skinned" and considered ancestors of modern Somalis, inhabited the Mogadishu areas.[29]

On the Somali Peninsula, Mogadishu became one of the most important centers of the new religion and its subsequent expansion to North Africa and along the East African coastal area. Over this period, Somali traders ran commercial expeditions 3,000 miles down to Mozambique, where they successfully established a colony to extract gold from the rich mines in Sofala. According to Arab and Somali chronicles, in about 1403, the small trading city of Adal in the southern Somali region of the Gulf of Aden was established by the newly converted African Muslim merchants as one of the fast-growing Muslim coastal trading enclaves.[30]

Inland, the new religion brought significant influence to bear on the nature and organization of the indigenous clan systems and the political grouping of the Somali people. In the fourteenth century, for instance, the Ajuuraan clan established a dynasty, which soon commenced control of the coastal cities and a lucrative trade across the sea. At this point, much of the Somali people were spiritually unified by Pan-Islamism, which became virulent especially among the inhabitants of northern Somalia. Somalia became integrated in the spiritual commonwealth of Muslims and by association, part of the global army of *Mujahideens* united in resistance against the Christian Crusaders.

In the sixteenth century, Adal or Awdal (c. 1415–1555) rose to prominence as a Muslim sultanate.[31] The Adal Sultanate stretching from Cape Guarddafui to Hadiya, was taken over by the expanding Ifat Kingdom with its capital at Zeila. As a new hub of a commercial empire, the Adalites prospered under the protection of the Ifat rulers who further sent their army to capture the ancient kingdom of Shoa in 1270 CE.

The Ifat army's conquest of Shoa or Shewa kingdom (at this period, an independent kingdom within the Abyssinian Empire) in 1285 set off a prolonged volatile relationship between Christian communities in Ethiopia and Muslim communities in the region.[32] Now bordered by a Muslim neighbor, the Ethiopian rulers were poised to collide with the people of Ifat, ignoring the centuries of cordial relations between the emergent Muslim and Christian communities on the Horn of Africa. After several devastating wars, Ethiopia momentarily gained a decisive but brief victory under the strong leadership of the Solomonic dynasty. Particularly under Amda Seyon I (r. 1314–1344), and Emperor Yeshaq I or Dawit (r. 1412–1427), who declared the Muslims "enemies of the Lord," the Ethiopians relentlessly attacked the sultanate of Adal now within Ifat's suzerainty. In 1415, according to, the *Walashma Chronicle*, an Ethiopian source, Emperor Yeshaq's army captured the Adal' Sultan, Sa'ad ad-Din II, in the capital city Zeila, and he was punished with death.

The Ethiopians celebrated their victory too early, because the war was anything but over. The eldest sons of Sa'ad ad-Din II, Sabr and Jamal, and his subsequent successors had escaped unhurt to Yemen during the war of 1415, taking refuge at the court of the Yemeni ruler Ahma bin al-Ashraf.[33] Here, they reconstituted under the leadership of Sabr, who built a new capital, Dakkar, to the east of Zeila, the former capital of Adal. Assuming the title King of Adal, Sabr ad-Din II continued the war with Ethiopia. With a ragtag army, Sabr defeated the Ethiopian soldiers at the battles of Serjan and Zikr Amhara, plundering the people.[34] The Ethiopians and Adalites waged several more destructive battles with truces arranged intermittently until Sultan Mansur, who succeeded his brother, Sabr ad-Din II, was captured in a battle along with his brother Muhammad by the Ethiopians in 1422.[35]

Yet the conflicts stretched on into the sixteenth century when Adal regrouped in 1527 under the leadership of Imam Ahmad ibn Ibrahim al Ghazi and attacked Ethiopia with the Ottoman leaders' assistance. The invading forces held an advantage with their possession of firearms. They caused serious damage to manuscripts and historic churches and looted the settlements up to the point of entering Tigray.[36] A total crushing of Ethiopia was averted by the intervention of a Portuguese army made up of 400 musketeers under the command of Christopher Da Gama, the son of the renowned navigator Vasco Da Gama. After initial setbacks, Portuguese and Ethiopian forces defeated the Muslims at the battle of Wayna Daga, which took place in the eastern part of Lake Tina, Ethiopia, on February 28, 1543.[37]

Over the period of warring between Ethiopia and the Adal/Ifat sultanates, life on the other parts of Somali Peninsula did not come to a standstill. Rather, the port cities of Barawa, Mogadishu, and Merca continued to grow as centers of international trade. These cities hosted traders from around the world: Arabia, India, Venetia, Egypt, Persia, Portugal, and China. While Mogadishu became famous for its thriving weaving industry (*toob*) produced for the markets in Egypt and Syria, Barawa and Merca served as transit ports for merchants from Mombasa and Malindi—both in modern Kenya. Jewish traders brought Indian textiles from the island of Hormuz (Persia) in exchange for grains and woods.

The Moroccan-born Berber-Muslim traveler Ibn Battuta (1304–1369), who visited the east coast of Africa in 1331, observed the markets in both Mogadishu and Zeila and left an eyewitness account of his impressions. Regarding Zeila, Battuta described it as "the town of the Berberah [Berbera], who are a Negro people," and a "large city with a great bazaar." Battuta goes on to say that Zeila was "the dirtiest, most abominable, and most stinking town in the world. The reason for the stench is the quantity of its fish and the blood of the camels that they slaughter in the streets."[38] Beyond the emphasis on the stench oozing from the fishing industry is a proof of Zeila's popularity as a major producer of seafood.

In reference to Mogadishu, Battuta described it in better words, as he spent more days there with his party, who were attended to with hospitality. "On the fourth day, a Friday, the qadi (judge) and one of the wazirs (minister or adviser) brought me a set of garments. We then went to the mosque and prayed behind the [sultan's] screen."[39] Battuta identified both Zeila and Mogadishu as hubs of fish, camels, and meat trade. He also noted that the wealthy merchants of these cities exported locally made clothes to places like Egypt, among others.[40]

While the eyewitness account of Battuta provides historians with a rare sourcebook, it is important to note that his accounts are sometimes biased. For instance, Battuta is often very critical of those Muslims who practiced their religion differently than he was accustomed to, particularly those outside his Tangiers birthplace, and especially Shiites.[41] Battuta's accounts speak little of Shiite women, but his disgust at their "detestable doctrine" is blatant.[42] He is horrified when he sees a Shiite perform ablutions backwards, hence he withheld no punches in his description of Zeila, a chiefly Shiite town, as the "dirtiest, most disagreeable, and most stinking town in the world."[43] One can then understand better why Battuta held Mogadishu, a predominantly Sunni city, in higher respect even when the two shared similar economic practices. This exemplifies his biases toward those who did not subscribe to the same lifestyle and ritual to which he was accustomed. Battuta's perceptions of the places and peoples were shaped not only by the North African culture he was born in, but also by how he was received and treated as a visitor in foreign lands. The respect and courtesy shown to him in Mogadishu obviously tempered his judgments of the people and the city.

The legendary Portuguese noble and explorer Vasco Da Gama (1460–1524) also visited Mogadishu in the fifteenth century and recorded an account of a prosperous city. Da Gama corroborated Battuta's recognition of Mogadishu as a big medieval metropolitan town with centrally located and imposing palaces, mosques, three-dimensional shaped minarets, and houses that went up to five stories high.[44] Duarte Barbosa (d. 1521), a Portuguese writer and merchant, further observed in 1485 on his way to Bahrain that the overseas trade across the Indian Ocean generated a lot of wealth for the merchants. Merchant ships came to Mogadishu with spices and cloths from the Cambaya kingdom of India. These goods were exchanged for gold, beeswax, ivory, and other commodities on which they made lucrative profit. Barbosa, like Battuta, noted the plenty of meat, wheat, barley, horses, and fruits on the coastal markets, including Zeila, Mogadishu, and other port cities: "It is a very rich place."[45] The point of convergence for the various sources of information on the Somali coastal towns in the fourteenth and fifteenth centuries is the agreement that these cities were hubs of commercial excellence. This reality is sharply in contrast with the economic downturn that marks the postcolonial Somali state today.

The rulers of Ming China (1368–1644) also commissioned trading expeditions across the Indian Ocean to East Africa, which made a historic stop at the port in Mogadishu in 1434. The Chinese sailors took back to China exotic curiosities like African giraffes, zebras, cinnabar, ambergris, and incense as gifts for their emperor. Other merchants from India who wanted to elude the Portuguese and Omani confrontations in East Africa regularly used the Somali ports of Merca and Barawa, which were beyond the influence of these two powers.

Watching from its relatively confined location in the highlands, it was natural for the Ethiopian rulers to desire unhindered access to the sea and the profits of the seaborne commerce. Meanwhile, the record of clashes between the Ethiopians and Portuguese on the one hand, and the Somali and Arabs on the other, was an indication of what to expect in the Horn region in particular and the entire East African coast in general in the coming centuries. The increasing influence of the Ottomans in the area greatly worried the Portuguese, who were not only concerned with their commercial interests in the region but also thought about the bigger purpose of attaining victory in the Crusades. Soon after, the Portuguese launched attacks on Mogadishu (the most prosperous of the coastal cities in the sixteenth century), with an aim to seize control. Although these attacks did not achieve the intended goal, they would eventually mark the beginning of a painful decline and fall of the Somali port city.

In 1580, a joint force of Somali, Arab, and Turkish fleets attacked Portuguese colonies in southeast Africa. The Portuguese fended off the attack with reinforcements from their military stations in India. Throughout the rest of the sixteenth century, Mogadishu continued to exert power over the Banadir areas (the territory around the city) through political, commercial, and Islamic influences. Of particular importance to the Muslims of Mogadishu was the proselytization of the nomads who inhabited the interior. This program of conversion was championed by a mystic sect, the Sufis, who began to move inland, establishing marital relationships with local women. Gradually the interracial unions resulted in tempering Somali ways of life with Muslim values.

AJUURAAN SULTANATE AND ITS SUCCESSOR STATES

One visible impact of Portuguese hostile relations with Mogadishu and the dynamism brought by increasing Muslim movement into upcountry vis-à-vis the shift of locus of intercommunication to the inland areas bordering the Juba and Shebelle rivers was the rise of the Ajuuraan Sultanate in the sixteenth century. The Ajuuraan state is regarded as the successor to its more influential and resilient predecessors such as the Adal and Ifat—both of which spearheaded resistance against Christian Ethiopian and Portuguese aggression on the Horn of Africa. The Ajuuraan state gradually became a notable and well-respected empire between 1550 and 1650, using a strong centralized administration and an aggressive army to project itself as a force in the region. This image helped to keep at bay any devastating outside assault.

Using its military strength to assure security and stability, the sultanate quickly revived old and defunct infrastructure, which in turn reinvigorated the declining Indian Ocean commerce. As a result, traders returned to the kingdom from Africa, Arabia, India, and China. The profits accruing to the Ajuuraan state from this trade were used to commission projects like castles, necropolises, pillar tombs, fortresses, cities, and other landmark architectures—some of which are still standing as historical sites today. Ajuuraan was also reputed for its water or hydraulic engineering. The empire's engineers put to good use the opportunities presented by the Juba and Shebelle rivers to construct limestone wells and cisterns. Some of these systems are still in use today as solid evidence of the quality of Ajuuraan's technology. Furthermore, the rulers developed new systems of agriculture and taxation that remained functional until the nineteenth century.

By the beginning of the eighteenth century, the Ajuuraan state had broken apart under constant Portuguese harassments. Part of the problems that brought about its fall were the tyrannical inclinations of its later rulers, whose style of leadership eroded internal unity and destroyed trust among its supporters. The result was the fragmentation of the kingdom into several smaller kingdoms and states such as the Gobroon Dynasty, the Warsangali Sultanate, and the Bari Dynasty. The new states and principalities continued with the entrenched tradition of seaborne trade and architectural constructions in the region.

Among the motley group of states that succeeded the Ajuuraan state, the Gobroon Dynasty stood out as the most successful. Under one of its sultans, know as Yusuf Mahamud Ibrahim, the third sultan, who ruled from 1789 to 1848, the kingdom entered into an era now called the Golden Age of the Gobroon Dynasty. Through a robust diplomacy and exercise of military power, the succeeding sultans of Gobroon were able to successfully quell internal oppositions and gained the respect of both neighboring and distant contemporaries. In 1843, Sultan Ibrahim's army came out victorious during the revolt of the Baardheere Jamaaca jihadists—a religious sect that sought to bring about religious purity among its neighbors. For clarity, the conflict was between Baardheere Jamaaca sects and the Geledi Sultanate. The ensuing violence disrupted the peace on which the seaborne trade prospered; hence Sultan Ibrahim of Gobroon decided to intervene in the war with a show of force involving 40,000 soldiers and comprising both professionals and volunteers.[46] The Gobroon army effectively subdued both sides of the combatants, thus restoring stability in the southern region. This in turn helped revive the lucrative East African ivory trade.

While much of the allure and splendor that marked the coastal trading enclaves was fading out, the Majerteen Sultanate of Somalia came into reckoning. In the northeast regions of present-day Puntland state is found the Majerteen clan, which is part of the Herti confederacy of the Darod family clan. This territory was the seat of the coastal Majerteen (Bari) people, who, between the middle of the eighteenth and nineteenth centuries, established two small kingdoms that played a significant role in the politics of the Somali Peninsula on the eve of European colonization. These kingdoms were the Majerteen Sultanate of Boqor Isman Mahamud and that of his cousin and rival Sultan Yusuf Ali Keenadiid of Hobyo (Obbia). Although the Majerteen Sultanate was founded in the second half of the eighteenth century, it only came into prominence in the nineteenth century following the time in power of the famous Boqor Isman Mahamud.

During his reign, Sultan Mahamud allied himself with the British, and through British patronage that came in form of trade subsidies, the Majerteen emerged as a prosperous coastal polity. Mahamud won the trust of Her Imperial Majesty's merchants for taking care of the British naval crews that were stranded periodically on the Somali coast. Mahamud was further liked by the British for what they generally perceived as his liberal trade policy that facilitated a prosperous trade in livestock, ostrich feathers, and gum arabic. The sultan's leadership talent was also revealed in the manner in which he piloted the kingdom's diplomatic affairs. For instance, while conceding a general subordination to the British Crown, the sultan successfully maintained the freedom of his kingdom until the latter half of the nineteenth century.

Boqor Isman Mahmud's sultanate almost capitulated in the middle of the nineteenth century during a tumultuous five years of dynastic war between him and his younger and ambitious cousin, Keenadiid. The end of the civil war only came after the challenger was driven into exile in Arabia. Those hoping they had heard the last of Keenadiid were mistaken. A decade later, in the 1870s, Keenadiid returned from Arabia with a sizeable number of Hadhrami (Yemeni) musketeers and a group of fiercely staunch followers. The foreign fighters helped Keenadiid seize control of portions of lands from the local Hawiye clans of the Majerteen country. Keenadiid renamed this new territory under his control the kingdom of Hobyo.

Given their strategic proximities to the coast, in the last quarter of the nineteenth century, both the Majerteen and the Hobyo kingdoms became the center of attention by European colonial powers, particularly the Germans and the Italians as these powers began to seek markets in the area. Ultimately, it was the Italians who outmaneuvered their competitors and systematically wrapped up the entire Majerteen territories into what became the Italian Somaliland.

At this time, the past splendor of the southern Somali coastal cities had neared their end. In fact, the decline of Mogadishu into a state of irrelevance in the nineteenth century closed an important chapter in the politics and economic history of the East African coastal peoples. From this point, the Omani Sultanate of Zanzibar had established control over the Benadir coast while the northern coast from the mid-eighteenth century came under the jurisdiction of the sheriffs of Mukha in modern Yemen. The Omani presence marked the dawn of a new era in the history of the region. As for Zeila, Lt. Richard Burton of the British India navy, who visited the coastal city in 1854–1855, was struck by the poor conditions of its rulers, who, according to him, were unable to practically exert any meaningful control beyond the walls of a fast-decaying city. Burton observed that the aged governor of Zeila, Sharmarke Mohammed of the Habr Yunis subclan, had by name become a commissioner of the Ottomans. Oblivious of his dwindling power and influence, Mohammed was still entertaining the hope of rebuilding the city with heaps of rubble and collapsing walls through military expeditions against the rebellious former vassals.[47] In 1875, anything left of this hope was completely erased following the occupation of Zeila and Berbera by the Egyptians under khedive (viceroy) Ismail Pasha. With the active encouragement of the British, the khedive's army pushed further into the interior, colonizing Harar, the border town with Ethiopia.[48]

The Egyptian occupation was, however, short-lived because of its financial woes following an expensive conflict with the Mahdists in Sudan. Thus, in the heat of the Berlin Conference on Africa in 1885, Egypt was forced to evacuate its troops from Harar. As history shows, movement means displacement. This explains the action of Menelik, the Ethiopian emperor's decision to attack and seize Harar two years later. As elaborated on in the next chapter, the dramatic partition of the Somali Peninsula by four foreign powers had begun.[49]

NOTES

1. This was the main focus of colonial scholars, whose works have influenced several other writings before the decline of the now discredited Hamitic hypothesis. See, for instance, Ralph E. Drake-Brockman, *British Somaliland* (London: Hurst & Blackett Ltd, 1912), 68.

2. National Archives Kew (hereafter NAK), CAB/129/85, Somaliland Protectorate and the Horn of Africa, dated February 15, 1957, 2.

3. Gene Gragg, "Etymology and Electronics: The Afrosiatic Index," *The Oriental Institute and Notes* 149 (1996): 1–5.

4. NAK, CAB/129/85, 2.

5. Bernd Heine, "Linguistic Evidence on the Early History of the Somali People," in Hussein M. Adam (ed.), *Somalia and the World: Proceedings of the International Symposium* (Mogadishu: National Printing Press, 1979), 23–33.

6. Peter Robertshaw, *A History of African Archaeology* (London and Portsmouth: James Curry and Heinemann, 1990), 105.

7. Marlene Felius, *Genus Bos: Cattle Breeds of the World* (Rahway, NJ: Merck and Co., 1985); Valerie Porter, Ian Lauder Mason, *Mason's World Dictionary of Livestock: Breeds, Types and Varieties*, 5th ed. (Abindgon, UK: CABI Publishing International, 2002), esp. 125–62.

8. *Somaliland Times*, "Rockshelters of Las Geel: Republic of Somaliland," October 15, 2005; X. Gutherz, J.-P. Cros, and J. Lesur, "The Discovery of New Rock Paintings in the Horn of Africa: The Rockshelters of Las Geel, Republic of Somaliland," *Journal of African Archaeology* 1, no. 2 (2003): 227–236.

9. Neville Chittick, "An Archaeological Reconnaissance of the Horn: The British Somali Expedition," *Azania* 4 (1975): 115–30.

10. See Mohamed Hussein Abby, "The Land of Poun (Punt)," Working Paper, Center for Research and Development, University of Hargeisa, n.d. 1–28.

11. See David Perlman, "Scientists Zero in on Ancient Land of Punt," *Chronicle Science*, May 8, 2010.

12. Ibid., 2.

13. See, for instance, M. F. Abdillahi, *The Best Short Stories from the Land of Punt (Somalia)* (Mogadisco: Author, 1970).

14. Joyce A. Tydesley, *Hatchepsut: The Female Pharaoh* (London and New York: Penguin, 1998), 147.

15. Peter A. Clayton, *The Chronicle of the Pharaohs: The Reign-by-Reign Record of the Rulers and Dynasties of Ancient Egypt* (New York: Thames and Hudson, 2006), 61.

16. Amelia Ann Blanford Edwards, "Queen Hatasu, and Her Expedition to the Land of Punt," in Amelia Edwards, *Pharaohs Fellahs and Explorers* (New York: Harper and Brothers, 1891), 261.

17. Björn Landstöm, *Bold Voyages and Great Explorers: A History of Discovery and Exploration from the Expedition to the Land of Punt in 1493 B.C. to the Discovery of the Cape of Good Hope in 1488 A.D.* (New York: Doubleday, 1964).

18. Herodotus, *The History of Herodotus by Herodotus* by George Rawlinson (New York: Appleton and Company, 1859), 153; and *The History of Herodotus by Herodotus Vol. 1*, trans. by G. C. Macaulay (Gutenberg Ebook Project, 2001).

19. Øystein S. LaBianca, "Subsistence Pastorialism," in Suzanne Richard (ed.), *Near Eastern Archaeology: A Reader* (Winona Lake, IN: Eisenbrauns, 2003), 120–23.

20. Malcolm McNeill with a chapter by Arthur Charles Hugh Dixon, *In Pursuit of the Mad Mullah: Service and Sports in the Somali Protectorate* (London: C. Arthur Pearson, 1902), 269.

21. Anonymous, "Periplus of the Erythrean Sea," in G. S. P. Freeman-Grenville, *The East African Coast, Select Documents from the First to the Earlier Nineteenth Century* (Oxford: Clarendon Press, 1962), 1–2; Cosmas Indicopleustes, *The Christian Topography of Cosmas an Egyptian Monk*, trans. and edited by J. W. McCrindle (London: Hakluyt Society, 1897), 49–54.

22. See Paul J. J. Sinclair, "Archaeology in Eastern Africa: An Overview of the Current Chronological Issues," *Journal of African History* 32 (1991): 179–219.

23. Anonymous, "Periplus of the Erythrean Sea," 1.

24. Indicopleustes, *The Christian Topography*, 49–50.

25. Richard Francis Burton, *First Footsteps in East Africa, or An Exploration of Harar* (London: Longman, Brown, Green, and Longmans, 1856), 175, 430, 502.

26. I. M. Lewis, *A Modern History of Somalia: Revised, Updated and Expanded 4th edition* (Oxford: James Currey, 2002), 10.

27. Raphael Chijioke Njoku, *Culture and Customs of Morocco* (Westport, CT: Greenwood, 2005), 24, 113–14.

28. Stuart Munro-Hays, *Aksum: An African Civilization of Late Antiquity* (Edinburgh: Edinburgh University Press, 1991), 56–60.

29. I. M. Lewis, *A Modern History of Somalia*, 20.

30. Nehemia Levtzion, "Islam in Africa to 1800: Merchants, Chiefs and Saints," in John L. Esposito (ed.), *The Oxford History of Islam* (Oxford: Oxford University Press, 1999), 501.

31. Levtzion, "Islam in Africa to 1800," 501.

32. Shoa was first established in the ninth century as a Muslim state with its capital at Walalah. See Charles Johnston, *Travels in Southern Abyssinia: Through the Country of Adal to the Kingdom of Shoa* vol. 1 (London: J. Madden and Co., 1844).

33. J. Spencer Trimingham, *Islam in Ethiopia* (Oxford: Geoffrey Cumberlege for the University Press, 1952), 74.

34. Richard Pankhurst, *Ethiopian Borderland: Essays in Regional History: From Ancient Times to the End of the Eighteenth Century* (Lawrenceville, NJ: Red Sea Press, 1997), 113–29.

35. Trimingham, *Islam in Ethiopia*, 75.

36. See Richard Pankhurst, *The Ethiopians: A History* (Somerset, NJ: John Wiley & Sons, 2001), 90.

37. The battle in particular and the war in general have wider significance in the Crusade between the Muslim Turkish (Ottoman Empire) and the European Christian positions.

38. Ibn Battuta, *Travels in Asia and Africa 1325–1354* (1929; reprint Oxford: Routledge-Curzon, 2005), 110.

39. Ibid., 109.

40. Ibid., 110–12.

41. Ross E. Dunn, *The Adventures of Ibn Battuta: A Muslim Traveler of the 14th Century* (Berkeley: University of California Press, 2005), 1.

42. Ibn Battuta, *The Travels of Ibn Battuta*, trans. H. A. R. Gibb (Cambridge: Cambridge University Press, 1962), 94.

43. Ibid., 373.

44. Vasco Da Gama, *The Diary of His Travels through African Waters, 1495–1499*, trans. with an introduction and notes by Eric Axelson (Somerset West, South Africa: Stephen Philips, 1998), 88; Castaneda, Herman Lopes de, *The First Book of the Historie of the Discoveries and Conquests of the East India by the Portingals* (London, 1582), in Robert Kerr (ed.), *A General History and Collection of Voyages and Travels* vol. II (London: T. Cadell, 1811, 1824).

45. Duarte Barbosa, *A Description of the Coasts of East Africa and Malabar in the Beginning of the Sixteenth Century*, trans. by Henry E. Stanley (1540; reprint London: Hakluyt Society, 1866), 16–17, 93, 185. See also Duarte Barbosa, *The Book of Duarte Barbosa: An Account of the Countries Bordering on the Indian Ocean and Their Inhabitants* (1518; reprint London: Hakluyt Society, 1902).

46. See Virginia Luling, *Somali Sultanate: The Geledi City-State over 150 Years* (Piscataway, NJ: Transaction Publishers, 2002), 229, 275.

47. Burton, *First Footsteps in East Africa*, 71, 308.

48. Mohammed Diriye Abdullah, *Culture and Customs of Somalia* (Westport, CT: Greenwood Press, 2001), 18–19.

49. See NAK, CAB/24/275, Anglo-Italian Conversations marked "Secret C.P. 50 (38)" and dated February 28, 1936, annex 2, 23.

3

Colonial Conquest

"In several respects, colonialism in Africa bequeathed a distinctively destructive legacy to its successor regimes."[1]

—Crawford Young

The connection between European colonial rule and the abiding crisis of the postcolonial state in Africa is a hot subject of debate among scholars, politicians, and other interest groups. Those who link colonialism with the present crisis in Africa have made the argument that Somalia is now in shambles because of its complex experience under the various European imperial powers. For example, in a vexed comment on the consequences of colonialism on the present situation in the country, a Somali writer, Imaan Daahir Saalax, indicted Britain, France, and Italy—the three European powers that exercised colonial rule in Somalia from 1900 to 1960—for the violent and enduring crises that have troubled the postcolonial state. Saalax argues that: "The presence of colonialism [in Somalia] still lingers today; it can be seen in the way we think, and the way we divide ourselves. We as a people have been violated on our land and in our minds. We are divided and therefore we are conquered."[2]

Such charges have been the dominant view among Africans, although a handful of others, among them economists like George Ayittey and Chika Onyeali, have begged to disagree with the popular opinion. Instead the opponents place the bulk of the blame on the African political elite and the people.[3] The controversy will persist unless political and socioeconomic institutions in the continent grow to be more stable. This chapter deals with British, Italian, French, and Ethiopian colonial intrusions on the Horn of Africa and their consequent impact on the Somali ways of life, particularly after 1960. The crucial issue is to understand how the processes of colonialism introduced new dynamics of conflict to existing ones and thus contributed to the problems of disunity and state collapse in the postcolonial era.

While all the blame for Africans' problems cannot be laid at the feet of the colonial overlords, everywhere the fact is that the brand of imperialism practiced by the Europeans in the twentieth century raised the propensity for disunity among the colonized people. In order to maintain colonial control and to discourage a united African front against alien control, the Europeans systematically applied the "divide-and-rule policy," which used unfair redistribution of rewards to create new lines of intraethnic and interethnic quarrels among the colonized groups that once lived side by side without much reason for fighting. This policy created a pattern of disunity and envy among the indigenous groups, while helping to consolidate the colonial agenda.

Among the Somali, colonization disrupted existing alliances and introduced new forms of competitions among the traditional communities, social groups, principalities, and kingdoms. The new sociopolitical relations brought by the Europeans left the Africans in a poor and volatile condition on the road to independence in 1960. To better understand the new dynamics introduced by colonialism, it is crucial to briefly describe the nature of society and politics on the eve of colonial rule.

BACKGROUND TO COLONIZATION

Before 1900, as discussed in detail in Chapter 2, the Somali were never organized in a monolithic statehood under one form of government. What the people had were systems of indigenous governments that differed from clan to clan, state to state, and kingdom to kingdom as these forms of political organization changed across time and space. In general, the Somalis organized their politics in forms of independent family clans with predominantly nomadic pastoralist and sedentary farming communities operating a highly decentralized system of government. While semblances of this indigenous system were found in different regions of the Somali Peninsula, it was most common along the southern region's river valleys. Along the northern and eastern coastlines were confederacies, principalities, rudimentary city-states, and sultanates of varied sizes such as the Ifat, Adel, Ajuuraan, Gabroon, Majerteen, Hobyo, Hargeisa, and Mogadishu, to mention but a few.[4]

As some have asserted in the historiography, prior to colonial rule, the Somali people had a strong sense of common cultural unity that was yet to translate into a purposely developed single statehood.[5] While most of the population spoke the Somali language as a marker of identity and homogeneity, there were also minority Bantu, Arab, and Yemeni populations living within the Somali Peninsula. The Somali Bantu (also called Jareer or Gosha) lived mainly in the south near the Juba and Shebelle rivers. The Arabs and Yemeni were mostly found in the coastal towns. Through the practice of marriage, Islam, and business relationships, the minorities and later migrants blended with their host society.

On a broad note, the various groups together formed what one may describe as two visible Somali "republics." The first comprised the majority rural dwellers and pastoralist nomads. This more pastoral/ rural group, who were nominal Muslims on the eve of colonial rule, were also almost indifferent to modernization; they retained much of their indigenous ways of life and independent spirit. The second "republic" comprised the coastal and more cosmopolitan population. Most of them practiced Islam, apparently because of the substantial Arab Muslims' presence in these cities. The two "republics" constituted the greater Somali through constant nomadic movements, the proselytization of the Islamic faith by Arab and native converts, the coming and going of local and foreign traders, and the increasing influx of Arabs into the economic commonwealth of East African littoral.

Since Ethiopia occupies an important place in the colonial history of Somalia, it is necessary to also highlight the nature of its relationship with Somalia on the eve of colonial rule. First, prior to the rise of the Muslim sultanates, the Somali and the Ethiopians shared a less conflicted relationship despite Ethiopia's designs for occupying the Ogaden territory—the area with the largest main Somali population concentrated around Dire Dawa.[6] The Ogaden territory, which became a tricky puzzle for the British in the colonial chess game, allowed Ethiopia, a landlocked country, to gain vital access to the Indian Ocean via Somalia's territory. In return, Ethiopia readily permitted Somali nomads access to the rich fodders of its eastern borders.[7]

The second point to keep in perspective, which is closely related to the first, is that on the eve of colonial rule, the Somali had neither come to an understanding of themselves as a distinct ethnic group nor expressed a Pan-Somali identity in the modern sense. If there was anything to be labeled such, it was rather founded on a broader ideology of the Islamic religion than on any ethnic, racial, or political sentiments. Islam played a definite role in the society as the Somali people embraced the alien religion whose appeal was reinforced by commerce, prestige, literacy, and of course the belief in their common descent from the lineage of the Prophet Mohammad.[8] The seed of a distinct Somali consciousness in the contemporary era was theoretically conjured up by the participants in the Berlin African colonization conference of 1884–1885.[9] During that meeting, the imperial powers drafted their rules of engagement, carved out African lands, and assigned them names that suited their imperial interests. The British, Italians, and French brought over the new constructs and applied them to Somalia as they went about pacifying the people in order to gain control of their lives and lands.

Third, in terms of regional politics and interethnic relations, the precolonial period may be described as the "age of innocence." This by no means suggests that there was an absence of intra and interethnic/clan conflicts. Rather, it suggests that a significant number of Somalis lived in the neighboring Ethiopia, Kenya, Djibouti, and Eritrea without much conflict with their hosts. It is noteworthy that whether in or outside their homelands, the natives of the Horn region may have organized their politics around the clan level but did not hold any overt perception of "we" and "they" consciousness. For the Somali, political loyalty rested on the individual's family clan that often had extensive networks of ties with other family clans and subclans. In a society where ancestral heritage was highly regarded, chieftains and clan heads gained power through respect, leadership, and honor within their own clans, and by demonstrating wisdom and leadership acumen, gained respect among rival clans.

In this way, the clan became the focus of government, and so the need for a centralized government was hardly necessary. Each clan lived by its own set of rules and regulations. The process of political decisions was conducted in a democratic manner, and indeed, as I. M. Lewis observed, all men were councilors and politicians in the

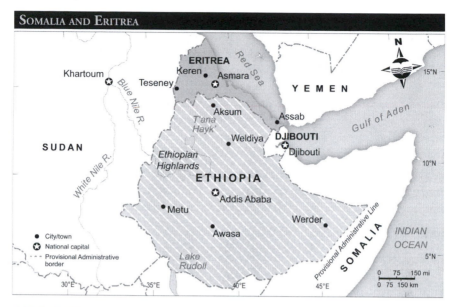

(ABC-CLIO)

people's assembly. Democratic principles were practiced "almost to the point of anarchy."[10] Chiefs or headsmen were voted into office by either the people or a select group of council of elders. Often elders were elected individuals or those nominated to the council because of their wisdom—a quality commonly assumed in the African culture to come with superior chronological age. As Victor Uchendu, the eminent anthropologist, illustrates with the example of his Igbo people of southeastern Nigeria, politics was approached as the mutual accommodation of differences; "the concept of sovereign power was understood as everybody's business"; the need to rotate power and authority among politically competing units was the philosophy of engagement; and the importance of political discourse among individuals was emphasized.[11]

Another key element of the clan's self-government was alliances with neighboring clans. These alliances were forged through marriage, blood oaths, blessings, or other forms of peace offerings. In periods of crisis, members of the alliance worked together to resolve the problem.[12] This arrangement enabled the Somali to settle local quarrels quickly before they got out of control. The effectiveness of the indigenous conflict resolution techniques, which was now being reinvented in the breakaway republics of Somaliland and Puntland, depended on the strength of members of the alliances, as well as the nature of the issue at hand.

This order of society came under attack in the late nineteenth century following the arrival of the Europeans. With a mindset the English poet Rudyard Kipling has aptly depicted as "the white man's burden," the Europeans assumed a self-entrusted "divine mandate" to civilize the indigenous peoples of the world they had come to perceive as uncivilized and inferior.[13] The real civilized human became synonymous with the generation of Europeans that emerged in the nineteenth century—self-assured, arrogant, rude, violent, and meddlesome. This view was implied in a secret report, received for British Cabinet Office by Norman Brook on March 23, 1956. The memo described the Somali population as being "in many respects backward."[14]

THE COMING OF THE EUROPEANS

Between 1491 and 1498, the Portuguese, led by Vasco Da Gama, plotted a course through the western to eastern coast of Africa. The Europeans navigated through the seas reaching modern Tanzania in the south in 1491 and moving northward to the coastal city of Mombassa in Kenya in 1498. At this early period, Portugal claimed only to be interested in finding a safe passage to harness the profits of the Indian Ocean–borne sea trade. Gradually, they were joined by the Dutch, the British, and the French merchants. The Europeans wanted to avoid the high taxes that were levied by the Ottomans, who firmly controlled the shorter route to India via the Mediterranean Sea and the Red Sea channels. The exorbitant tariffs levied by the Ottomans had left the European merchants with high-priced goods that consumers in Europe could hardly afford. Only the nobility desired the imported commodities like silk, spices, cloths, and curry in order to demonstrate their wealth and maintain their elite status. An unhindered access to the Indian Ocean trade became urgent for the merchants to expand the market in Europe for more profit.

As was the case with the Spanish-led explorations in the Americas in the late fifteenth century, Portuguese-led exploration for new routes to India marked the genesis of colonial aggression that ended in the colonization of the entire continent in the late nineteenth century. As the new route to East Africa, the Far East, and China became entrenched, the Europeans made frequent stops off the African coasts, interfering in the local politics of the East African coastal states, including the Somalia coasts. Such imperial encroachments coincided with expansions of the American plantation colonies, which brought the coastal enclaves of Africa closely and more vigorously integrated into the new global trade. In this new trade, Africa would serve as a vital source of a highly demanded slave labor in the Americas. The Arab/Indian Ocean slave trade had been in existence prior to the European arrival, but the new impetus from Europe expanded the slave market, with every African port turned into a major slave supply route. Most of the victims were captured from the hinterlands of the contiguous territories known today as the Great Lakes Region, comprising Uganda, Democratic Republic of the Congo, Ethiopia, Rwanda, Burundi, and Tanzania. The Europeans also traded in gold, ivory, ambergris, wax, and spices throughout the sixteenth and seventeenth centuries.

Often, the Europeans stayed on the coast and used African chiefs and individual traders to acquire their victims. Some African rulers cooperated with the slave merchants because it gave them an opportunity to attack their adversaries, sell them off, and make some profit out of the enemy. But the victims of the horrendous trade were not only prisoners of war. In some cases, those sold as slaves were victims of kidnappers. Some others were pawns of debt and condemned criminals who had committed acts like murder, incest, and other things considered an abomination in the local culture. These categories of people were traded for European-made goods.

Economically the slave trade both facilitated and hurt the Somali society. While the trade brought immediate wealth to the handful of local dealers, it brought misery to the African victims and their families, disrupting village life, the local manufacturing industries, and the sociopolitical order. In the Somali region, for instance, slave trading negatively affected existing clan alliances, pitting clan against clan through wars and hostage taking. More notably, it affected the quality and quantity of agro-allied goods that were produced and exchanged for foreign products off the coastal cities as the human cargo took top priority.

As a result, by the end of the trans-Atlantic slave trade in the first half of the nineteenth century, the local economy of the East African coastal cities had taken a serious downturn because of overdependence on the hated trade across the sea. The once vibrant and prosperous trading enclaves would never recover from the consequences of the European commercial presence. Yet this was the beginning of what was to come as the European control increased, entrenching this pattern of economic and political subservience.

COLONIAL CONQUEST AND AFRICAN RESISTANCE

The desire of Britain, France, and Italy to claim territories in Somalia in the late nineteenth century was motivated first by each country's political, diplomatic, military, and nationalistic interests. In other words, the economic considerations were secondary to the strategic and military considerations. The material motive was nonetheless a big factor, particularly for economically poor Italy. Somalia's strategic location on the Horn of Africa was magnified through a number of political developments on the global stage during the nineteenth century. First, the opening of the Suez Canal in 1869 increased or rather renewed the European powers' long-standing interests in the region.[15] The major participants in the Berlin Conference on African colonization in 1884–1885—Britain, France, Italy, Portugal, Belgium, and Germany—all arrived at the meeting with clear aims to secure some measure of power and control in Africa.[16] In regard to Somalia, the equations were complicated by similar designs nursed by Ethiopia and Egypt as internal colonialists. These African powers were determined not to be outplayed by the Europeans in a region particularly considered by the Abyssinian emperor as his top priority. As Menelik II (1844–1913), the emperor of Ethiopia, had unequivocally declared in a letter of 1891 addressed to the European powers, "I have no intentions at all of being an indifferent spectator, if the distant Powers hold onto the idea of dividing up Africa. For the past Fourteen centuries, Ethiopia has been an island of Christians in a sea of pagans."[17]

The emperor of Ethiopia was serious in his words, especially with his stated belief that "in the past, the boundary of Ethiopia was the sea."[18] By the late 1800s, the partition and formal colonization of Somalia had been completed on paper. Ethiopia was joined by three foreign powers: Britain, Italy, and France. In the words of historian Angus Hamilton, the Horn of Africa became the subject of a Triple European Alliance.[19] Egypt's colonial interests in the area suffered an irreparable setback following its entanglement with the Muslim Madists in the Sudan in 1884. The heavy financial and military costs the revolt placed on the khedive's army forced Egypt to quickly evacuate the region, thus giving Britain enough reason to step up its presence and establish ultimate control of the territory. Originally, Britain had wanted to commit fewer resources in the Somali Peninsula, using Egypt as a source of vital security in the region.

BRITAIN AND THE NORTHERN SOMALILAND

In the 1880s and 1890s, Britain's major colonial policy in regard to additional territorial acquisition was the defense of its Indian colony. In order to guard the spinal cord of British trade and empire, tropical African and Pacific claims were repeatedly sacrificed as pawns in the higher game of imperialism.[20] In the heat of the Berlin Conference in 1884, for example, the Foreign Office decided that the security dangers facing Britain in Egypt weakened the ability of the country to successfully compete with other European powers in West Africa. In this regard, the Foreign Office considered it wise "to confine ourselves to securing the utmost possible freedom of trade on that [west] coast, yielding to others the territorial responsibilities ... and seeking compensation on the east coast ... where the political future of the country is of real importance to Indian and imperial interests."[21]

Thus, Britain's primary interest in the Somali lands arose from this need to protect its colonial territory of India, and to this end, it intended to secure a steady supply of food—specifically beef—needed by Her Majesty's soldiers stationed in the Yemeni port of Aden. The British first seized the strategic Aden seaport by force in 1839.[22] In 1869, the port of Aden became even more vital for the British navy following the opening of the Suez Canal that year.[23] This meant that the canal would witness more traffic, more trade, and obviously more conflicts. For the British to successfully protect the route that led to Her Majesty's Indian dominion, Somali meat was needed to feed the army. Prior to 1839, Aden had procured its meat exclusively from its Somali neighbors on the other side of the sea. In other words, what the British needed at this time was to simply strengthen and safeguard this existing supply route. As long as the meat supplies were uninterrupted, the British government did not seriously consider an outright colonization of the territory. This modest need was reminiscent of the Dutch presence and subsequent colonization of the Cape colony in South Africa after initial arrival in 1652. By implication, prior to 1887, the British considered Somalia a secondary concern in relation to Aden. This attitude would change after almost fifty years.

The question arises as to what eventually led the British to launch a Somaliland Protectorate from 1887, three years after the Berlin conference. Part of the explanation is tied to the nature of relations between the Egyptians and the Somalis. I. M. Lewis argues that Egypt's presence in the Somali Peninsula was ignited by a determination to protect its interest from foreign powers as invested in it by the Ottomans, who from the fifteenth century established a strong presence in the region. Early in 1866, Turkey had transferred the Red Sea ports of Suakin (modern Sudan) and Massawa (modern Eritrea) to its Egyptian provincial government under khedive Ishmail Pasha (1830–1895).[24] From these positions, the khedive promptly claimed that his jurisdiction in the region also embraced the Somali coast.[25] In an aggressive move, Pasha attempted to consolidate his presence with a military expedition launched in 1875. Part of the bold move on the part of Egypt was also aimed to confront the Omani authority in the southern Somali coast as well as on the island of Zanzibar.

The Somalis welcomed the Egyptians in an apparent show of distaste for what they had perceived as Zanzibari-British collaboration to colonize and exploit the Somali coast. At this point, the British decided that Egypt's presence in the region, and the security its forces provided actually helped to maintain British interests in the region. Perhaps this crucial recognition prompted khedive Ishmail's self-indulgent 1876 declaration that: "My country [Egypt] is no longer in Africa; we are now part of Europe. It is therefore natural for us to abandon our former ways and to adopt a new system adapted to our social conditions."[26] In 1877, the British signed an agreement with the khedive Pasha formerly recognizing Egyptian jurisdiction as far south as Ras Hafun, a small low-lying territory in the Bari (Majerteen) region of northern Somalia. One of the crucial terms of the agreement was that Egypt should not, under any pretext, cede any part of the Somali coast to a foreign power.[27]

But Egypt's hopes for empire in the Somali lands was shattered by the Sudanese anti-Egyptian Mahdist revolt in 1884, which compelled the Egyptians to request British assistance in evacuating their troops trapped on the coast.[28] To fill the vacuum created by Egypt's forced withdrawal, Britain, between 1884 and 1888, concluded several treaties with local rulers of northern Somalia. This marked the beginning of formal British colonization of northern Somalia. According to Hamilton, although the British had secured these treaties of protection with the Somali chiefs, they would have still preferred to maintain their titular control of the Zeila, Berbera, and Bulahar seaports, while the Egyptians maintained authority in the region. But the hasty manner in which the local Somali leaders signed these treaties with the British indicated that they were tired of Egyptian influence in the area and needed British protection from them.[29] The formal inauguration of the "Protectorate of Somalia" in February 1884, which the Italians formally ratified in the Anglo-Italian Protocol of 1894 (vide "spheres of influence"), came on the heels of mounting French and Italian imperial advances into the areas.[30]

For the next 14 years, the British ruled northern Somalia from their Indian colonial territory using the indirect rule system. The system, as explained by Sir Donald Cameron in the *Native Administration Memorandum* of 1930, recognized that the British "must first endeavor to teach the people to administer their own affairs, and it seems obvious . . . the wise course . . . is to build on the institutions of the people themselves, tribal institutions which have been handed down to them through the ages."[31] This strategy allowed Britain to use local Somali chiefs, the *akili*, as middlemen in the administration of the colony. Under the indirect rule system, the judicial structure, *qadi*, as well as the powers of the *akili*, was reinforced with new powers in order to meet the expectations of the new order.

Like elsewhere in Africa where the British applied the indirect rule model originally developed in colonial India, the newly appointed Somali traditional official began to assume unusual despotic powers. This was possible because the chieftains were now no longer accountable to the people as had been the case in the past. The ordinary Somali were more or less shielded from direct contacts with the colonial overlords given that the day-to-day running of the colony remained in the hands of the *akili*, the very local rulers the people had been dealing with. Somali scholar Mohammed Abdullahi eloquently argues that this seeming magnanimity of the British in the northern region of Somalia should be considered inconsequential in a country that had at this time "neither gold nor verdant lands suitable for European settlements such as the green lands of East Africa or Southern Africa."[32] True, such approach is consistent with the idea that colonies should be self-supporting—a policy consistently maintained by the British as a dictum guarding British taxpayers' money from the developmental needs of the colonies.

FRENCH SOMALI COAST

Although the French and the British had been jostling for territorial control in Africa since the eighteenth century, the two powers began to fight for the Horn of Africa as a result of French intrusion into the port of Obock in Afar (Danakil) country in 1862. However, British colonial policy was strategic, deliberate, and not driven by indiscriminate land-grabbing as was the case of the French in Africa. Indeed, the British penetration into Uganda and their securing of the rest of the Nile Valley was a highly selective program, insofar as it gave up "some British West African claims to France and transferred part of East Africa to Germany."[33] The French, who had been evicted from Egypt by the British, sought to have a coaling station on the Red Sea to strengthen its naval logistics to their colonies in Indochina. Early on in 1859, the local Afar had ceded the territory to France, but the French did not immediately set up a direct colonial administration over the port until they paid a sum of 10,000 *thaler* as compensation to the Danakil in 1862. Subsequently, France constructed a seaport in the area and then a railroad to the highlands to enable its merchants to gain access to Ethiopian coffee, gum, ivory, hides, and skins.

For nearly two decades, the French did not endeavor to further consolidate their presence in the Horn region until after the British outmaneuvered them and established claims to Zeila, one of the major port cities in the north. In response to this development, the French expanded the pre-1862 land to include a strip of area on the coast belonging to Somalis who the French mistook as the same as the Afar. Although they share a common history of genealogy, the Somali are distinct from the Afar people. This oversight on the part of the French resulted in the creation of a new country, French Somaliland (later Djibouti), with the Somalis constituting half the population. In 1881, the French then established the Franco-Ethiopian trading company at Obock, and even at this time, the region was still not a high priority for the French.

The French were rather consolidating control of their newly acquired possessions in Madagascar and Indochina. French attitude or rather complacency was changed quickly after the British declined French ships permission to berth at the port of Aden. Consequently, the French turned Obock from a trading post to a coaling station. In 1884, Léonce Lagarde (1860–1935) was made governor of Obock and later the entire French Somaliland; his appointment would greatly influence the course of French expansion in the region, ultimately leading to the formal establishment of French Somaliland by 1900.[34]

ITALY: ROMANS, FASCISTS, AND COLONIAL PACIFISM

In his study of Italy's colonial policy in the Horn, Said Samatar, one of the doyens of English Somali studies, argues that Italy was amateurish in the conduct of its imperial politics in Africa and that it was careful to stake out a territory without antagonizing its more powerful European competitors. The truth is that Italy was newly unified as a state in 1861, and thus its cautious approach to colonial acquisition was conditioned by its economic, military, and political fragility rather than the lack of experience and its "reluctance" to colonize, as is often emphasized in the historiography.[35] A more accurate report is that Italy pursued its colonial ambition in a more aggressive manner, while wisely avoiding a fight with its more formidable competitors Britain, France, and Germany. Factors driving Italian colonial moves were both economic and political. On the economic front, the government wanted to use the new colonies in Africa as an emigration outlet for its increasing and impoverished population. Additionally, the colonies were to provide Italy a secure market for its manufactured goods. Politically, colonies were desired by Italy for national pride. This was best revealed in the nationalists' expression of pride in their Roman heritage. The common idea implicit in the race for colonies was that Italy had to emulate the other colonial powers in order to be taken seriously by its critics and to attain continental respect.[36]

As a late bloomer in the scramble for African lands, Italy's opportunities were, however, limited. With sections of Somalia left out of the so-called Conventional Free Trading Area in East Africa, Italy immediately saw an opportunity to grab a territory that not only provided a strategic link with the Eritrean colony, but also shared a border with Ethiopia—a country that had since the fifteenth century caught the imaginations of many Europeans as the legendary land of Prester John—a mythical figure popular among the Europeans.[37] In a letter addressed to Prime Minister Depretis by Macini, an Italian colonial agent, it was revealed that with Eritrea in their hands, Italy would have unhindered access to products from Ethiopia if the Benadir coastal area in the south of Somalia was added to Italian control.[38] In February 1885, the Italians seized control of Massawa in Eritrea, following the withdrawal of Egyptian troops under the fire of the Mahdist army.

In 1876, Antonio Cecchi (1849–1896), an ardent imperialist, had carried out an expedition from Zeila in Somalia all the way to the Kaffa region of Ethiopia. In 1885, Cecchi landed in Zanzibar in the company of Cmdr. Matteo Fecarotta of the Italian navy, declaring to the world that Italy wanted to conclude a commercial treaty. Assisted by Sir John Kirk (1832–1922), the British administrator in Zanzibar, Cecchi signed the treaty on May 28, 1885. Cecchi, however, failed to disclose to Kirk his ulterior motive about Sultan Barghash's readiness to cede Kismayo on the condition that Italy and Zanzibar were going to split the revenue equally.

In a diplomatic manner, Sultan Barghash asked Cecchi to make a formal application with no intention to respect his request. Cecchi rightly doubted the sultan of Zanzibar was going to honor his request, and so he did not bother to make the application.[39] Throughout the early 1880s, Cecchi continued to detour through the Benadir (Banaadir) littoral—that broadly included the long coastal plains stretching from the Gulf of Aden in the north to the Juba River in the south and encompassing the Mogadishu area.[40] In September 1886, Capt. Vincenzo Filornardi, the Italian who would later become the administrator of the Benadir coast (from 1889 to 1893), declared to the British and Germans that Sultan Barghash had offered to cede Kismayo to Italy on the same terms Cecchi has earlier proposed.

Both Britain and Germany hotly contested this claim, but in the end, it became the basis on which Italy began to press on Barghash's successor, Sultan Khalifa ibn Sa'id of Zanzibar, in May 1888 to conclude the "agreement" with the new sultan's predecessor. The first step in the rigorous and lengthy process toward actualizing the Italian designs for Somali lands began with the April 1889 agreement reluctantly signed by Sultan Khalifa in which he accepted to transfer the Benadir ports to the British East African Company.[41] This was the result of a prolonged negotiation among the Italian, British, and German agents with the sultan of Zanzibar, who had signed the documents in understanding that Britain could reassign the deeds of concession to Italy. It took another two years to make another significant step as further negotiations centered on issues such as compensations, terms of the agreement, and boundary adjustments. In March 1891, the sultan of Zanzibar endorsed an amendment to cede control in perpetuity for a fixed annual settlement of $80,000. Yet this did not end here as expected because of more delays by the Italian Chamber of Commerce. Italy finally ratified the agreement in July 1893. The responsibility of managing the Benadir coast was given to the Royal Italian East African Company, controlled by Filonardi.

While the battle for the possession of Kismayo was going on, the Italian agents were concurrently targeting the sultanates of Majerteen and Hobyo (Obbia) in the northeast. In the initial period of the scramble, four major imperial powers, Germany, Britain, France, and Italy, were locked in a contest to win protectorate treaties with the two sultans. Situated on the tip of the Horn and bordered to the north by the Red Sea and to the east by the Indian Ocean, the sultanates were defined by the Nugaal Valley which runs through the middle of the territories to the south. To the western border was British Somaliland. The Majerteens and Hobyos operated their separate polities with diversified degrees of centralized and decentralized authority systems. In the latter part of the 1880s, Germany had gained some advantage in the race for control of these two strategically located sovereignties, having established a unique liaison with their rulers.

In the end, it was the Italian agent Vincenzo Filonardi who turned things around with an unexpected treaty of protection, concluded first with the Hobyo in December 1888 and with Majerteen Sultanate in April 1889. In April 1895, the treaties were renewed without much trouble. The terms of the agreements unmistakably specified that Italy was not to meddle in the domestic affairs of either of these two kingdoms, and in order to better consolidate their relations through closer and regular liaisons, Italy appointed envoys to both sultanates.

The truth about Italy's unanticipated success with the local rulers is that the sultans had been suspicious of each other and therefore wanted to use Italy's friendship to secure an edge over the other. For instance, Sultan Yusuf Ali of Hobyo signed the 1888 treaty in order to lock in Italy's support in a quarrel with the sultan of Zanzibar over the border region of Warsheekh in the north. Sultan Yusuf Ali further figured that he could use Italy's friendship as cushion to outmaneuver his rival, Boqor Osman Mahmud of the Majerteen, in the race for control of the strategic Nugaal Valley. Coincidentally, Boqor Osman Mahmud also accepted Italy's protection to counter Yusuf Ali of the Hobyo Sultanate. Also implicit in the moves taken by the indigenous rulers was an attempt to avoid direct European occupation of their territories by force. In the end, Italy was the biggest winner as it succeeded in establishing a strong foothold on the two territories and soon after informed its rivals in accordance with the laws of engagement determined at the Berlin Conference in 1884–1885.

To reiterate, Italy had engaged in tricky maneuvers to gain control of the Benadir coast proper since 1886, gaining some measure of presence in April 1889. However, it was not until 1893 that the Benadir lands were finally taken from the rule of the Omani rulers of the Zanzibar. The new acquisition enabled Italy in 1893 to hoist its flag in Merca (Marka), which lies between Mogadishu and Barawa. This marked the formal establishment of the colony of Italian Somaliland on the Somali Peninsula.[42] The Italians followed their successes with an aggressive participation in the local trade, to the displeasure of Somalis and at the risk of conflict with the Omani rulers of Zanzibar, who retained a tenuous sphere of influence in the Benadir areas prior to the European scramble. Similar incidents were witnessed on the individual levels, too. For instance, in October 1893, a local feud involving an aggrieved Somali ended in a deadly fight as the man attacked and killed an Italian soldier before he was shot dead by Italian guards who were close by. This incident and other similar ones implicate the nature of the Italian presence and the dynamics of economic competitions. However, colonization remained a slow process due to Italy's lack of confidence in its capacity to build a viable overseas territory in the manner of the Romans or even to the ability of its British, French, and German competitors.

As often witnessed in the colonial period, African rulers who collaborated with the colonialists enjoyed all the privileges associated with such cooperation as long as they avoided direct altercations with their European masters. In April 1903, a deviation from this unwritten code of protectionism endangered the friendship between Hobyo and

Italy when Sultan Yusuf Ali and his son Yusuf (Jr.) were deposed and deported to Assab in Eritrea by the Italian officials. Trouble started when Sultan Ali adamantly rejected an appeal by the Italians to allow British forces to use Hobyo as a passage in the anticolonial war led by Seyyid Hassan and his Dervish fighters. At this point, it became clear to the Somali indigenous rulers that colonial protectorate agreements were good as long as the local parties respected and protected the Europeans' interests.

Having decided the fate of the Hobyos, the Italians next began to cautiously target the sultanate of Majerteen, mindful not to provoke conflict with Britain. In this regard, it was important for the Italians to work with the British in clearly defining their separate zones of influence. The result was the signing of the Anglo-Italian Treaty of May 5, 1894, which defined the Majerteen Sultanate as being to the east of Taleh and Baran. In 1906, Cavalier Pestalozza of Italy and Gen. Swayne of Britain concluded a follow-up agreement that formerly accepted Baran as part of the Majerteen Sultanate.[43] Among other things, the Anglo-Italian treaty, negotiated without input from the Somalis, predetermined that the Italian administration would bear responsibility for any act perpetrated by the Majerteen against the people under British protection.

Prior to 1903, the Majerteen rulers had somehow avoided any direct collision with the Italians in the region. However, with the sacking of Sultan Yusuf Ali of Hobyo in April 1903, Majerteen's Boqor Osman Mahmud started to test the strength of the treaty of protection. Early on in 1901, Boqor Osman had extended his border by capturing two small towns in the Mudug region. Although this area originally was under the suzerainty of the Majerteen Sultanate, it was seized by Osman's rebellious cousin Keenadiid in the 1870s with the aid of foreign mercenaries. The result of Sultan Boqor's adventure was the ultimate overrun of the Majerteen Sultanate by Italy on its own terms.

THE ETHIOPIANS

While the British, French, and Italians were busy organizing and consolidating power in their newly acquired territories on the Somali Peninsula, Ethiopia's Emperor Menelik II declared his intention not to sit aside and watch the Europeans endanger his country's strategic interests in the Horn region. As a landlocked territory, Ethiopia desperately needed to safeguard its access to the coastal ports of Somalia, particularly the Ogaden passage to the northern port city of Zeila. In Menelik's calculation, the only possible way it could be able to fulfill this need in the context of colonization was to carve out and try to enforce its own part of Somalia. Emperor Menelik II not only tried to keep the European powers from encroaching on Ethiopia territory, but he also tried to extend his sovereignty over the Ogaden region of Western Somalia. Between 1887 and 1897, the Ethiopian army carried out devastating raids, leaving the Somali communities along their path devastated and starved as the invading troops looted and plundered the area.

Actually, this was not anything entirely new to the Somalis. Somalia's history has long been interlocked with Ethiopia's imperial expansions. While the two nations, for the greater part of their existence have had their periods of mutual relations, they have also been in a state of conflict over religious, economic, and political matters. The history of these conflicts goes back to the thirteenth century.[44] In this regard, historian of Africa Lee Cassanelli argues that for the Somali, the European presence, particularly Italy's claims to the ports of Benadir, presented less danger compared to Ethiopia's long-standing threats. In fact, the Somalis had every reason to see their Ethiopian neighbors as more dangerous than the Italians, who at this early period of their arrival were still confined to the coastal enclave.[45] The Somali were intimidated by Emperor Menelik II, who in 1891 had declared that "I do not think for a moment that He [God] will divide Ethiopia among foreign [European] powers."[46] Indeed, Ethiopia lived up to its ruler's declared intentions with a devastating defeat of Italy at an epic colonial battle of Adowa in 1896.[47] The emperor also forcefully seized control of what he claimed was Ethiopia's "seacoast."[48] As a secret British memo rightly stated, "Menelik, the greatest figure in modern Ethiopia, was the first Ethiopian Emperor of whom it might be said that he was facile princeps; not only did he extend Ethiopian territory considerably by the conquest of Galla and other territory, but in the later years of his reign there was no serious threat to his authority from any quarter; and his commanding position was naturally strengthened by the prestige gained by his victory over Italy in 1896" [sic].[49]

By 1897, Menelik had brought the Muslim Emirates of Harar and the Ogaden (western Somalia) under Ethiopian rule.[50] By dint of diplomacy and a strong military presence in the occupied lands, Ethiopia sought to make the Europeans recognize its claims in the Horn. Between 1894 and 1908, Menelik II successfully negotiated treaties with England, Italy, and France. The terms of these treaties effectively recognized Ethiopia's position with a guarantee they would not challenge Menelik's rights over the Somali lands.[51]

SOMALI RESPONSE

Across the continent, Africans' reactions to the European colonial presence took several forms, including diplomacy, emigration, spiritual response, pure silence, and war-making. Most centralized African states with standing armies, such as Samori Toure's (1830–1900) Islamic Mandingo kingdom in West Africa, fought out-and-out wars with the European colonialists.[52] Decentralized societies had no such defense mechanism but also resisted as best they could. The duration of resistance spanned the entire colonial era and one of the important aspects of Africans' response is that the early resistances formed the foundation on which the later and more coordinated anticolonial/nationalist movements were built. For the moment, we are only concerned with the first phase of the resistance lasting approximately from the 1880s to the 1920s.

In most cases, the African indigenous ruling elite whose positions were directly threatened by the alien presence led this early phase of resistance. The indigenous elite figures were often victims of the colonial wars, hence most of the early forms of resistance were directed against mere alien presence. It was later when that presence became more obvious that the resistance was directed against the most intolerable aspects of the colonial rule. It is difficult to provide a comprehensive overview of Somali resistance in a single chapter like this. The following is a brief example of the nature of Africans' initiatives in the face of the alien threat.

In his *A Modern History of the Somali*, Lewis argues that the Somali had in large part acquiesced to the new imperial intrusions by the turn of the twentieth century, except for Sheikh Muhammad Abdille Hassan, who led his Dervish (or *Daraawiish*) followers against the European presence.[53] To this view should be added the contention that such resistance against a formidable enemy needed not always be violent. The Somali used different kinds of strategies, including emigration and indifference. However, the most elaborate and sustained resistance was led by the man the British branded the "Mad Mullah." Hassan and his fighters put up a valiant effort, and without a doubt, the resistance collapsed in the 1920s because of the willingness of the Europeans to act as a common front. This was best expressed in 1888 when the British and the French signed an agreement that recognized each other's separate areas of influence. Later, another border would be drawn up between the British and the Italians by the Anglo-Italian Protocol of May 1894.[54]

Whatever course of action or expression the Africans embarked upon, the European colonial aggression was at this point virtually unstoppable—given the Europeans' advantage over weaponry. By the turn of the twentieth century, the Somali Peninsula has been partitioned into British Somaliland, French Somaliland, Italian Somaliland, and Ethiopian Somaliland (the Ogaden).[55] The nature of partition and the policies pursued by the colonizing powers determined the historical currents of Somalia's evolution for the next two decades. Indeed, a wary Somali poet, Farrah Nurh, best captured the mode of his countrymen about the whole dramatic process of partition: "The British, the Ethiopians, and the Italians are Squabbling. The country is divided and snatched by Who ever is stronger!"[56]

LIFE UNDER COLONIAL RULE

Under colonial rule, the Europeans tried different styles of administration in accordance with the colonial power's goals in the colony. Whether it was the direct or indirect rule system, it was designed to exploit the colony while making the colonized subjects inferior to the colonizers. In the first two decades of the colonial era, the major challenge for each of the imperial powers was to gain firm control of the colony. To this end, the Europeans achieved limited and often varied successes depending on who was the colonizer, the colonized, and in what sociopolitical environment they operated. To better understand the dynamics, it is crucial to approach the history from a geographical standpoint.

In British Somaliland, the colonial order created two "republics": subjects and citizens. The subjects were those in the cities and coastal town like Zeila and Berbera where the colonial influence and authority were mostly exercised. The citizens of British Somaliland were in the hinterlands, where they continued with life as usual with little or no direct contact with the Europeans. Given the circumstances, Somali culture and politics remained largely unaltered in the countryside as they had been prior to colonial invasion. The clans of the countryside continued to function as the center of sociopolitical organization, and family hierarchy was the most common social structure. Somali chieftains "formed a well defined autonomous community with a distinctive way of life, language, and culture."[57] The native people continued to live as nomads, maintaining loyalties to their local clan rather than to Her Majesty's agents who supposedly "owned" them. In other words, colonial influence was limited to a slow pace in contrast to that of the urban centers.

The colonial subjects were found mostly in the cities. This group had been systematically initiated into the colonial system through Western education, cash economy, and new colonial administrative structures. The impact of these colonial institutions on the ability of the individual to resist the process of cultural Westernization and thus be alive to indigenous identity has been aptly summed up by Jean and John L. Comaroff with the experience of Tswana people of Southern Africa as "the colonization of consciousness and the consciousness of colonization."[58] For the individuals who took up residence in the cities, the major attraction was to avail themselves to the new opportunities to earn a living within the global capitalist economy. The colonial urbanites attempted, sometimes with limited success, to emulate European city lives. The anticipation that the local economy would be developed did not materialize due to several factors including lack of natural resources, the predominantly nomadic population, and of course the Europeans' vested economic interests.

In slight terms, Italian interests in the Horn of Africa including Somalia were not exactly similar to the British. While the British downplayed their overall intent of making a formal colony, the Italians did not make any pretense of their intentions. Rather, they wanted to use Somalia as a source of raw materials for their industries. As one of the key policies of the Portuguese, the Italians planned to use their African colonies as a reprieve for Italy's growing and impoverished population. Thus, the government encouraged Italians to migrate to the colony to help develop plantations on the Shebelle and Juba Rivers.[59] The river valleys were favored as the most convenient site of the plantations for irrigation purposes. Italian settlers did not come into the areas in droves because the imperial government lacked the strategy to recruit Italians for supervisory duties in Africa. The African laborers coerced to work on the plantations were watched by armed guards, and most of the workers were Somalis of Bantu origin.[60]

After he landed in 1919, Prince Luigi Amedeo of Savoy, duke of Abruzzi (1873–1933), launched the plantation system in Somalia with the fascist administration of Governor Cesare Maria de Vecchi de Val Cismon (the governor of the Somaliland Protectorate from 1923 to 1928) providing the crucial logistic support. The plantations produced cotton (the first Somali export crop), sugar, and bananas. Although Somali bananas were first exported to Italy in 1927, overall, plantation agriculture attained primary significance in the colony in 1929, after the world cotton market collapsed.

From 1929 to 1936, banana plantations covered more than 3,975 hectares of land. From 1935, the Italian government authorized the Royal

Banana Plantation Monopoly (*Regia Azienda Monopolio Banane*, or RAMB) to take charge of all banana exports as a monopoly. In 1950, when the United Nations (UN) granted Italy the administration of the Somalia trust territory, RAMB was reorganized and renamed the Banana Plantation Monopoly (*Azienda Monopolio Banane*, or AMB). This was part of the move to resuscitate the moribund Somali economy almost destroyed by the war. The Italian monopoly was a mixed bag of blessings for the local economy. Whereas it made possible the initial penetration by Somali bananas into the Italian market, it also eliminated incentives for Somali producers to become internationally competitive or to seek markets elsewhere.

In comparative terms, the investment in cotton brought fewer dividends than bananas. Although cotton showed some promise in 1929, it experienced serious problems following the 1930 world commodity crisis. The impact was such that exports fell from nearly 1,400 tons in 1929 to just 400 tons by 1937. In the 1950s were years of marginal success but no consistent growth. Matters were complicated by lack of Somali wage labor for cotton harvesting—a problem that the Italians tried to reconcile without a significant result.

Among all the plantation crops, sugarcane was the most profitable. First, the sugar business was different from the banana and cotton economies because it was produced for domestic consumption under control of the Italo-Somali Agricultural Society (*Societa Agricola Italo-Somala*, SAIS), based in Genoa. Launched in 1920, the SAIS estate near Giohar started with a modest size of land under cultivation. In 1950, the output had attained about 80 percent domestic demand with 4,000 tons of harvest. Seven years later, the output had met 100 percent domestic demand of 11,000 tons.

In order to solve the acute labor shortages that beleaguered the plantations, the administration changed from forced labor to paid wages. It also granted some extra incentives to workers in the form of permission to maintain private gardens on some of the irrigated lands. As a result, a relatively permanent workforce developed for the plantations. In 1957, the plantation contributed about 59 percent of total exports, thus creating the postcolonial structure of the Somali economy.

NOTES

1. Crawford Young, *The African Colonial State in Comparative Perspective* (New Haven: Yale University Press, 1994). See also Gale M. Gerhart, Review: "Crawford Young, *The African Colonial State in Comparative Perspective*," in *Foreign Affairs* (Sept./Oct. 1995): 185–186.

2. Imaan Daahir Saalax, "The Colonial Impact on Somali Politics," *Somaliland Guardian* (Hegeisa), Oct. 9, 2009.

3. George B. N. Ayittey, *Africa Betrayed* (New York: St. Martin's Press, 1992); and *Africa in Chaos* (New York: St. Martin's Press, 1998); Chika A. Onyeka, *Capitalist Nigger: The Road to Success: A Spider Web Doctrine* (New York: Timbuktu Press, 2000), 63–82.

4. Mark Bradbury, *Becoming Somaliland* (London: Progressio, 2008), 23.

5. Lee V. Cassanelli, *The Shaping of Somali Society: Reconstructing the History of a Pastoral People 1600–1900* (Philadelphia: University of Pennsylvania Press, 1982), 3–12.

6. I. M. Lewis, *Understanding Somalia and Somaliland: Culture, History, Society* (New York: Columbia University Press, 2008), 29.

7. See National Archives Kew (hereafter NAK), CAB/24/256, Italo-Ethiopian Dispute (file marked "Secret C.P. 161" 35), dated August 16, 1935, 6–13; and NAK, CAB/129/12, British Somaliland: Proposals by Ethiopian Government for an Exchange of Territory (marked "Top Secret C.P. 46 319"), dated August 6, 1946, 2–5.

8. Across the Islamic world, such claims are common as identification with the Holy Prophet's lineage accords the claimants a sense of nobility.

9. NAK, CAB 24/3 Fourth Report of the Sub-Committee on Territorial Changes (marked "Secret G-11 8c"), dated July 17, 1917.

10. I. M. Lewis, *A Modern History of the Somali: Nation and State in the Horn of Africa*, 4th ed. (Athens: Ohio University Press, 2002), 10.

11. Victor C. Uchendu, "Ezi na Ulo (The Extended Family in Igbo Civilization)" in *1995 Ahiajoku Lecture* (Owerri: CDMICYSO, 1995), 25–26.

12. Cassanelli, *Shaping of Somali Society*, 19–21.

13. Rudyard Kipling, "The White Man's Burden: The United States and Philippines Islands," *McClure's* (New York), Feb. 12, 1899.

14. NAK, CAB 129/80, The Horn of Africa: Memorandum by the Secretary for Foreign Affairs and the Secretary of State for the Colonies (marked "Secret C. P. 56 84"), dated March 24, 1956, 1.

15. For a synopsis of this interest among the European powers, see NAK CAB 129/86, The Suez Canal of 1888 by Reginald E. Manningham-Butler, dated March 6, 1957.

16. NAK, CAB 24/3, Fourth Report of the Sub-Committee on Territorial Changes (marked "Secret G-11 8c"), dated July 17, 1917.

17. Menelik II, The Emperor of Ethiopia, Letter to Great Britain, France, Germany, Italy, and Russia, 1891.

18. Menelik II, Letter, 1891. See also NAK, CR 2017/C1217, Menelik II [Emperor of Ethiopia] to Colonel [Sir John L.] Harrington [agent and consul-general at the court of Menelik II c.1898-1908] a letter written in characters.

19. Angus Hamilton, *Somaliland* (Westport, CT: Negro Universities Press, 1970), 2.

20. John Gallagher and Ronald Robinson, "The Imperialism of Free Trade," *The Economic History Review* 6 no. 1 (1953): 1–15.

21. NAK, Foreign Office (hereafter FO), Confidential Print (East Africa), 5037. See also NAK, CAB 24/3 Fourth Report of the Sub-Committee on Territorial Changes (marked "Secret G-11 8c"), dated July 17, 1917.

22. NAK, CAB/129/93, Aden Protectorate: Memorandum by Secretary of State for the Colonies dated June 24, 1958.

23. NAK, CAB 129/86, Report, dated March 6, 1957.

24. Although now in ruins, the Suakin seaport served as a hub of international commerce for over 3,000 years.

25. See Khedive Ishmail to Admiral MacKillop, Secret Letters from the Khedive of Egypt in Connection with the Occupation of the East Coast of Africa, dated Sept. 17, 1875.

26. Khedive Ishmail Pasha cited in Robert T. Harrison, *Gladstone's Imperialism in Egypt: Techniques of Domination* (Westport, CT: Greenwood Press, 1995), 53.

27. Lewis, *A Modern History of the Somali*, 42.

28. Said S. Samatar, "Historical Setting," in Helen Chapin Metz (ed.), *Somalia: A Country Study*, 4th ed. (Washington, DC: Library of Congress, 1993), 11–12.

29. Lewis, *A Modern History of the Somali*, 47.

30. NAK, CAB/24/256, 24.

31. Sir Donald Cameron, *Native Administration Memorandum, No.1* (Dar es Salaam, 1930), 4–6, 18–19.

32. Mohammed Diriye Abdullahi, *Culture and Customs of Somalia* (Westport, CT: Greenwood Press, 2001), 20.

33. Gallagher and Robinson, "The Imperialism of Free Trade," 12–13.

34. Lewis, *A Modern History of the Somali*, 41, 44.

35. See, for instance, Paolo Tripodi, *The Colonial Legacy in Somalia: Rome and Mogadishu: From Colonial Administration to Operation Restore Hope* (London: Macmillan Press, 1999), 9–28.

36. Robert Hess, *Italian Colonialism in Somalia* (Chicago: University of Chicago Press, 1966), 2–3; R. J. B. Bosworth, *Italy and the Wider World 1860–1960* (London: Routledge, 1996), 94–97.

37. Actually, this European fantasy goes back to the twelfth century.

38. Archives of the Ministry of African Italian (hereafter ASMAI), pos. 65, f.1, Letter from Mancini to Prime Minister Depretis.

39. NAK, FO, 84/1928, Memo, Kirk confidential, Sept. 24, 1888.

40. The etymology of the name "Benadir" is from the Persian word *bandar*, which means port. In connection with Somali history, it was used in reference to the northern ports of Barawa, and Mogadishu. This fact mirrors the region's importance to Persian and Arab traders during the European Middle Ages. Benadir is renowned for a special breed of goats.

41. Rhodes House Oxford, Salisbury Papers, FO, 84/1980, Portal to Salisbury, Sept. 23, 1889; Salisbury Papers A/179, Portal to Barrington, Sept. 24, 1889.

42. Samatar, "Historical Setting," 11.

43. See Charles G. Herbermann et al., *Knight of Columbus, the Catholic Encyclopedia: An International Work of Reference* (New York: Encyclopedia Press, 1910), 245.

44. Mohamed Haji Mukhtar, "Ethiopia," in *Historical Dictionary of Somalia*, new ed., African Historical Dictionary Series, no. 87 (Lanham, MD: Scarecrow Press, 2003), 82.

45. Menelik II, the emperor of Ethiopia, Letter to Great Britain, France, Germany, Italy, and Russia, 1891; see also Cassanelli, *Shaping of Somali Society*, 200.

46. Menelik II, Letter to Great Britain, France, Germany, Italy, and Russia, 1891.

47. NAK, CAB/24/256, Italo-Ethiopian Dispute, 7–8.

48. Samatar, "Historical Setting," 12–13.

49. NAK, CAB/24/256, Italo-Ethiopian Dispute, 7.

50. Samatar, "Historical Setting," 12–13.

51. NAK, CAB/24/256, Italo-Ethiopian Dispute, 8–10. This memo details the various agreements concluded with the various European colonial powers. See also Cassanelli, *Shaping of Somali Society*, 30.

52. Ibrahim Khalid Fofana, *L'Almina Samor Touré Emperor* (Paris: Présence Africaine, 1998).

53. Lewis, *A Modern History of the Somali*, 62.

54. For details of the terms of these agreements, see NAK, CAB/24/256, Italo-Ethiopian Dispute, 8–10.

55. NAK, CAB/24/256, Italo-Ethiopian Dispute, 8–10. See also Samatar, "Historical Setting," 13.

56. Nurh Farrah, *Sweet and Sour Milk* (St. Pauls, MN: Graywolf Press, 1979/1992).

57. Lewis, *A Modern History of the Somali*, ix.

58. Jean and John L. Comaroff, "The Colonization of Consciousness in South Africa," *Economy and Society* 18 (1989): 267—96.

59. Lewis, *A Modern History of the Somali*, 85–92.

60. Ibid., 93.

4

The Model Colony at War and the Aftermath, 1900–1960

"Decolonization is always a violent phenomenon."[1]

—Frantz Fanon (1925–1961)

Frantz Fanon, a radical race theorist and leader of the Algerian struggle against French colonial rule, argued that the only way to get rid of colonialism and its effects on the colonized society is through violence and bloodletting. In Somalia, violence welcomed colonialism in the first two decades of the twentieth century. Violence has been also prevalent since independence in 1960 despite the fact that a more peaceful order reigned in the country between the end of the First World War and throughout the decolonization period in the 1940s and 1950s. It is now time to closely examine the nature of Somali people's resistance against colonialism and the struggle for freedom, which saw the unification of the ex-Italian Somaliland and the ex-British Somaliland under a self-government on July 1, 1960. The temper and course of the Somali nationalist movement in the post–World War II era was structured not only by all that transpired on the Horn of Africa in the immediate period before and after the Berlin conference of 1884–1885, but also by a variety of developments that transpired during the six decades of colonial rule.

Among these factors were the influence of the Islamic religion on individuals like Sheikh Muhammad Abdille Hassan—the man his countrymen called the "Seyyid" ("Master")—and the legacy he left behind as a champion of anti-imperialism. Other issues included the nature of colonial rule itself, which through exploitation and domination tended to provoke disobedience in the colonized people, and the impact of Western education and the ideologies and lifestyles it inculcates in the learner. Some of these benefits include the power of literacy, the rise of a new social class, and a new brand of nationalism. There are also the varied effects of the First and Second World Wars, which inspired colonized peoples to question the right of aliens to control their destinies. Such radical questions were best articulated in the cities where colonial servants constituted the emergent leaders of opinion—espousing a newly honored public unity.

In general, historians of Africa are divided on the debate about whether the early resistance movements of 1900 to the 1920s inspired the later and better-articulated nationalist movements that eventually led to colonial freedom. For example, Africanist scholars like Coleman, and Robinson and Gallagher have tried to dismiss the early resistance movements by categorizing them as foolish, "romantic," and "reactionary"—thus asserting that the efforts of the early-stage resisters provided no motivation for the later nationalist movements against colonialism.[2] But historian Terrence Ranger strongly contends there is an undeniable connection between primary resistance and the development of nationalist movements in Africa.[3] In East Africa, the Europeans, to their surprise, encountered some of the most formidable struggles often led by elites of the indigenous religious order such as Sheikh Hassan.

However, Mohamed Abdullahi, a Somali historian, strongly refutes any meaningful connection between Sheikh Hassan's Dervish (*Daraawiish* or monks as in Christianity) anticolonial struggle of 1899–1920 and the post–World War II nationalist agitations. For Abdullahi, the Dervish leader "had no grasp of the wider implications of Somali nationhood in the order of [modern] nations; his movement and rhetoric . . . were parochial in nature."[4]

Writing in 1964, eminent British historian Robert Hess acknowledged the mistakes of Hassan that resulted in serious hardships and deaths to the very people whose cause he claimed to be championing; however, Hess described Hassan as the undisputed pioneer of Somali anticolonial nationalist agitation.[5] It is therefore helpful to look at the legacy of Sheikh Hassan and his movement—a struggle the British had waved aside at the onset as an expression of religious fanaticism. Understanding Hassan is critical to understanding how his ideology intersects with the post-WW II nationalist movement that finally brought freedom to the Somalis.

SHEIKH (SEYYID) MUHAMMAD ("MAD MULLAH") ABDILLE HASSAN (1856–1920)[6]

As the Ottoman Empire, representing Muslim might from the early modern period, was breaking up in the nineteenth century following the rise of Europe as a global force, a Euro-Christian fear gripped many Islamic cultures. A combustible mixture of the manner in which the Europeans went about grabbing Asian and African territories as well as the colonizers' Christian identity created a sense of alarm among Muslims around the world. The fright often gave rise to a violent form of anticolonial movements in several parts of Asia and Africa under the banner of jihad or "struggle" against what the Muslims perceived as undue aggression from the "Christian infidels."[7] In Somalia, the leader of this violent anticolonial, anti-Christian sentiment was a self-made legend called Sheikh Muhammad Abdille Hassan. His activities would enthrone a new sense of Pan-Somalism quite unknown to the people prior to his rise.

In spite of his critics, Sheikh Hassan is today widely acknowledged as the father of contemporary Somali nationalism. The mullah, or "Muslim savior," best known to the British authorities as "the Mad Mullah," was born on April 7, 1856, in the Sacmadeeqa valley, a small village between Wudwud and Kirrit in the Buuhoodle of Ogaden desert region of Western Somalia. The family descended from the Darod family clan comprising the Marehan, Ogaden, and Herti confederate (Majerteen, Dulbahante, and Warsangeli). Hassan was the eldest son of Abdullah Hassan and Timiro Seed. His father was an Islamic scholar who had many wives. According to his biographers, young Hassan's family was known for their tradition of Islamic learning.[8] In line with his family tradition, Hassan took to the study of Quran seriously and was also versed in Islamic traditions and jurisprudence, which he sought to apply in a strict and often violent manner among his people.

Die-hard anti-British and anticolonialist, Hassan affiliated himself with the radical Wahhabi School in Islam, which Jeffrey Bartholet in a 2009 commentary pointed out also inspired Osama bin Laden

(March 10, 1957–May 1, 2011).[9] Hassan's mentor in the Wahhabi Order was Sheikh Mohamed Salah or Salih (1853–1917), whom he met in the course of his many traditional pilgrimages to Mecca. Sheikh Salah from Sudan was the founder of the Salahiya mystic order (an offshoot of the Ahmadiyya Order), which was gaining significant influence in the Arabian Peninsula and across the East African coast in the late nineteenth century. A couple of years later in 1895, Hassan appeared on the Somali scene presenting himself as the ambassador of the Salahiyas.[10]

As a young man, Hassan had sailed to Cairo and Alexandria (in Egypt), where he availed himself of the teachings of the Mahadi—a Sudanese radical Islamic religious leader best remembered for his victory over Charles George Gordon in Khartoum, Sudan, in January 1885, which prompted "The Gordon Relief Expedition" of 1884–1885 carefully documented by Sir Charles W. Wilson and widely reported in British newspapers.[11]

On his return to Somalia in 1895 after one of his several trips to Saudi Arabia, Hassan sought to establish an Islamic state in his home-land free from European/Christian/ Ethiopian control. There are stories about how he came to be called "Mad Mullah." One common understanding is that on his arrival at the seaport of Berbera from the trip of 1895, a British officer demanded customs duty. Hassan insisted the officer justify why he should pay a foreigner to enter his own homeland. Other Somalis who served in the colonial administration at the port asked their superior to ignore the man they then called "crazy mullah." Eventually, the term "Mad" was assigned a popular use in colonial writings in 1899 when J. Hayes Sadler, the first British consul general of the Somaliland protectorate, wrote in an official correspondence that reports from Hassan's hideout in the southwestern region indicate that he "had gone off his head."[12]

However, it is important to point out that the Somali word *waalam* or "mad" connotes concepts like renunciation of material or worldly pursuits as with the Sufi mystic order; death-defying recklessness of a warrior; and, of course, genuine insanity. In other words, each of these concepts or all of them could have been implied in reference to the word "crazy." This view is corroborated by accounts of those who had firsthand knowledge of the sheikh. According to a local historian, Aw Jama Omer Issa, who interviewed some of Hassan's former lieutenants, the Master was both charismatic and cruel, and was simply overwhelming with his extremist inclinations. Hanging around him, "You would lose your senses. . . . To whomever he hated, he was very cruel. To those he liked, he was very kind."[13] By the turn of the twentieth century, Hassan had gradually established a reputation as a holy man and sheikh.[14] In a manner reminiscent of the Maji Maji (1905–1907) revolt in Tanzania against the Germans, Malcolm McNeill who served in Her Majesty's Somaliland protectorate in the 1900s, observed that prior to an attack, Hassan was in the habit of working up his followers into a spiritual frenzy by hammering it into their senses that the enemy's bullets would all melt into water upon contact and be rendered useless.[15] In 1912, for instance, British colonial administrator Douglas Jardin narrates an episode in which a Dervish fighter "crawled to Berbera with a bullet wound on his leg and a spear wound right through his body. When the doctor probed the first, the patient gasped 'do not worry about that, but please have a look at the spear wound; it hurts me when I laugh.'"[16]

Hassan first started preaching sedition in the port city of Berbera in 1895, but when he realized that there was little or no chance of making any significant progress among the predominantly Qadiriyya Brotherhood in northwest Somalia who were hostile to other sects in Islam, he began planning to relocate his base. Two years later, Hassan transferred his headquarters to be among the Dulbahante, his maternal kinsmen, in the interior village of Kob Faradod in the Nugaal Valley.[17] It was here that Hassan started to preach strict Islamic practices in line with the teachings of the Salahiya Order. Here also, Hassan familiarized himself with the politics of Ethiopian colonial overtures in the Ogaden territory. Earlier in 1895, Emperor Menelik II of Ethiopia had instructed Ras Makonnen, the governor of the Harrar Province of Ethiopia (from 1887 to 1906) to send occupying forces to the Ogaden as the British began to systematically pull their troops out of the territory.[18]

Thus, in the initial period of the struggle in 1897, Sheikh Hassan's Dervish movement aimed to flush out the Ethiopian occupation force from his Ogaden native land. But with the British's hostile attitude toward the Dervishes' cause, the struggle expanded to include the Europeans as targets following an incident in 1899 that involved an illegal sale of a gun to Hassan by a corrupt Somali constable named Ilaalo, who was in the employ of the British colonial administration. On his return to Berbera, the corrupt officer, who wanted to save himself, apparently lied in a report to the authorities that his gun had been stolen by Hassan. The report prompted the British vice-consul in Somaliland to dispatch a stern and insulting memo alleging that Sheikh Hassan has stolen the gun and that he should immediately return it. Instead, on September 1, 1899, Sheikh Hassan replied in a letter challenging British rule in the country. The defiance brought the sheikh to the attention of the British authorities. At this point, the mullah found enough reasons to rightly interpret the Ethiopian aggression in Ogaden as a conspiracy between the Abyssinians and the British. The mullah's perceptions were justified as was later revealed in a top secret memo from the Ethiopian government addressed to the British Cabinet and dated August 1946 where the officials discussed about an opportunity "of rectifying the injustice done to the British Somali tribes by the treaty with Ethiopia in 1897."[19]

For the mullah and his followers, the dawn of a long struggle had kicked off. In his speeches and writings, Hassan repeatedly argued that the British infidels "have destroyed our [Islamic] religion and made our children their children."[20] He further alleged that the Christian Ethiopians and British were bent on destroying the Somali tradition of religious and political freedom. Therefore, every Somali must rise to resist this new development. It was in this mindset that Hassan wrote to the British in 1897 demanding respect for his "country" and to be taken seriously as the leader of a sovereign nation. "We are a government. We have a sultan, and emirs, or princes, and chiefs and subjects."[21]

At the inception, the Dervish movement attracted a small number of followers from different regions of the Somali Peninsula. Most supporters, however, came from among his Ogaden kinsmen. Portraying himself as a champion of Somalis religious and political freedom, Hassan declared a sacred ordinance that anyone who spurned his call for Somali unity and independence would be considered a pagan or unbeliever (*kafir* in Arabic; *gaal* in Somali). He appointed ministers and advisers for different parts of Somalia and began to procure arms from Sultan Boqor Osman Mahmud of Majerteen Sultanate (in the northeast part of Somalia). He also got arms from the Ottoman Empire and Sudan to enable him to launch a jihad to free his people.

Organization of the jihad faced numerous challenges including training, logistics, weaponry, food, and other material supplies. These crucial resources were not simply at the Dervishes' disposal. While some Somalis voluntarily donated a few of the critically needed materials, the Dervishes often resorted to brigandage in order obtain some critically needed materials such as camels, provisions, and rifles for their cause. These violent raids increasingly alienated Hassan from the people and thus eroded his respect among the greater population, including Sultan Boqor of the Majerteen Sultanate, who initially revered and supported his cause.

In 1899–1900, Hassan launched coordinated attacks against both the Ethiopian and British troops stationed in the Ogaden territory. For instance, Capt. Malcolm McNeill, who commanded the Somali Field Force against the mullah, reported in his diary that in "March, 1900, he [Hassan] attacked, with a large force, an Abyssinian frontier outpost near Jig Jigga, but was completely defeated, being repulsed with heavy loss which the Abyssinians stated amounted to 2,800 in killed alone."[22] The reported number of deaths appears suspicious because in regard to the same battle, MacNeill wrote that the attack was reportedly carried out by "Hassan's 1,500 Dervish troops equipped with 20 modern rifles."[23] Despite his losses, similar spectacular and bloody raids would be repeated across northern, central, and western Somalia until 1920. In fact, Captain McNeill noted that "toward the end of June 1900, Mahomed Abdullah had, by all accounts, made his position even stronger than before his defeat in March, and he practically dominated the whole of the southern portion of our Protectorate."[24]

The overall commander of the British Somaliland forces was Lt.-Col. (later Brig.) Eric John Eagles Swayne (1863–1929), and he bore the full brunt of the mullah's wrath after he was dispatched from India in late 1900 for the Somali assignment.[25] Swayne left a vivid account of his horrific experience commanding troops hunting for Hassan and his Dervish fighters. In one report, Swayne narrates: "We were in an extremely dense bush, so I decided to move slowly, hoping to find a clearing, which was confidently reported by prisoners, but the bush became thicker. Soon the Dervishes were advancing from all sides. Men and beasts fell around, as great shouts of "Allah! Allah!" rang out. Somali "friendlies" panicked and fell back. Pack animals stampeded—a thousand camels with water tins and ammunition boxes jammed against one another . . . scattering their loads everywhere."[26]

The tenacity of the Dervishes' struggle was unwavering, according to Douglas James Jardin (1888–1946), who served as secretary to the administration in the Somaliland protectorate between 1916 and 1921. Jardin recorded that after one humiliating defeat, the British forces "imagined that they saw a 'white man' fighting alongside the Dervishes—how else could these 'natives' be inflicting so much pain."[27] Similar "visions" were recorded by McNeill, who took part in the war and recounted spending several sleepless and jumpy nights in anticipation of when the mullah's fighters might take his battalion by surprise.[28] Such nightmares in the hands of the mullah forced the British to rethink the map of British Somaliland—which saw concessions made to the Ethiopians and the Italians in order to secure their help in the war against a formidable enemy.

In 1901, a joint Anglo-Ethiopian force began to coordinate massive plans to eradicate the jihadists and/or at least confine the movement farther west to the Ogaden and/or the frontier borderland of northern Kenya.[29] It soon became clear to the British that stopping the Dervishes' challenge was not going to be easy in a land that lacked such common necessities of life as fresh drinking water and food. The inclement weather and the arid/semiarid terrains offered no easy consolation for the Europeans. In contrast, Hassan and his fighters knew the rugged terrain and the networks of caves and trenches. In the manner of the Mongols' army, the Dervishes adapted to the depredations of the desert conditions by eating carcasses of beasts and drinking water from the dead bellies of animals. Until 1905, the Anglo-Ethiopian expedition was still struggling to gain a hold on the revolt despite the advantage of possessing superior weapons, which included the dreaded Maxim machine gun invented by American-born British inventor Sir Hiram Maxim in 1884.

Meanwhile, the Dervish movement was attracting supporters as Hassan incrementally seized more territories. One of his designs was to gain access to the sea through the Illig corridor so that he could obtain supplies. In 1903, the Dervishes stormed the sea in an attempt to take possession of the port there. The Italians saw themselves in the middle of a desperation battle. In April 1904, British forces came to the rescue to engage the fighters, who fought "in a determined manner in which stone zaribas and towers were defended by the Dervishes who lost heavily."[30] In March 1905, following the Illig Treaty of 1904, for instance, the entire Nugaal Valley, a large shallow drainage territory lying between the sultanates of Hobyo (Obbia) and the Majerteen in the Northeast of the country, was conceded to Hassan by the Italians as a way of placating his unrelenting threat.[31] The hope was that this concession would make the Dervishes turn their interest away from the rest of the Italian Somaliland, and by so doing allow the Italians to give the needed attention to the administration of the territory. The plan failed because Hassan could not be appeased, now having built a solid support base among those who had identified with his ideology. To this crowd of followers, the mullah was everything: an icon of revolt, killer of colonialism, and a symbol of freedom and liberty.

Pressing on with the struggle was not by any means easy as one of the greatest hurdles that dogged Hassan's progress was the efficacy of the imperial divide-and-rule canon. Hassan's greatest undoing was the brutal manner he went about trying to build a unique centralized state that had never been seen before on the Somali Peninsula. As a result, Somalis were mostly opposed to the Dervishes. Yet some of the raids, killings, stealing, and other acts perpetrated by the

Dervishes could hardly be associated with any sane religious practices. Consequently, many concerned individuals and groups began to question Hassan's moral convictions. The opposition received a boost when some members of the Dervish made public a memo condemning Hassan's excesses against fellow Muslims from the founder of the Salahiya order, Sheikh Mohamed Salah, who lived in the Arabian Peninsula. The letter that was secretly circulated among the Dervishes dealt a serious blow to Hassan's reputation as his mentor Sheikh Salah (the founder of the Salahiya *dariqa*) renounced him completely in 1909.

Following this episode, 600 Dervishes consulted secretly at Gubad, a small village south of Eyl to plot against the mullah. The meeting, which took place under a tree, was to be called *Canjeel Talawaa* (the Tree-of-Bad-Counsel). The participants deliberated on three options: (1) to kill Hassan and replace him with another sheikh who could continue the holy war; (2) to strip him of the honor and responsibility of the Dervish and replace him with another sheikh; (3) to completely cripple the struggle.[32]

The third option was endorsed by the plotters, and the decision was to simply desert the movement en masse. But no sooner did the meeting end than one of the participants, Shire Cumbaal, alerted the mullah. The result was a bloody battle between the loyalists and the conspirators' clans. The mullah emerged victorious after decimating several Dervish clans, like the Majerteen and Dulbahante. The loyalists also slaughtered many holy men, a desperate action considered a heinous crime in Islamic teaching.[33]

At this point, the British, who had experienced serious frustrations at the hands of the mullah, hoped that the worst was over, hence the commanders ordered that their forces be pulled out of the interior of the Somaliland protectorate. But they acted in haste, for no sooner had the British forces vacated their positions than Hassan took over the empty areas, causing enormous fear that the entire peninsula could fall under his control. Total anarchy had ensued in the years following the abandonment of the English interior, and according to British estimates, had caused the death of one-third of the Somaliland protectorate's population during the reign of the Seyyid.[34] Again the actual number of casualties may never be determined because the British used the inflated figures for anti-Dervish propaganda. At this point, Hassan had gained the upper hand, and the British needed to take prompt action in order to avoid further damages.

The response was the first successful Anglo-Italian cooperation, which came in December 1910 when the Majerteen and Warsangeli clans readily joined forces with the British to stop the reign of Hassan. The joint operation was crucial as it also enabled the Italians to start regaining control of the northeastern territories and found the peace critical for a social order that was compromised by the jihadists. Also, some of the Dervish supporters turned against the movement in a show of respect for the European rule.[35] Under pressure, Hassan's followers retreated into the British Somaliland, establishing a new Dervish headquarters at Taleh (Taleex), a small enclave in northeastern Somalia. With the retreat, the Italians turned indifferent to the rebellion, which they now conceived of as a purely English problem.[36]

Soon new battles erupted between the Dervishes and the British forces. In 1913 at the battle of Dul Madoba (which means "Black Hill" in Somali), the British forces suffered one of their most embarrassing defeats in the struggle. Basking in this victory, the poet, soldier, and scholar authored a poem in which he taunted Richard Corfield, one of Her Majesty's commanders of the expedition against the Dervish fighters who was killed in the battle: "You have died Corfield and are no longer in this world. A merciless journey was your portion." In the same poem, Sheikh Hassan instructed Corfield on what he should tell those who will judge him in hell: "Answer them how God tried you. Say to them: From that day to this the Dervish never ceased their assault upon us."[37]

Among other things, the mullah's poem continued to taunt his victim. "Say: 'When pain racked me everywhere / Men lay sleepless at my shrieks.' Hyenas eat Corfield's flesh, and crows pluck at his veins and tendons." Toward the end of the poem, Hassan asked Corfield to tell the angels of God at the gate of hell that the mullah's fighters "are like the advancing thunderbolts of a storm, rumbling and roaring."[38]

Between 1913 and 1920, Britain launched at least two major assaults aimed at either killing or capturing Hassan. Although they almost succeeded, these efforts did not achieve their desired results. At a point, Hassan sensed a demoralized and confused Britain and in a correspondence addressed to the British, he teased them thus: "I wish to fight with you. I like war, but you do not."[39] As *The Times* of London newspaper summed it up in a 1923 review of Hassan's correspondence, it "suggests that—mad or sane—he was intelligent enough to grasp the essential factor and sincere enough to state it in plain terms."[40]

Indeed, historians may not know to what extent this pugnacious declaration may have informed the British Cabinet's approval of air operations against the Dervish fighters. In fact, the challenge of the

Dervishes in Somalia presented the British with testing grounds for its new doctrine of war, which stressed the use of aircraft as the primary arm, usually supplemented by ground forces, according to particular requirements.[41]

The formidable "Force Z" under the command of Group Capt. R. Gordon landed in Berbera in December 1919 to take a crack at the warmonger.[42] After 19 long years of pain and anarchy, the end of the Dervishes was near. The unit comprised 12 Havilland DH.9 aircraft, 10 Ford trucks, two Ford ambulances, six motorcycles, two Crosley light trucks, 36 officers, and 183 men.[43] Maj. A. B. Russell, who was with the Force Z of the RAF unit, acknowledged that it was difficult to achieve a decisive victory against Hassan until the aerial assault was launched.[44] The RAF's unparalleled aerial bombardments in Taleh, lasting about 23 days, shocked and awed the fighters.[45]

The entire air attack, which eliminated thousands of the Dervish forces, claimed only the lives of two British soldiers and left four others wounded.[46] Hassan and the remainder of his followers vacated their headquarters, moving to a neighborhood of Gorrahei close to the Fafan River. Here, the British-commanded Camel Corps thought they had finally cornered the very elusive man. In the violence that ensued, the Camel Corps killed most of his remaining followers, including six sons, four daughters, and two sisters. But for the final time they lost complete sight of Hassan.[47] In February 1921, news reached the British in Mogadishu that Hassan had died of pneumonia in December 1920, following the worldwide influenza epidemic of the previous year, which got to the region in that year.[48]

CONNECTION BETWEEN THE MULLAH AND THE RISE OF THE LATER NATIONALIST CONSCIOUSNESS

Contrary to what some of his critics might say, the immediate and longer impact of Hassan's Dervish anticolonial struggle was vast and profound in the broader contexts of colonial rule and modern Somali nationalism. For Britain, the direct and successful outcome of the aerial assault marked the beginning of a new small-war doctrine that would witness the use of airpower to prosecute military operations especially in its imperial dominions. The new doctrine inspired the declaration by Winston Churchill in December 1919 that "the first duty of the RAF [Royal Air Force] is to garrison the British Empire."[49] Yet, throughout the decades that colonialism lasted, Britain was extremely careful not to provoke the rise of another "Mad Mullah"-style uprising in Somalia. For instance, in February 1922, when a high-ranking British officer, Captain Gibb, was shot dead by those described in a telegraph to the Colonial office by Governor Archer of Somaliland as "miscreants," the governor advised caution, noting that "the trouble is strictly localized. . . . Am waiting arrival of Pinder before determining necessary action and will telegraph again."[50] Such a guarded approach explains why a more cordial atmosphere marked the decolonization program in Somaliland from the postwar period to independence.

For the Somalis, the question lingers as to whether Sheikh Hassan practiced tribalism or nationalism. In 1993, Somali scholar Abdisalam M. Issa-Salwe argued persuasively that Hassan was "a Somali nationalist hero and father of modern Somali nationalism." According to Issa-Salwe, Hassan "envisaged the Somali state as being a unified political unit and nurturing a political ideology surmounting clanism. Both attributes were part of the modern Somali nationalism when it reawakened in the early 1940s."[51]

Perhaps there may be no common agreement on Hassan's place in history as a symbol of Somali nationalism. From his writings and proclamations, however, an unbiased judgment of him is that the mullah was a cultivated nationalist who arrived far ahead of his time. Said Samatar authoritatively asserts that the mullah earned himself a special place "in the history of the Horn as the George Washington of Somali nationalism and the Shakespeare of the Somali language."[52] Samatar further lauds Hassan for his ability to forge a centralized state, which is a very difficult task for Somalis today. This sense of patriotism could be seen when Hassan repeatedly called for Somali unity against the alien invaders. They "have destroyed our [Islamic] religion and made our children their children."[53] Such language of nationalism often arises when a people, a group is confronted with a common danger, especially when the danger is coming from outside.

It was very rare to find Africans like Sheikh Hassan in this early period of colonial conquest who fully understood the implications of the Europeans' colonial aggressions. Hassan compares well with King Tewodros II (1818–1868) of Ethiopia, who fought against British imperialism in Ethiopia and committed suicide in the war rather than be subjected to humiliation in the hands of the colonialists.[54] Hassan further reminds us of the tenacious Berber anticolonial leader Abdul Karim (1882–1963) in Morocco, who sustained a brutal war against the French and Spanish imperialism for over two decades. Each of these early African leaders of anticolonial movements was judged "mad" for questioning the Europeans' acts of injustices meted out to Africans. Indeed, as the Europeans aspired to dominate the world with the advantage of superior technology, the thought of an African leader demanding respect from the conquerors sounded to them like an act of impudence.

Hassan's exploits and his ability to evade capture have been represented in Somali poetry and mythologies vis-à-vis its intersection with modern Somali nationalism, particularly in the context of decolonization. These writings evoke passions in the minds of the reader, while reinforcing the myths and legends that were cultivated in the mullah's memory. One of the myths remains the belief among the Somalis that Sheikh Hassan possessed supernatural powers. The tradition claims that the "Master" always wore a protective amulet, which contained a Koran donated by the *shaitan* (or devil) on the request of a lady lizard. According to this legend, Hassan had on one occasion spared the life of the lizard, who was actually the wife of the devil. In gratitude, the lizard told Hassan the same night that her husband, the *shaitan*, would be visiting him to express his thanks and that he (Hassan) should request the devil give him the amulet with a promise that whatever he asked for would be granted.[55]

This legend is reinforced with many other stories. Ralph E. Drake-Brockman, a colonial scholar who was in Somalia in the early 1900s, encountered one of these stories repeated among the people. An Ogaden man hatched a plan to assassinate Hassan when no one was around besides the two. The mullah soon became aware of his intentions and at once confronted his would-be assassin. Then pointing to the man's rifle, Hassan said, "Now is your time." The would-be killer raised his rifle, pulled the trigger, but nothing followed. He reloaded and attempted again, but there was a misfire. At this point the Master exposed his amulet that the *shaitan* had instructed him to wear every day and night.[56]

In whatever light one may cast him, the truth remains that the Dervish soldier, poet, and religious figure resisted foreign control for 20 long years while attempting to spread the Wahhabi brand of Islam throughout the Horn of Africa. This effort endured as a counter ideology to European colonialism. The mullah's leadership gave rise to a new form of Pan-Somali nationalism which cut across clan feelings. In a society where clan identity has proved so resilient, there is no debating the fact that some of his fellow Somalis, particularly certain rivals to his Darod clan, rejected and despised the Dervishes. Yet it is clear that the legacy of the movement portrays contemporary nationalism as a struggle against foreign invasion as well as a struggle against interclan conflicts and disputes. The importance of the stories and poems Hassan's activities inspired cannot be underestimated.

THE ITALIANS AND THE NORTHEASTERN SULTANATES

After the collapse of the Dervish rebellion, no comparable coalition of Somalis materialized against foreign rule throughout the duration of colonial rule. The only other notable resistance movement was the struggle between the Italians and sultans of the northeastern sultanates of the Majerteen and Hobyo. Trouble began in April 1901, when Boqor Osman Mahmud, the Majerteen sultan, acted against the treaty of protection between his kingdom and Italy by seizing two small towns in the Mudug region. Although this area was originally under the suzerainty of the Majerteen sultanate, it was seized by Osman's rebellious cousin, Keenadiid, in the 1870s, and since then had become an independent breakaway sultanate of Hobyo.

Given that both regions were under Italian protection, Giulio Pestalozza, the Italian consul at Aden pressed the Majerteen ruler to withdraw from the occupied lands in order to avoid conflict with the Hobyos. This entreaty made little or no impression on Boqor Osman, who flatly rejected the appeal. The disagreement bred deep-seated distrust between the Italians and the Majerteens. Consequently, the Italians decided that if Osman were to get away with this action, it might embolden him to do something worse. Events took a new twist when an Italian officer in Cairo, Egypt, intercepted a secret letter from Boqor Osman seeking Ottoman protection against the Italian presence in his kingdom.

Under these circumstances, Italy launched a preemptive assault on Boqor Osman. The heavy artillery bombardments directed toward the coastal villages of Bareeda and Bender Khassim (Boosaaso) crippled Osman's modest cache of arms and ammunitions. Osman fled to the interior, as the Italians seized the coastal towns of Alula, Bender Khassim, Bareeda, and Muranyo. Finding himself in an awkward position, Osman decided to seek reconciliation with Italy. This was happening in the heat of the Dervish anticolonial movement, which also put both the Italians and the British on edge. For his own part, Osman had previously enjoyed a more cordial relationship with the Dervish leader until constant Dervish raids on Majerteen settlements caused strains in their relationship.

But as is well known in history, fear creates strange bedmates. The ominous threat presented to both the Europeans and the Majerteen sultan prompted both sides to seek a resolution to their quarrel. In March 1910, following prolonged discussions, the protectorate agreement between Italy and Majerteen was renewed with modifications that secured for Italy a more rigid and effective control.

The dawn of fascism in the early 1920s implied a radical change of strategy for Italy as the northeastern kingdoms were soon fenced within the boundaries of *La Grande* Somalia in accordance with the designs of the Italian fascist government. With the arrival of Governor Cesare Maria De Vecchi on December 15, 1923, things began to change fast for the Benadir parts of Somaliland. Prior to the 1920s, Italy had some degree of presence, but secured direct rule over these territories. However, the final crushing of the Dervishes in January 1920 altered Italy's approach to the colony. Implicitly nullifying previous treaties, Benito Mussolini gave the green light to De Vecchi on July 10, 1925, to commence a direct takeover of the two separate northeastern sultanates.

Governor De Vecchi began to carry out the plan without delay. Haunted by their experiences with the Ethiopians, the Italians' original plan was to disarm the sultanates. In order to see that his plan succeeded, the governor began to reconstitute the old Somali police corps, the *Corpo Zaptié*. The pressure engendered by the new development forced the two rival sultanates to settle their differences over Nugaal possession—forming a united front against their common enemy.

The Italians' attack on Hobyo commenced in October 1925, and the entire territory was completely overrun in a month with minimal resistance. But the conquest of the Majerteen kingdom did not come as easy. No sooner had the Italians turned their attention to the Majerteens than a new setback arose. On November 9, 1925, a mutiny led by Omar Samatar, one of the military chiefs of Sultan Ali Yusuf of Hobyo, would not only upset the original battle plans of the Italians but also forced them to first deal with the new threat. After two years of devastating war, the Majerteen Sultanate was overrun and Sultan Osman took refuge in British Somaliland. In November 1927, formal surrender was observed in Hurdia where the sultan dramatically handed over his sword to Governor De Vecchi.

THE INTERWAR YEARS

From the 1920s, following the end of the WWI, the colonial authorities, particularly Britain, settled down for the first time to create a functional colonial bureaucracy. This new administration was composed of both European and Somali peoples. The former occupied the top administrative and supervisory positions, while the newly educated Somalis occupied secondary or lower positions.

As the "new men" mingled with their colonial superiors, they developed new tastes, new words, and new ideologies. The result was that a revival, albeit in a more temperate manner, of Somali nationalist consciousness began to spring up in the urban areas like Mogadishu in the south and Berbera in the north. This development first began to manifest at a slower pace in the 1930s. It gathered momentum in the 1940s and became more noticeable in ways never before seen. At this time, the population of the ancient cosmopolitan port city of Mogadishu had doubled in the colonial century—that is, since 1900.[57] Although unionism or any forms of political gathering was outlawed by the Europeans, there were new political and social attitudes and ideas concerning the future of Somalia as a free nation. Most of these new ideologies were being championed in Italian Somaliland by the new generation of a small young, educated, and urban working African middle class who had been given access to Western education and occupied positions of privilege in the colonial civil service.

At the same time, such feelings had begun to manifest in the British Somaliland protectorate, although at a measured pace given the absence of encouraging conditions such as urbanization in the colony.[58] One of the earliest examples of an influential Somali colonial civil servant who sought to spread the ideology of political and social unification of the Somali people was Haji Farah 'Omar, who became active in the 1920s. Omar was soon exiled to Aden, where he participated in founding the Somali Islamic Association (SIA). Together with his associates, Omar strived hard to present Somali problems and concerns to the people of Britain. Through their activities, the SIA sowed the seed for the development of modern Somali nationalism and new dreams of a unification of all Somali people, including the idea of creating Somali orthography.

In other cities, such as Berbera, Burao, and Hargeisa, small groups of agitators of Somali nationalism emerged around 1935. The Somaliland National Society (SNS) was established in 1936. The society focused on promoting the importance of modern educational progress in general and to seek avenues to transcend clan consciousness, which continued to divide Somalis. In 1938, the first government school opened to the male public, but it was not until the 1950s that females were first admitted in any public school. Although Western education was gaining more popularity, Islamic traditions and system of education that had long been connected to a large population of the Somalis were upheld by the new generation of nationalists.

Italian troops raise their flag on the roof of the British post of Jirreh in British Somaliland during World War II. (AP Photo)

POST WORLD WAR II PERIOD AND THE COUNTDOWN TO INDEPENDENCE

On May 5, 1943, the Somali Youth Club (SYC) was founded by Seyyid Abdullah (who later became the first prime minister of his country). The party grew in leadership and membership to emerge as one of the first major political associations in the period. In 1947, the SYC became known as the Somali Youth League (SYL). At its inception, the members of the party retained some of the old parochial loyalties, drawing its main support from the Darod and Hawiye family clans. However, the SYL had goals similar to the SIA, and soon its leaders began to advocate for the elimination of the ancient interclan and communal frictions. The leaders also called for the expansion of educational opportunities to enable young people to gain access to Western-style schools, while also calling for adoption of a Somali language. British administrations encouraged the SYL largely because it supported the unity of all Somalis under a single (and most likely British) government structure.

It might be recalled that in 1947, following Allied victory in the Second World War, the British foreign secretary of state for the colonies, Ernest Bevin, on February 9, 1959 at Hargeisa, implored members of the Four Power Commission comprising the United States, Great

Britain, France, and Russia, to support the unification of all strands of Somali lands under a single government—"i.e., those in the Protectorate, Kenya, Ethiopia and French Somaliland."[59] This appeal was denied by the other members of the commission charged with the task of deciding the future of Italy's former colonies. At the same time, the pro-Italian lobby group launched an intense campaign for 30 years of trusteeship under an Italian administration. Early in 1947 the United Nations had mandated Italy to renounce all its colonial possessions in Africa, including Somalia.

In 1950, just three years after it had acted in accordance with its mandate, the United Nations permitted Italy to take over the administration of its former Somalia as a Trust Territory. Under the agreement, the UN Advisory Council based in Mogadishu, supervised the activities of *Amministrazione Fiduciaria Italiana della Sommalia*, or AFIS, which was assigned to prepare southern Somalia for independence over a 10-year period.

The SYL was strongly opposed to Italy's new role as the Administering Authority for southern Somalia. For the SYL members, this was apparently difficult to comprehend, considering the sudden twist of events—perhaps a diplomatic move aimed to reward the same Italy (that fought with Axis Germany against the rest of the world) for a future expected compliance with Western-prescribed ways of behavior.[60] The SYL suspected that Italy was attempting a return to colonial rule under the guise of diplomacy. This suspicion amplified nationalist rhetoric and the desire for freedom from colonial rule.

In the 1954 municipal elections, the SYL won 141 of the 281 seats. Another political party, the Hisbia Dighil Mirifle, which was the only running party of that year established on a clannish basis, won 57 seats. Both the National United Front and the United Somali parties also held tight to the idea of an independent and united Somali territory.[61] In 1959, the Somali Youth League, which under the leadership of Seyyid Abdullah had gained a reputation as a pro-Western political party, won a general election in the UN Trust Territory. Full of nationalist vigor, the SYL advocated a single state embracing all areas populated by Somalis. This would mean parts of Ethiopia, Kenya, and French Somaliland (now independent Djibouti). The appeal for amalgamation of the North and South was well received by the nationalists in British Somaliland, where such ideology had been on the rise.

In the British Somaliland (north), nationalists focused their anger on the transfer of the Haud and Reserved Areas in 1954 to Ethiopia under Emperor Haile Selassie. The British agonized over how best to settle the situation without antagonizing their Ethiopian allies as well as not provoking the anger of Somali nationalists. Besides the political and historical implications of the transfer of this Somali-inhabited region to Ethiopia, the economic consequence was that an area that had provided rich fodder for the clans in British Somaliland had been pulled out of their reach. From this point, northern Somalia would enter into a period of nationalist sentiment described by Mohammed Abdullahi as "paroxysms of nationalism that took them to independence."[62] In 1957, the first Legislative Council of the British Somaliland Protectorate was formed, and Somalis began to replace expatriate officials at the national government level. On June 26, 1960, British Somaliland was granted independence under leadership of the Somali National League (SNL) headed by Mohamed Ibrahim Egal. Although Somalia was being hastily geared for political independence by foreign powers, these humble beginnings of Somali political successes helped to frame the scheduled independent picture not even one decade into the future. When Somaliland finally became free from British control in 1960, it was officially merged with the UN Trust Territory on July 1, 1960, to form the Somali Republic.

It is therefore clear that on the eve of Somalia's unification and independence, a unique and virulent brand of nationalism, infused with traditional cultural unity, proindependent, and promodern advancements in all lands inhabited by the Somalis, had emerged among the people. The new aspiration reechoed the struggle first campaigned for by Sheikh Muhammad Abdille Hassan. His legacy and influence as the father of Somali nationalism had continued to influence nationalist thinking. This spirit eased the newly independent nation into the postcolonial order.

The effects of colonialism and the brand of nationalism it inspired from that point on had significant effects on the troubled Somalia independent state. This is best attested to by a British secret memorandum dated March 24, 1956, and jointly released by the secretary of state for foreign affairs and the secretary of state for the colonies. The memo highlighted some of the sociopolitical and economic problems that were considered likely to break the proposed new state; it was unequivocally noted that "the natural resources of Somalia are insufficient to make her [Somalia's] economy viable without outside help."[63] Additionally, there was an acute shortage of teachers to execute development programs, and it was noted that "if independent Somalia is to be prevented from coming under influence of Egypt or the Russians, the West will need to subsidize her and provide advisers and technical help."[64] Yet, more revealing is the realization on the part of the British that the Ogaden question needed to be resolved for peace to prevail in postcolonial Somalia. As Norman Brook, Her Majesty's official, stated in a report on Somaliland's proposed independence, "The problem here turns entirely upon a settlement of the difficulties which have arisen in the Haud and Reserve Area. The prospect of the cession of these territories to the protectorate (which would be the only real solution of the immediate and limited problem) must be regarded as extremely remote."[65]

From the foregoing, it becomes clear that the colonialists fully understood the precarious conditions of Somalia and that it was going to hinder the state building project in the postcolonial era. The argument is not whether the British and Italian colonial rulers did not do enough to prepare the Somalis for self-rule; the concern is that by error or commission, Somalia, like most former colonial territories, was programmed for failure even before it reached the promise land of freedom. This left the Somalis with the question of *"Que faire?"*

NOTES

1. Frantz Fanon, *The Wretched of the Earth, Preface by Jean-Paul Sartre* (New York: Grove Press, 1963), 99.

2. James S. Coleman, *Nigeria: Background to Nationalism* (Berkeley, University of California Press, 1963), 172; R. E. Robinson and J. Gallagher, "The Partition of Africa," in *The Cambridge Modern History* (Cambridge: Cambridge University Press, 1962), xi.

3. Terence O. Ranger, "Connections Between 'Primary Resistance' Movements and Modern Mass Nationalism in East and Central Africa," *Journal of African History* 9, no. 3 (1968): 437–53.

4. Mohamed Diriye Adbullahi, *Culture and Customs of Somalia* (Westport, CT: Greenwood Press, 2001), 23.

5. Robert L. Hess, "The 'Mad Mullah' and Northern Somalia," *Journal of African History* (1964): 419.

6. The date of Hassan's birth has been a point of controversy. While some sources put it at 1864, others, like his native Somali biographer Ciise, put it at 1856. See Aw Jaamac Cumar Ciise, *Taariikhdii Daraawiishta iyo Sayid Maxamed Cabdulle Xasan, (1895–1921), Wasaaradda Hiddaha iyo Tacliinta Sare* (Muqdishu: Akadeemiyaha Dhaqanka, 1976), 4.

7. Abdisalam M. Issa-Salwe, "The Daraawiish Resistance: The Clash between Somali Clanship and State System," paper presented at the fifth International Congress of Somali Studies, Holy Cross College, Worcester, Massachusetts, Dec. 1–3, 1993, 1, 5, 18.

8. See I. M. Lewis, "In the Land of the Mullah," *Sunday Times* (London), Aug. 30, 1992, 8–9; and Robert L. Hess, "The Poor Man of God: Muhammed Abdullah Hassan," in Norman R. Bennett, ed., *Leadership in Eastern Africa: Six Political Biographies* (Boston: Boston University Press, 1968), 63–108.

9. Jeffrey Bartholet, "It's a Mad, Mad, Mad, Mad World: How Somalia's Legendary 'Mad Mullah' Prefigured the Rise of Osama bin Laden—and the 'Forever War' between Islam and the West," *Newsweek*, Oct. 1, 2009, 43–47.

10. One aspect of the story said that Sheikh Salah had appointed Hassan his representative in Somalia. Another version claims that a group nominated Hassan for appointment. See Ciise, *Taariikhdii Daraawiishta*, 8.

11. See Sir Charles W. Wilson, *From Korti to Khartum: A Journal of the Desert March from Korti to Gubat, and the Ascent of the Nile in Gordon's Streamers* (Edinburgh and London: William Blackwood and Sons, 1885), vii–viii; *The Times*, "The Fall of Khartoum" (London), Feb. 6, 1885; and *The Times* "The War in the Soudan" (London), Feb. 11, 1885.

12. NAK, Sadler to Salisbury, Correspondence, No. 5, July 16, 1899, Cmd 597, 901. See also NAK, CAB 127/1, Lectures given at the Staff College Quetta, "Somaliland 1884–1919," Life of Mohamed Abdulla Hasan (the 'Mad Mullah') 1864–1918.

13. Jama Omer Issa, cited in Bartholet, "It's a Mad, Mad, Mad, Mad World," 44.

14. Hess, "The 'Mad Mullah' and Northern Somalia," 419.

15. Captain Malcolm McNeill, *In Pursuit of the "Mad Mullah" (Mohamed Abdullah): Services and Sport in the Somali Protectorate . . . with a Chapter by Lieutenant A. C. H. Dixon* [with illustrations and a map] (London: C. Arthur Pearson, 1902), 142. For the Maji Maji account, see Source: German military officer, account of the 1905 Maji Maji Rebellion in German East Africa, *German Military Weekly Newspaper*, 1906. See also Jamie Monson, "Relocating Maji Maji: The Politics of Alliance and Authority in the Southern Highlands of Tanzania, 1870–1918," *Journal of African History* 39, no. 1 (1998): 95–120.

16. Douglas J. Jardine, Review in *The Times*, "The Mad Mullah: A Twenty Years Struggle," (London), May 8, 1923, 19.

17. Ralph Evelyn Drake-Brockman, *British Somaliland* (London: Hurst & Blackett, 1912), 177.

18. NAK, CAB/24/256, Italo-Ethiopian Dispute (marked "Secret C.P. 161 35"), dated August 16, 1935, 18.

19. NAK, CAB/129/12, British Somaliland: Proposals by Ethiopian Government for an Exchange of Territory (marked "Top Secret C. P. 46 319"), dated August 6, 1946, 2. See also CAB/129/12, Annex: Ethiopian Proposal for Exchange of Territory with British Somaliland, 4–8.

20. Issa-Salwe, "The Daraawiish Resistance," 3–4.

21. NAK, Foreign Office (hereafter FO), 78/5031, Consul General for the Somali Coast. Hayes-Sadler. District Officer at Bulhar. Jones. Egypt. Diplomatic. Dispatches, 1899.

22. McNeill, *In Pursuit*, 5.

23. Ibid., 5–6.

24. Ibid., 6.

25. Bodleian Library of Commonwealth and African Studies, Rhodes House Oxford (hereafter BLCAS), Eric John Eagles Swayne, Mss. Africa s 424 British Empire s 279 Memoranda and Papers 1902–1914.

26. Eric Swayne cited in Bartholet, "It's a Mad, Mad, Mad, Mad World," 44. See also McNeill and Arthur Charles Hugh Dixon, *In Pursuit*, 17–21.

27. Douglas J. Jardine, *The Mad Mullah of Somaliland* (London: Jenkins (1923; reprint New York: Negro Unit Press, 1969). See also Bartholet, "It's a Mad, Mad, Mad, Mad World," 45.

28. McNeil, *In Pursuit*, 17–19.

29. See *The Times*, "The Abyssinia Expedition against the Mad Mullah," Oct. 19, 1901, 12.

30. *The Times*, "The Somaliland Expedition: Bombardment of Illig," (London), Oct. 26, 1903, 6; and *The Times*, "Capture of Illig. Stronghold Stormed by a British Force," (London), Apr. 28, 1904, 5.

31. Illig was a village about 160 miles from Obbia. It was then the operational base of the Mullah. For details, see Ciise, *Taariikhdii Daraawiishta*, 188–89.

32. Ciise, *Taariikhdii Daraawiishta*, 187.

33. See Said S. Samatar, *Oral Poetry and Somali Nationalism: The Case of Sayyid Mahammed 'Abdille Hasan* (Cambridge: Cambridge University Press, 1982) 48–149.

34. Hess, "The 'Mad Mullah' and Northern Somalia," 431.

35. Ibid., 427.

36. Ibid., 429.

37. Hassan, quoted by Bartholet, "It's a Mad, Mad, Mad, Mad World," 43.

38. For a detailed read of this poem and others, see B. W. Andrzejewski and I. M. Lewis, *Somali Poetry (An Introduction)* (Oxford: Oxford University Press, 1964), 70–74.

39. "The Mad Mullah: A Twenty Years Struggle," 19.

40. Ibid.

41. Royal Air Force Staff Memorandum No. 52, Air Ministry, June 1933, 3.

42. Lieutenant Colonel David J. Dean, "Air Power in Small Wars: The British Air Control Experience Air University Review" 34, no. 5 (July-Aug. 1983): 24–31,

43. Flight Lieutenant F. A. Skoulding, "With Z Unit in Somaliland," *The Royal Air Force Quarterly* (July 1930): 390 [387–398].

44. Major A. B. Russell, OBE Memoirs of Major A. B, Russell ABR/I ca. 1978.

45. Wing Commander W. Turrel's Paper, Imperial War Museum, Department of Documentations, London, Sept., 1920.

46. Royal Air Force and Civil Aviation Record, Sept. 1920.

47. NAK WO 106/272, History of the King's African Riffle and the Somaliland Camel Corps, including the final overthrow of the Mad Mullah, 1912–1936.

48. *The Times*, "The Mad Mullah: His Death Confirmed" (London), Sept. 18, 1921, 7.

49. Winston Churchill cited in Charles Sims, *The Royal Air Force: The First Fifty Years* (London: Adam and Charles Black, 1963), 38.

50. NAK, CAB/24/136, The Somaliland Disturbances dated Apr. 11, 1922, 1.

51. Issa-Salwe, "The Daraawiish Resistance," 1.

52. Said S. Samatar, "Genius as Madness: King Tewodoros of Ethiopia and Sayyid Muhammad of Somalia in Comparative Perspective," *Northeast African Studies* 10, no. 3 (2003): 27–32.

53. Issa-Salwe, "The Daraawiish Resistance," 3–4.

54. NAK, FO 401, Confidential Print Abyssinia (Ethiopia), 1846–1956.

55. See B. W. Andrzejewski, "Muhammad Abdille Hassan and the Lizard: A Somali Legend," *Sonderdruck aus: Afrikanische Sprranchen und Kulturen—einQuersch-nitt* 14 (1971): 298–304.

56. Drake-Brockman, *British Somaliland*, 185.

57. I. M. Lewis, *A Modern History of the Somali: Revised, Updated & Expanded* (Oxford: James Currey, 2002), 113.

58. Some of the other dire conditions have been documented. See NAK, CAB 129/80, The Horn of Africa: Memorandum by the Secretary of State for Foreign

Affairs and Secretary of State for the Colonies (marked "Secret C.P. 56 84"), dated Mar. 24, 1956, 1–3.

59. NAK, CAB/129/101, Cabinet: Policy in the Somaliland Protectorate: Memorandum by the Minister of State for Colonial Affairs, dated Apr. 4, 1960, 1–2.

60. Correspondent Report, "Greater Somalia Demand Opposition to Return of Italians," *The Times* (London), Aug. 20, 1949, 3; and NAK, Home Office (hereafter HO) 401/2 1986–2000.

61. Mark Bradbury, *Becoming Somaliland* (London: Progressio, 2008), 31.

62. Adbullahi, *Culture and Customs of Somalia*, 26.

63. NAK, CAB 129/80, Horn of Africa, 1.

64. Ibid.

65. NAK, Cab 129/65, Somaliland Protectorate and the Horn of Africa (marked "Secret C. 57 38"), dated February 15, 1957, 1, 3.

5

Independence and Nation Building, 1960–1969

The immediate period following independence was one of optimism as well as unrealized dreams for most African countries, including Somalia. The widespread feelings of euphoria and sense of optimism arose from the assumption on the part of Africans that self-rule would enable the people to harness the abundant natural and human resources and thus bring about socioeconomic improvement of the continent and a better standard of life for them. Unfortunately, the emergent political elite grossly underestimated the nature of the task ahead, not least that involved in building a new nation out of nothing.

The project of nation building perhaps was more daunting in postcolonial Somalia than in any other African nation. The Somali political elite had very meager resources at their disposal for a successful execution of the job before them. The so-called gains of independence, as often debated among scholars, included: the self-indulgent feeling that at last power had been restored to Africans which, to a certain degree, restored the self-confidence considerably eroded through the practice of colonial racism. Other circumstantial gains were improvements on infrastructures like roads, railways, seaports, schools, hospitals, and dispensaries, as well as participation of Africans in modern banking, insurance, and wholesale and retail trade.[1]

In fairness, it is reasonable to assert that the disadvantages of colonial rule far outweighed the "incidental gains," to use the words of the radical Pan-Africanist and scholar Walter Rodney.[2] Among the problems was the task of crafting a modern democratic system out of the authoritarian political culture inherited from colonial rule. Commentators often forget that throughout the continent, modern democratic practice was only tried on the eve of independence, and Africans were not allowed enough time to experiment with the rules and strictures of the political game. As if that was not enough, there was also the herculean task of developing socioeconomic and administrative institutions critically needed in order to meet the yearnings of a generation of Africans that suffered diverse kinds of deprivation under the alien rule.

For a fuller appreciation of the challenges of the immediate postcolonial period that would eventually upset and break the newborn Somali nation, it is crucial to approach the narrative normatively and in light of the relevant theories. This approach promises to shed some light not only on the very complex Somali history but also the general trends emerging in other parts of the continent. It is difficult to prioritize either which of the problems comes first or what aspects to focus on. For the purpose of organizing, the transition approach, the modernization approach, and the structural approach are discussed in that order. The other important aspect of the theories explored also includes the paradigm of external factors in political and democratic consolidation. The external approach is even more important considering the Cold War climate of the world order in which African countries operated at the end of colonialism. Again for the purpose of organizing, the effects of external factors on the outcome of the Somali postcolonial state would be better considered in the next chapter.

THE TRANSITION APPROACH

The initial symptom of disaster was obvious with the emergent political order. Although the precolonial Somalis did not live under a single monolithic polity, at independence, the country's political elite favored amalgamating all parts of Somalia. In other words, building a united country was widely considered by the nationalists as the right direction to go. But the crisis of the coming years would reveal that this decision was at best a leap of faith. The transition theorists emphasize a number of factors that would either encumber or make a smooth and successful transition from an authoritarian rule (in this case such as practiced under the British and Italian colonial rules) to a more democratic and stable government. These are: (1) the historical sequences in political development of a nation-state; and (2) the behavior of its ruling elite in terms of their disposal to accept consensus and make compromises. These factors are crucial in any successful transition to democracy, particularly for such a new nation as Somalia. In order to logically assert the centrality of interelite relations in the immediate period following Somalia's transition from colonial rule to independence, first, the historical sequence of development must be discussed.

Sequences in Political Development

The transition theorists, among them Dankwart Rustow, state that when political development proceeds in phases—with national identity established in phase one, internal feuds burning out in phase two, and groups in conflict agreeing to reach a compromise in phase three—prospects for a stable polity are enhanced. In phase three—that is, "the historical moment"—the political elite resolve to concession and to abide by democratic rules of the game. Afterward, a particular nation-state moves into the final phase, "the habituation phase," which witnesses the emergence of a new generation of elites holding steadfast to the democratic ideals bequeathed them by their predecessors with a firm commitment to defend those principles as national ideals.[3] Rustow's model has a striking similarity to that by Leonard Binder and coauthors, who posit that achieving a common identity is crucial in nation building, which "refer to the subjective, but not always emotional, basis of membership in a political community."[4]

Next is the question of "legitimacy," which refers to change in the nature of ultimate authority and to which political obligation is owed. This transitional change demands shifting of allegiance from a traditional authority system to a national authority system. At this stage, if the question of who is entitled to rule and how they should obtain office is settled, the next in sequence becomes "penetration" of the established order of legitimacy, with manifestations observed in increased demands for political participation, and judicious redistribution of resources.[5]

Applied to Somalia, one immediately perceives a problem of abnormality in the sequences of the country's historical and political development. The role of colonialism in forcibly fencing in the various precolonial independent Somali family clans into a single political entity stands out as a huge problem. Although they inhabited the same stretch of territory, spoke the same language, and shared a common history of origin, each of the various family clans—Isaaq, Dir, Hawiye, Darod, Digil, and Rahanwein—considered itself as a nation and did not willingly submit to join the others under one government. This problem informs Wole Soyinka's argument on "a flawed origin" in the evolution of African states, although the playwright quickly asserts that the African case is not entirely "worse than [the experiences] of others."[6] Through one process or the other, perhaps some kind of integration would have been forged among the Somalis if colonial rule had not intruded in their history. This could be seen from the emerging trend with the rise and fall of diverse sizes of sultanates, kingdoms, and principalities like the Adal, Ifat, and so on—mostly starting from the fourteenth century.

It is difficult to speculate now whether the modern Somali state would have evolved along the same trajectory enthroned by colonialism. Perhaps, there could have been some similar problems, but one issue stands out—namely the various family clans in conflict today could have only come into a common national union on their own terms rather than on the terms of the Europeans.

Elite Behavior

Among other theorists, Dankwart Rustow also puts the emphasis for stable democracy in particular and stable politics in general on a readiness of political actors to concession by subscribing to political rules. While social science theorists Almond and Verba put more emphasis on the collection of individual attitudes, Rustow stresses the groups as collective bodies or the elites leading the groups.[7] In Rustow's model, a protracted struggle between groups ends when solution proved impossible through expulsion, or genocide, or secession. At this point, the necessity to resolve the situation peacefully through the adoption of democratic rules, including the appropriate checks and balances, and the protection of rights is appreciated. Realization of the desired behavior is usually not automatic, but once the foundation has been laid, it may be consolidated by subsequent generations of politicians and voters and may be adapted to accommodate previously excluded groups into the political process.[8]

As seen from its history, the way the emergent political elite handled or rather mishandled the wealth of challenges facing the new nation in the 1960s went a long way to set the tone of what was to come in Somalia. One can also argue that the preceding colonial era determined the course of the postcolonial history. In fairness, the emergent elite deserve some commendation for their courageous attempts to address the flawed route that gave birth to the new republic in 1960. The immediate task for the Africans after independence was nation building, which could be defined in this context as the process of creating a cohesive, united, and stable political and cultural community with its own character or identity.

The tricky aspect of the new Somali state is that the stakeholders now included the former colonial masters—Britain, Italy, France, and Ethiopia. Any political permutations that fail to carefully consider their interests are doomed to crash. This is the complex crisis of development that James Coleman describes as "the development syndrome," which demands an interface of "a continuous interaction among the processes of structural differentiation, the imperatives of equality, and the integrative, responsive, and adaptative capacity of a political system."[9] In other words, the Somali nation-building project in the 1960s was in dire need of appropriate and acceptable political structures and functional socioeconomic and political institutions that would command the primary loyalty of the citizens. For success, the people, the political leaders, and the former colonial overlords must work in harmony.

The historic merger of 1960 between ex-British Somaliland and the UN Trust Territory remains a milestone in the practice of elite compromise and consensus. Filled with nationalist vigor, the leaders of Somali Youth League (SYL), the major political party that eventually led the ex-Italian Trust Territory to independence, advocated a single state embracing all areas populated by Somalis—including parts of Ethiopia, northern Kenya, and the former French Somaliland (now independent Djibouti).[10] In a commendable spirit of elite cooperation, the representatives of the two Somalis—that is, the north and south—came together to appoint Dr. Aden Abdullah Osman (1908–2007) the country's first president. The two dominant parties in the former British protectorate joined with the SYL to form a coalition government.[11] Dr. Abdirashid Ali Shermarke of the SYL, and a member of the Darod family clan, became prime minister following Abdullah Isa's resignation.

The readiness of the Somali political elite to make consensus and accept compromises for the sake of the new country was unparalleled in comparison with most of the emerging countries in Africa and Asia. It is particularly telling that while new nations like Morocco, the Democratic Republic of the Congo (DRC), Sudan, and Nigeria, to mention but four, were dealing with the secessionist movements of the Western Sahara, Katanga, Southern Sudan, and Biafra respectively, the Somalis were pushing for the reunification of all Somalis. Nonetheless, in view of the way things turned out for the worst starting in the mid-1960s, and attaining a crescendo in the 1980s and 1990s, it is left for posterity to judge whether the Somali nationalists acted wisely or foolishly with the merger of 1960.

Retrospectively considering the paucity of Somalia's economic resources and poor level of development, it appeared that bringing the entire Somali Peninsula under one country was dangerously idealistic. In a sarcastic retort in the London British *Daily Herald* newspaper (1912–1964) of June 29, 1960, Victor Anant had called Northern Somalia (i.e., ex-British Protectorate of Somaliland) "The Colony That Rejected Freedom." In his commentary, Mr. Anant noted that, "Somaliland, a British Colony for nearly 80 years, became independent last Sunday. And on Friday, after four days of freedom, this British outpost will surrender its sovereignty and merge with Somalia. . . . Now it has become an area of historical significance. And the reason is that its merger with Somalia is unique, as Somalia itself is not yet free."[12]

Obviously, the article of 1960 was a reaction to the quickness with which the northerners sought a union with the southerners. While such comments expressed by Anant indicated some kind of colonial doubt over the ability of Africans to govern themselves in the postcolony, it remains a gauge of the feverish decisions made by the Somali nationalists without giving deeper thought to the likely consequences. If observers in London were worried about the future of Northern Somalia, those in Southern Somalia were scarred to the marrow about the prospects of losing their political and economic advantages to the North. This sense of apprehension is best captured in the secret meetings held in Mogadishu by the Southern political elite on the eve of the union, during which the southerners hurriedly arranged a set of conditions the northerners must accept as terms for the unification. These conditions included the understanding that the president and the prime minister must be southerners. Additionally, the capital city must remain in Mogadishu, and the national flag must remain the one originally designed by the southerners.[13]

One would wonder why the northerners had accepted this inflexible set of conditions presented to them by the southerners. The truth of the matter is that the north was desperate to conclude the merger, among other reasons because of the precarious state of its economy. Indeed, a British cabinet on Somaliland admitted the fact in a memo dated April 1960: "Apart from the fact that the Somaliland Protectorate is not administratively and economically ready for independence, the outstanding political problems which need be resolved are: legal and constitutional, financial, transfer of administration for the Somali scouts, arrangements to secure the pension and other benefits of the civil service, arrangements for the tribesmen from the protectorate to continue to move into Ethiopian territory to graze their herds; currency," and lots more.[14]

In other words, the consensus building among the Somali nationalists was in reality a marriage of expediency. In the merger talks, the southern politicians had conspired to raise the stakes so high that it would disfavor and frustrate the North to a point where they might abandon the entire idea. The plan fell through simply because the northern delegates had been mandated by their people to strike the deal at all costs. While the mandate best represents the level of extreme anxiety in the North, the precarious economic conditions of the northerners are the only rationale a group would have to accept such a crooked deal.

The differences between the North and the South as shaped by British and Italian colonialist regimes continued to manifest in the dual monetary systems—the North was in the sterling zone and the South in the lira area.[15] Other differences remained: the operation of two customs and exercise regimes, two different official languages (Italian in the south and English in the north), and two different educational systems. Also, Mogadishu, the national capital located in the former Italian territory, continued to command the bigger voice in any decision affecting the entire nation. Troubled by the imbalances in the affairs of the country, a referendum was called in 1961 by one of the main northern region's parties. The referendum aimed to invoke the court of public opinion in an attempt to address the inequity between the two regions. The results of the referendum in both regions favored the union. However, suspicions were rife that the outcome in the south would have been a resounding "no" but for the political leaders' vested interest and manipulation in order to entrench all the advantages already enjoyed by the southerners. In such a national community, it is only a prosperous economy that would be able to sustain the politics of unequal partnership. Regrettably, the Somali economy was not healthy enough to weather the unfolding situation.

THE MODERNIZATION THEORY

Success in any nation-building project, especially in the context of a transition from an exploitative alien rule to a democratic self-rule requires sufficient resources. Unfortunately, colonial rule failed to

The main square of Mogadishu, Somalia, including a white minaret on a mosque, twin spires of Roman Catholic cathedral, and a memorial arch to Italians. (AP Photo/Miniclier)

establish a solid economic foundation under which the governing elite of Somalia could craft an enduring national unity. The question is not whether the infrastructures left after colonial rule were either better or worse than what was available in the precolonial era. Rather, the point is that at independence Somalia was left in worse shape than it had ever been because colonial rule introduced new bureaucracies, new tastes, new institutions, new ideologies, new practices of capitalism, and new patterns of consumption. These new trends were all alien to the culture. To efficiently manage and moderate the emergent trends in tastes and lifestyles, and thus stave off a system breakdown, a substantial amount of resources was required. The poor economic situation of Somalia more than anything else best explains why the transition into an independent statehood that was started on a peaceful note soon exploded in a violent and bloody conflict.[16]

In *Political Man*, Seymour Lipset found a strong relationship between stable democracy and a country's level of economic development or modernization.[17] Obviously the correlation is also true with other forms of political systems, including monarchical and totalitarian regimes. As long as there is enough money to buy off the opposition and sustain loyalties, politics and leadership usually run with a temperate tone. Modernization theorists presume that with "greater access to education, improved communications, and the shifting of people from the slumbering 'traditional' rural sector economy to the vibrant 'modern' industrial sector," ethnic consciousness will give way to national consciousness.[18] Lipset saw such variables as urbanization, industrialization, per capita income, and the level of education as harbingers of democracy.[19] The interests of the "lower class" are more likely to be protected in an economically viable state—thus allowing very slim chances for them to turn to opposition or counter ideologies. This illuminates some critical reasons why heated competition for power in Somalia in the 1960s became too difficult to moderate.

Somalia was encumbered with a difficult politics in the 1960s because of its rickety economy. Precolonial Somalis shared rural and agro-pastoral customs, which compelled the nomadic pastoralists to move constantly in search of fodder and water. Under colonial rule, the prevailing ways of life came under stress not only because of the boundaries imposed by colonial powers, which divided clans and confined them to a sedentary life, but also by the attempt by Britain to appease Ethiopia that seized the Haud, a strategic reserve for animal grazing and food production for most Somalis.[20] Although both the British and the Italian colonial governments were fully aware of the precarious economic situation posed by Ethiopia's imperial interests, they further compounded the problems by failing to provide Somalis enough developmental incentives like educational and job opportunities—avenues through which ordinary people could have been better integrated into the modern economy. This practice of indifference and oversight enthroned alienation of the masses while delaying emergence of a substantial middle class whose labor and productivity support the modern democratic state system everywhere.

It was not until from the Second World War that the colony began to see some meaningful consideration for educational expansion. For instance, when the British took over the administration of Italian Somaliland in 1941 there were only 13 government-supported elementary schools in operation. These schools were serving the needs of both children of Italian settlers and Somalis. Within a decade from 1941, the British colonial administration added twenty-one new schools, bringing the number of elementary schools to 34. Together, there was a student population of 1,800 with an additional 1,000 in mission schools in the former Italian territory of southern Somalia. In the northern region (British Somaliland), three elementary schools were opened in 1942—each located in Hargeisa, Berbera, and Burao. By the end of the Second World War in 1945, there were seven elementary schools with a total student population of just 400 pupils.[21]

In time, the new expansions engendered a popular quest for Western education, and it was in light of this that in 1952, the UN Trustee government pressed the Italian Administration to launch a five-year program for educational development. Funds for the program came from the United Nations Educational, Scientific and Cultural Organization (UNESCO). The plan was to build 140 new primary schools targeting an annual enrolment population of 22,000 pupils. This was estimated to meet about 10 percent of the estimated school-age population. The plan also included provisions for secondary, technical, and vocational schools; teacher training schools; and institutions of higher education.

Just before independence in 1960, 135 primary schools had been established, and the attendance stood at 16,000 pupils. Meanwhile, one out of two pupils who entered school completed the five-year primary school program. The 50 percent dropout rate was attributed to the nomadic mode of production, which remained a way of life for the children the schools were built for. Another problem was the acute shortage of professional teachers, which remained a problem even up to the 1970s. In order to address this issue, a Teacher Training Institute was established in Mogadishu in 1953. On the eve of independence, there were about 470 Somali teachers. Out of this number, 290 had teaching diplomas; the rest qualified as assistants. Additionally, there were about 200 expatriate teachers recruited from Britain, Italy, and the United Arab Republic. By independence in 1960, the total number of primary schools for boys stood at 2,000, and there were only three institutions for girls.

Opportunities for secondary education expanded at a slow pace, especially in the UN Italian-administered Trust Territory. The first was opened in Mogadishu in 1950, and by 1959, there were altogether four secondary schools. Although there were also opportunities for vocational and technical education, these only became popular in 1957. On the eve of independence, about 220 students were enrolled in the only Vocational Training School in Mogadishu. At the level of higher education, the Higher Institute of Economics and Law, created in 1954, became the University Institute of Somalia (UIS) in January 1960. Between 1955 and 1960, 58 students received their diplomas out of a total number of 336 enrolments.

Overall, on the eve of independence, development of the educational sector in the whole of Somalia was grossly inadequate. It is noteworthy that a secret report of March 24, 1956, by the British administration observed that "the Egyptians were showing an increasing interest in [Italian] Somaliland and also in the [British] Protectorate. Because of lack of Arabic teachers elsewhere the Italians have imported large numbers of Egyptians and Egypt is also represented on the United Nations Advisory Council for Somalia. [Col. Abdul] Nasser [Egyptian leader] is therefore in a good position to carry on intensive propaganda among the Somalis." The same report expressed deep concerns over the possibility of having "an independent Somalia under Egyptian influence, which must now be reckoned to carry with it the probability of Russian infiltration."[22] It is important to emphasize that this trend in Egyptian/Russian infiltration was brought about by the poor socioeconomic condition of Somalia on the eve of independence. Despite the expressed intention of Britain to halt this evolving trend, Russia's presence in Somalia continued to expand, blossoming under Siad Barre's rule from 1969 to 1977, when the Ogaden war with Ethiopia strained Somalia's relations with the USSR.

The educational sector of the Somali economy experienced a concerted effort for development at the end of colonial rule. From 1963 to 1966, more giant steps were taken to consolidate expansion at all levels of Western education in line with the growing popular demands. For example, there was a significant increase in the number of primary school enrollment from 15,400 in 1959, to 23,000 in 1966. In secondary education, the number rose from 1,100 in 1964 to 3,100 in 1969. The University Institute of Somalia remained the only tertiary institution in the country, although plans were underway to expand this level of education. Even more bold steps would be taken to expand the education sector from 1969 under Barre's Supreme Revolutionary Council (SRC), but for now there are enough facts to conclude that the paucity of socioeconomic institutions, particularly in regard to the low level of literacy in Western education, placed a serious premium on the ability of the country to develop in the modern capitalist economic sphere. The handful of educated people under colonial rule constituted the new petty bourgeoisie whose level of sophistication and productivity was too poor to sustain and nourish a new democratic order.

The modernization theorists hold that the middle class in a country can be reinforced by socioeconomic development, which is good for democracy, because it "tempers conflict by rewarding moderate and democratic parties and penalizing extremist groups."[23] More importantly, Lipset argues that a legitimacy crisis may arise if rising social groups were denied political access, or if new class divisions

reinforced older divisions based on ethnicity and confessional affiliations.[24] The insight offers lenses on the circumstances in which the
nascent democratic national government of the 1960s was transformed into a more parochial game of clan politics amid fears of the
unlikely sustainability of the political union. In other words, Somalia
inherited a somber crisis of political legitimacy from the colonial
economy. According to Lipset, "to attain legitimacy, what new democracies need above all is efficacy, particularly in the economic arena,
but also in the polity."[25] Similarly, political science theorist Samuel
Huntington authoritatively asserts that "In short if you wish to produce democracy, promote economic growth."[26] The Somali elite did
express their dreams, but mere wishes were not enough to meet the
challenges of the time.

It may be recalled that in anticipation of the economic problem, in
1952, a United Nations Technical Assistance Program (UNTAP) survey had reported a morbid economic condition.[27] The agriculture sector that was once the foundation of the society had suffered a stunted
growth. The sector remained in the hands of the rural producers who
raised livestock and cultivated food crops barely enough for subsistence living. With the intention to assist in the development of the
agricultural sector of the economy, UNTAP suggested the creation of
farming stations—something that had been brought up before and that
recorded limited success.[28] In the 1950s, the Italian administration
attempted to improve the weak economy and level of literacy with a
200 billion lire investment, which a British memo of March 24, 1956, corroborated with a statement that the Italians' subsidy to the Territory
stood at "£2–3 millions per year; they get nothing in return for this
and there are reports that they wish to withdraw."[29] But Britain tried
to persuade the Italians to keep the subsidy in hope that economic
improvement would go a long way in ameliorating interclan and
intra-lan conflicts. Much of this effort did not bring the desired results
on the economy as a whole and the agricultural sector in particular.

In a report by James F. Keim, Agricultural Extension Advisor for the
USAID who studied Italian Administrations project in Somalia, it was
noted that:

> While there must be an overall country program to give coher-
> ence and define objectives. In Agricultural Extension, this plan
> should begin with individual projects, planned and executed on
> the level at which they will be understood by the people. The dif-
> ficulties of communication, transportation or the lack of teaching
> and demonstration materials, or adequately trained personnel

must not be overlooked. It is here that the principle of self-help comes in. The project must be on a subject consistent with their experience to appreciate its value, within their ability to take part, so that they may be encouraged to participate in its growth and contribute to its support.[30]

The report further stated that one of the major reasons why food production was grossly neglected in the 1950s plan was because the Italians invested solely in cash crop production in order to realize enough money through export to defray the external loans taken from various creditor nations.[31] The cultivation of cash crops like cotton, sugarcane, and banana depleted the soil nutrients and thus made the cultivation of other staple food difficult. Other factors that hampered agricultural production included communal farming and system of land ownership, which does not easily permit the tradition of open-field mechanized agriculture, lack of market-based planning, and the various problems of drought and famines beginning from the 1980s. As the case of Kenya has shown, the problem of droughts and famines in Somalia were the direct consequences of the colonial emphasis on cash crop production. The impact of the agricultural shortages became more overwhelming in a country that lacked natural resources like gold, diamonds, and oil—some of the resources that have cushioned off economic situations in some other African countries.

In the year following the 1969 coup d'état, Siad Barre, the incoming military dictator, declared Somalia a socialist state. He then went on to establish a large-scale public works program. The program implemented an urban and rural literacy campaign, which dramatically helped to increase the literacy rate within a space of 10 years. Nonetheless, the fact remains that the level of economic development or lack of it could not have been adequate to support the rocky political climate that emerged in the 1960s with deep clan consciousness.

THE STRUCTURAL APPROACH

It is now auspicious to consider the structures of the Somali society and how intergroup relations intersected with elite behavior and economic conditions to push the emergent state over the brink.

Social Structures and Interactions between Social Groups

Like other theorists, Barrington Moore focused his explanation on long-term processes of historical change as a factor in the development of a stable democracy. However, contrary to the transitional approach, Moore explains the democratization process as a function of interaction between groups in society—that is, on whole social groups and primarily "structures of power" rather than by the agency of political elites.[32] David Potter and others interpret the nonfigurative concept of "structures of power" as "the particular interrelationships of certain structures of power—economic, social, political—as they gradually change through history, providing constraints and opportunities that drive political elites along a historical trajectory leading towards a liberal democracy."[33] This view is strongly supported by Geraldo L. Munk, who argues that political actors make choices but not in circumstances of their own choosing.[34]

Thus, while others perceived democracy evolving out of reconciliation, Moore sees it as emerging out of revolution. He cites the victories of the Puritans in England, the Jacobins in France, and the antislavery states in the United States as revolutionary forces that paved the way for democratic development in the aforementioned societies. One might perhaps add the people's revolt against Milosevic in Yugoslavia; and more recently the 2011 Arab Spring mass uprisings against Zine El Abdine Ben Ali in Tunisia; Hosni Mubarak in Egypt; and Muammar Gaddafi in Libya as something that might corroborate this theory if they lead to a stable democracy in the Middle East.

The five general conditions for democracy offered by Moore are: (1) the development of a balance to avoid too strong a state or too independent a landed aristocracy; (2) a turn toward an appropriate form of commercial agriculture; (3) the weakening of the landed aristocracy; (4) The prevention of an aristocratic-bourgeoisie coalition against the peasants and workers; and (5) a revolutionary break from the past.[35] Moore's theory contrasts with the communist model used by Siad Barre in 1969, where the aristocracy remained indifferent to commerce with the survival of a large peasant mass, facilitating a revolution in the absence of the safeguards of bourgeois democracy. It also contrasts the fascist model, where the upper class used political and social levers to sustain the labor force while making the transition to commercial farming.[36] With the absence of market forces to moderate industrial growth, as against a liberal order, there is limited room for an autonomous bourgeois.[37]

One of the most interesting aspects of this Marxist angle to democratization in regard to Somalia is that Siad Barre took the country along that path with initial success but soon encountered a disastrous outcome. The end result of Somalia's experiment raises questions on Huntington's position that countries with a tradition of fairly unwavering dictatorships (as was the case with Spain and Portugal, for example) are more likely to evolve into relatively stable democracies than countries which have frequently swung between despotism and democracy.[38]

Like fascism and communism in earlier times, democracy has been propagated in other lands through acts of conquest and contagion, including places where authoritarianism seemed entrenched. Lipset argues that democracy has never developed anywhere by plan, except when it was imposed by the allies on Germany and Japan after the Second World War. Obviously, the institutionalization of freedom, suffrage, and the rule of law grew in a piecemeal, not in planned fashion.[39] Each country will have elements in its history and culture, which can be exploited as democratic assets, whether they are the tradition of civic engagement in the United States, egalitarianism and participation in Scandinavia, or nonelitist cultures of Somalis of the Horn of Africa or Igbos of southeastern Nigeria.[40] Also, the historical and cultural element could equally present inhibitions and encourage authoritarianism.

In regard to Somalia, it is an interesting point of debate whether the structures of authority and interclan relations undermined the authority of the emergent elite in the 1960s and their efforts at building a united nation. Of course, the answer is anybody's guess. The various hitherto independent clans and cultural groups—the Darod, Dir, Hawiye, Isaaq, Digil, and Rahanweyn, along with their respective sub-groups—had never had the free hand under colonial rule to test the strength of their unity. At the end of colonial rule, they were confronted with a difficult responsibility for organizing social, economic, and political activities and a struggle to create a unified nation. Also, the new Somalia society harbored more than just Somalis. Besides its known minorities like the Bantus, Arabs, and others, it now harbored new migrants such as Indians, Italians (who remained behind after independence), and Pakistani peoples. Additionally, there was a wide gulf of difference between those without Western-style education who were in the majority, and those with the advantage of Western education who were in the minority. Each group was living in its own separate communities within the country. In such a multicultural polity, there must be an accommodative system of managing inter and intra-ethnic relations in order to prevent eruption of anger and inter-class and interclan hatred.

This brings us to the question of the type of political system banqueted by colonialism. First, whether in the north or south, the Western concept of centralized government imposed under colonial rule and retained by the postcolonial leaders in a society that continued to exhibit strong particularity for loose political arrangement was a recipe for anarchy. This error of choice was prevalent across the continent. A confederate system with a very loose center, as discussed fully in chapter eight, would have been more accommodative of differences among the diverse social classes and rival clans. It could have also permitted a more successful experimentation with the indigenous and alien political traditions of government. Rather than pursuing this hybrid, the Somalis continued with modified versions of the Western-style parliamentary democracy that ended up derailing national aspirations through inefficiency and practices of corruption and nepotism. The experiment failed because clan consciousness remained as an organic product of autonomy guided by traditional law—a stock of social and political capitals that were not harnessed for sociopolitical progress.

Reflecting an escalating drift toward long-established clan divisions, about 1,000 candidates, representing 68 political parties emerged. The majority of these parties were one-man associations that were encouraged by their family clans and subclan supporters to vie for 124 seats in the March 1969 elections. This was slightly different from the March 1964 elections when 973 candidates from 21 political parties vied for a total of 122 posts.[41] Individuals behind this multitude of parties saw them as a front for bargaining and gaining access to the spoils of state power. As was the case in the independence elections, once again the Somali Youth League (SYL) dominated the polls, and Mohamed Haji Ibrahim Egal was reappointed prime minister amid serious allegations of fraud.[42] Unfortunately, the existing divisions and widespread sense of disillusionment had run deep, and as such the newly reconstituted government was no longer representative of the more cautious and subtle politics in the early 1960s.

Soon after the 1969 elections were over and the new parliament sworn in, on October 15, 1969 President Abdirashid Ali Sharmarke was assassinated by one of his own bodyguards while Prime Minister Egal was on a foreign trip.[43] The reason behind the assassin's action is still unclear to many. The popular assumption is that the killing may have been connected with the manner in which the government had mistreated the aggrieved assassin's clan, particularly during the conduct of the 1969 elections. From this point, things moved dangerously fast as the most coveted political position in the land was up for grabs. The situation demanded an urgent action in order to arrest what many had come to see as dangerous. The confusion and politicking with which the political group went about handling the problem set the stage for the army and their Soviet Union advisers to stage a military coup on October 21,

1969. Basking in this atmosphere of uncertainty and apprehension, General Siad Barre, declared, "There was no choice," in justification of the coup in his maiden speech to the nation on October 24, 1969.[44]

Students of Somali studies have yet to carefully articulate the details of the planning and execution of the October 1969 coup. One of the popular understandings remains that the army commander Maj.-Gen. Siad Barre was apparently angered by Prime Minister Egal's disdain for him as an officer without good education in military sciences and had pressured him to retire. If this is true, it was a dangerous path for the premier to take in a new country where survival of the fittest had become the rule for both the individual and the group. Against the notion that General Barre had much to do with the military takeover, the underlying suspicion is that he acted in line with the Machiavellian principle of self-survival and secretly perfected a plan to topple the civilian administration with the help of his trusted junior officers as well as the Russian military and technical instructors that had begun to infiltrate the country in the early late 1950s.[45] Being a former police officer, the police, his loyalists, and other coopted political figures and senior officers in the army came behind him to sack the civilians and suspend the constitution.

In a tradition common to the politics of the emergent new nations in Africa, Latin America, and the Middle East, the coupists formed the Supreme Revolutionary Council (SRC) with Barre as the chairman of the new ruling body. A few days later, Barre was proclaimed the president of a new country now branded the Somali Democratic Republic. Somalia has entered a new era of optimism that will later turn into a huge national disillusionment.

As the problems facing the country deepened amidst intra- and interclan struggles for power and access to the meager resources, Siad Barre and his cohorts thought that they had found a solution in their adoption of socialism as the pathway to addressing all the issues on the table. In the next three decades, General Barre would dictate the course of the country's history in a way no other Somali had ever done in the past or would ever do in the future. It is therefore necessary to closely provide a succinct account of Barre's years in power and his efforts to right the wrongs of his country. One primary focus would be to understand the context in which nationalist consciousness and political rhetoric lost out to parochialism and anarchy.

NOTES

1. For a synopsis of this, see A. Adu Boahen, "The Colonial Impact," in Boahen, *Perspectives on Colonialism* (Baltimore: Johns Hopkins University Press, 1987), 94–122; L. H. Gann and Peter Duigann, "The Burden of Empire," in

R. O. Collins (ed.), *Historical Problems in Imperial Africa* (Princeton, NJ: Markus Wiener, 1994), 271–79.

2. Walter Rodney, "Colonialism as a System of Underdevelopment," in Walter Rodney, *How Europe Underdeveloped Africa* (Washington, DC: Howard University Press, 1972), 223–61.

3. Dankwart A. Rustow, "Transitions to Democracy: Towards a Dynamic Model," *Comparative Politics* 2 (April 1970): 337–66; and Dankwart A. Rustow, "How Does a Democracy come into Existence?" in Paul G. Lewis and David C. Potter, eds. *The Practice of Comparative Politics* (Harlow, UK: Longman, 1973), 117–32. See also Robert Pinkney, *Democracy in the Third World* (Buckingham and Philadelphia: Open University Press, 1993), 24–25.

4. Leonard Binder, James S. Coleman, Joseph LaPalombara, Lucian W. Pye, Sidney Verba, and Myron Weiner, *Crises and Sequences in Political Development* (Princeton NJ.: Princeton University Press, 1971), 53.

5. Ibid., 53–64.

6. Wole Soyinka, *The Open Sore of a Continent: A Personal Narrative of the Nigerian Crisis* (New York and Oxford: Oxford University Press, 1996), 17–60.

7. Rustow, "How Does a Democracy Come into Existence?" 117–32.

8. Pinkney, *Democracy in the Third World*, 24.

9. James S. Coleman, "The Development Syndrome: Differentiation, Equality, Capacity," in Binder et al., *Crises and Sequences*, 74.

10. NAK, CAB/129/101, Policy in the Somaliland Protectorate: Memorandum by the Minister of State for Colonial Affairs, dated Apr. 4, 1960, 1–4.

11. Steve Bloomfield, "Aden Abdulle Osman: First President of Somalia," *The Independent* (London), June 11, 2007.

12. Victor Anant, "The Colony That Rejected Freedom," *The Herald* (London), June 29, 1960.

13. Mohammed Diriye Abdullah, *Culture and Customs of Somalia* (Westport, CT: Greenwood Press, 2001), 27.

14. NAK, CAB 129/101, Policy in the Somaliland Protectorate, 2.

15. Ibid.

16. Ibid.

17. Seymour Martin Lipset, *Political Man: The Social Basis of Politics* (London: Heinemann, 1960), 1–54.

18. Leroy Vail, "Introduction: Ethnicity in Southern African History," in Leroy Vail, ed., *The Creation of Tribalism in Southern Africa* (Berkeley and Los Angeles: University of California Press, 1991), 1.

19. Seymour Martin Lipset, "Some Social Requisites for Democracy, Economic Development and Political Legitimacy," *American Political Science Review* 53, no.1 (1959): 69–105. See also Seymour Martin Lipset, "The Social Requisites of Democracy Revisited," *American Sociological Review* 59 (Feb. 1994): 1–22.

20. NAK, CAB 129/80, Horn of Africa, 2.

21. Irving Kaplan, Margarita K. Dobert, James L. McLaughlin, Barbara Marvin, H. Mark Roth, and Donald P. Whitaker, *Area Handbook for Somalia second edition* (Washington, DC: U.S. Printing Central Office, 1977), 118.

22. NAK, CAB 129/80, Horn of Africa, 1.

23. Lipset, *Political Man*, 51.

24. Lipset, "Some Social Requisites," 87–97.

25. Ibid., 1. Lipset asserts that governments that defy the elementary laws of supply and demand will fail to develop along democratic systems.

26. Samuel P. Huntington, "After Twenty Years: The Future of the Third Wave," *Journal of Democracy* 8, no. 4 (1997): 5.

27. See United Nations Technical Assistance Program (UNTAP) Report, The *Trust Territory of Somaliland under Italian Administration* (New York: United Nations, 1952), 8–15.

28. Ibid.

29. NAK, CAB 129/80, Horn of Africa, 1.

30. James F. Keim, "Agricultural Extension–A Project Approach for its Development in Emerging Countries," 1962, 5.

31. Ibid., 5–6.

32. Moore, *Social Origins of Dictatorship*, esp. 8–14, 19, 31–49, 494.

33. Potter, *Democratization*, 18–19.

34. Geraldo L. Munk, "Democratic Transitions in Contemporary Perspectives," *Comparative Politics* 26, no. 3 (Apr. 1994): 357 [355–75].

35. Moore, *Social Origin of Dictatorship*, 430–31.

36. Pinkney, *Democracy in the Third World*, 26.

37. Moore, *Social Origin of Dictatorships*, 413–22.

38. Samuel Huntington, "Will More Countries Become Democratic?" *Political Science Quarterly* 99, no. 2 (1984): 193–218.

39. Lipset, "Social Requisites of Democracy Revisited," 4.

40. G. T. Basden, *Among the Igbos of Nigeria* (1921; reprint London: Frank Cass, 1966).

41. *African Contemporary Record*, Annual Survey and Documents 1968–1969: Somali Republic (London: African Research Limited, 1969), 104.

42. NAK, HO 401/2 1986–2000.

43. "Abdi Rashid Shermarke: President of Somalia since 1967" (Obituary), *The Times* (London), Oct. 16, 1969, 14.

44. Mohamed Siad Barre, "Revolutionary Speech by Mohamed Siad Barre to the Nation," Oct. 24, 1969.

45. Special Correspondent, "Somalia Planning Army of 20,000 with Russian Aid," *The Times*, (London), Nov. 11, 1963, 10.

6

Mohamed Siad Barre and the "New Era," 1969–1991

YES, it's a NEW ERA in the Horn of Africa! Since the Revolution, Somalia has looked at its priorities, and formulated new plans that will take it confidently into the decade of the seventies—and the future.

Ministry of Information and National Guidance.[1]

The above statement from Somalia's ministry of information and national guidance in August 1970 captured the general mood of the nation when the army announced the bloodless coup d'état of October 21, 1969, which ushered in a political order branded a "New Era" in the government-controlled popular press. President Mohamed Siad Barre (1919–1995) led Somalia for 22 long years. The new regime was announced with lots of promises and high expectations from the people. By way of populist proclamations, and a deft, swift response with which the new government went about tackling national issues in the early years, Barre's ascension to power brought great anticipation at a time when the average Somali perceived the country to be in a state of confusion and sociopolitical decay—a situation *The Times* of London editorial of October 22, 1969, described as "astonishing."[2] Sadly, all the high expectations and hopes of the people were soon replaced by national desolation and despondency.

On the strength of the evidence, one could describe Barre as a Somali patriot and nationalist. His initial intentions were genuine, at least if he is judged only by the record of achievements that were made in the first five years of his rule. Still, nothing could justify Barre's corrupt leadership and failures and the numerous atrocities he perpetrated on his real and imagined enemies. Among other things, the follies of Barre's regime included his dictatorial emasculation of the opposition and civil society networks, an ill-advised and damaging war with Ethiopia between 1977 and 1978, a desperate switch from reliance on the Soviets to reliance on Americans, and a litany of human rights abuses in which he used state power to bring about the deaths and incarceration of tens of thousands of Somalis.

These dysfunctional tendencies ended up destroying the very foundations of civic and political capital most Somalis had hoped Barre was going to use in building national unity and peaceful development. At the collapse of his despotic regime in 1991, practices of ethnic chauvinism, personal greed, and widespread violent and bloody political culture turned Somalia into a lawless land, a "failed state."[3] Under Barre, civil war, contested sovereignties, and criminality became the order of the day rather than the exceptions. To understand what happened in Somalia in the Siad Barre years, it is crucial to begin with the tasks the Marxist revolutionary junta assigned to itself and the methods through which it aimed to accomplish these goals after the 1969 coup d'état.

THE SUPREME RULING COUNCIL AND THE "NEW ERA"

A few days after the first republic's civilian government was sacked, the leaders of the October 21, 1969, coup published the names of a 25-member Supreme Ruling Council (SRC). The council's personnel consisted of officers picked from diverse ranks. The most senior members of the cabinet included Maj.-Gens. Siad Barre (president) and Jaama Ali Khorshel (or Qoorsheel), a member of the Warsangeli subclan of the Darod family and former deputy police commissioner, who was named co-vice president with Brig.-Gen. Mohamed Ainanshe. There were altogether two major-generals, two brigadier-generals, and seven officers at the ranks of lieutenant-colonel, major, and captain each.

A secondary 14-member Council of the Secretaries of the State, officially known as the Secretaries (instead of Ministers as was the case in the previous government), served as the national cabinet. The cabinet was comprised mostly of doctorate degree holders, "young men who have been trained academically and provisionally for the office they hold," who were responsible for the supervision of day-to-day operations of government business.[4] The only army officer in the 14-member council of secretaries was Maj.-Gen. Jaama Ali Khorshel, who held the portfolio of secretary of interior along with vice president and membership in the SRC. In a speech at the swearing-in ceremony on October 31, 1969, Barre told the newly appointed officers: "We have handed over the country to you and we hope that you shall fulfill and follow the principles of the revolution. . . . I wish you good luck and hard work, and I am sure the Somali people will get what they are expecting from you."[5]

Filled with revolutionary ardor—a familiar inclination among the postcolonial African armies as witnessed in Egypt under Gamal Abdel Nasser (r. 1956–1970), and in Guinea under Sékou Touré (r. 1958–1984), to mention but two—the SRC described their mission as a Marxist revolution in the Leninist tradition. Ironically, the young officers who had been trained by Soviet instructors in Somalia and who were better schooled in the Marxist-Leninist principles were barred from any key position within the ruling hierarchy. It is often commonly assumed among the African cohorts of the postcolonial order that Marxism is a recipe for radicalism and a practice of wickedness, but a closer look at the classical Marxist doctrine reveals that it is indeed a humanist ideology of state organization and economic existentialism. The original vision of Karl Marx, the architect of the ideology, had been the expectation that a more humane society would materialize where exploitation of the means of production by a few privileged elite would give way to a socialist workers' republic where those whose labor produces the wealth would enjoy the fruits of their hard work. This doctrine, first tested in Russia following the October Revolution of 1917, achieved limited success in the classical sense. Thus, it is important to know that the version of socialism that was instituted in the defunct Union of Soviet Socialist Republic (USSR) and that most African Marxists embraced in the period of decolonization differed from the original principles of Marxist ideology. Lenin and Stalin refurbished Marxism to suit their own brand of politics and societal organization.

Similarly, Siad Barre and his comrades would adapt socialism to serve their preferred kind of politics and notion of what the ideal society should be. As the government's official voice, the *New Era* explained in an editorial of March 1972 that "Socialism stems from the community of man. It means man working, not as an individual, but as a group or in groups for the betterment of the whole community, and therefore the entire country. Socialism postulates the principle that when an individual withdraws into himself and shuns his fellow beings, that is the beginning of selfishness that sets one person apart from another. This concept and practice has no place in the Socialist doctrine."[6]

Whether the military junta understood the complex nuances and varied interpretations and practices of their self-appointed mission in Somalia remains anybody's guess. Their actions and methods, not their public pronouncements, seem to suggest otherwise. The SRC commenced a reorganization of the political and legal institutions of the country, with its own peculiar ideology grounded both in the Quran (the holy book of Islamic religion) and on Marxism. This is a unique mix of ideologies in the sense that the Soviet model of Marxism the Somali leaders aspired to emulate abhorred any form of religion in society. The revolutionary council then proclaimed that their populist mission was to bring about a radical transformation of the society through the application of scientific socialism as the "only way for Somalia."[7]

The Somali leaders were not alone in the wider context of Africans' search for a potent formula to steer their various new nations on the road to progress at the end of colonial rule. In the framework of colonial rule and the decolonization struggles, the African nationalists and immediate postcolonial leaders had in a sense come to equate capitalism with colonialism, the practice of racial injustice, and exploitation. Perhaps this idea was best captured by Siad Barre himself in a speech to the nation in 1969 when he declared that "Freedom with hunger is far better than to be humiliated by others."[8]

Socialism, on the other hand, was perceived as coterminous with freedom, equality, and justice. With Africans' new focus on socialism, orthodox economics founded on the analysis of the market and private capitalism was considered improper for moving forward a nonindustrialized economy. At this juncture, most postcolonial African leaders started steering their country toward state communism. The more adventurous states like Tanzania under Julius Nyerere (1922–1999) adopted a middle course between the West and East ideologies in the name of *Ujamaa* or family-hood.[9] Kwame Nkrumah, who ruled the West African country of Ghana between 1957 and 1966, adopted scientific socialism.[10] There is no little doubt that the common African trends informed the actions of the Somali revolutionary leaders.

Yet none of the ideologies established on the socialist principles met the overall goals for which they were adopted in Africa. Perhaps the major reason may be connected with the leaders' belief that only governments possessed the political power to overcome the enormous challenges of development and force the pace of growth. To demonstrate its seriousness, the Somali SRC purged the country's civilian administrators, who were not favorably disposed to the new order. Army officers who were not open to the Siadism (i.e., socialism as interpreted by Barre) were either compromised or eliminated. For instance, Maj.-Gen. Mohamed Ibrahim, aka "Lii-liiqato" (Shiikland), the second-highest-ranking officer in the armed forces, was sent on a diplomatic mission to Germany, and Col. Adbullahi Farah Hooley (Marjerteen) was dispatched on a similar mission to Egypt. Mohamed Farah Aideed (Habar-Gidi), who would later be a major player in the civil unrests of the late 1980s and 1990s, was also offered a diplomatic position because of his misgivings about the regime. When Aideed declined his ambassadorial posting, Barre ordered his arrest, and he was incarcerated for six years.[11]

In its pronouncements, the SRC also targeted for eradication the practices of tribalism and client-patron political networks, including nepotism and other forms of favoritism based on family or clan affiliations. In 1971, the council further promised to phase out military rule after the establishment of political parties. The idea was that a new civilian order would proceed from the fresh foundations it was laying for the country and that civilians would take over from the SRC within a reasonable time. To better judge the performance of the SRC and Barre's regime, it is helpful to discuss the government's stated objects, achievements, problems, and failures.

STATED GOALS AND ACHIEVEMENTS

In his address to the armed forces on November 9, 1969, President Siad Barre began to articulate the goals of the SRC: "We have launched the Revolution to eradicate the colonial hangovers in all its forms . . . to work for our people in all sincerity."[12] One of the major programs of the new administration was to bring about a new culture of work ethics and patriotism. In line with the very familiar rhetoric often associated with populist socialism, the government promised to enthrone a culture of justice and reward based on merit and hard work. "We have to eliminate the unpleasant features that have been foisted on the Somali people—the injustice, the shameful goings-on, the rampant corruption, nepotism, favoritism and unjust discrimination, the sitting on one's hands and expectations of timely rain from heaven, the fanning of troubles among people, and the putting of some people in

For 20 years, Mohamed Siad Barre presided over Somalia. (AFP/Getty Images)

the position of servitude—a direct remnant of colonialism."[13] Slogans such as *Hardal yar hawl badan horumar lagu gaadhaa* ("Less speech and more work is the way to progress") adorned all public places.[14] The state-run media was put to good use in the condemnation of corruption, rumor-mongering, and practices of tribalism.[15]

To its credit in the effective use of propaganda, the regime identified women as the cornerstone of progress and development. As such, several programs were designed to educate, respect, and motivate women to actively participate in the execution of developmental programs—whether through family orientations, farm cultivations, health care, literacy campaigns, and numerous other activities and life pursuits. These ideas were cultivated and publicized through the electronic media and artistic posters and billboards well designed and strategically erected across Mogadishu to catch the attention of the public. For example, a picture depicting ceremonies marking observation of the "International Year of the Child" dated March 15, 1979, honored the role of women in society.

Others like the billboard of March 8, 1979, declared *"Ha Guuleesto Sannad Caruureedka,"* ("May the year of the children triumph."), and that of March 8 1981, was intended for the celebration of "World Day for Women." Even paintings primarily commissioned to honor the efforts of men also incorporated images of women. For instance, one of the slogans for the 10-year celebrations of the 1969 socialist revolution in 1979 was captioned *The Toban sano oo halgan ah nin ka soo baxay baa la dooranayaa* ("A man who had gone through ten years of struggle will be elected"). This together with another that depicted a special session of the Somali Socialist Revolutionary Party (XHKS) were intended to convey the message that the revolution represents a stage in the struggle for socialism and social progress. All the billboards marking historic events had images of women in the background. Overall, one of the most popular posters was the *8da Maarso 1980 Waa Maalinta Haweenka Horusocodka Ah*, which declared "8th of March is the day of the progressive woman."

In light of the low level of literacy in Somalia, the government pledged "liquidation of illiteracy and to develop an enlightened patrimonial and cultural heritage of the Somali people."[16] Barre positively identified education as the vehicle for national development, affirming his government's determination to provide educational opportunities for everyone as a force par excellence in national development. "The foundation of every nation's economy, its prosperity and aspirations, is education. We should, therefore, give education the important role it deserves. People of knowledge, in every aspect of Learning, can lead a nation out of the quagmire in which it has been bogged down for so long." Then Barre posed the rhetorical question: "If education has been neglected and consigned to a limbo, how do we expect to emerge as an advanced nation politically, socially and economically?"[17]

The propagation of mass literacy was one of the major areas in which Barre's regime attained remarkable success. To accomplish its dreams of education and national development, the regime abolished privately owned institutions—most of which were run by foreigners. This brings back memories of Julius Nyerere's educational policies in Tanzania that by the 1970s shot the level of literacy in that East African country to 76 percent. To create opportunities for the people, foreigners were also barred from posts that could be filled by Somalis. This period witnessed a rapid expansion of educational infrastructures at all levels. Scholarships were made available to students, and the government established the first Somali Institute of International Studies.

The government also founded the Somali National Academy of Arts, Sciences and Literature (SNAASL). The SNAASL soon became the second most important institution after the Somali National University. Through the SNAASL, further progress was made in regard to the native orthography through a Somali language dictionary and the writing of grammar books. This was in line with the new government's pledge in October 1969 "to constitute, with appropriate and adequate measures the basic development of the writing of Somali language."[18] In fact, the enforcement of Somali Script for the written language under the administration remains one of the sterling achievements of Barre's government. The new institute was further leading the way in a new effort to emphasize nationalist historiography. Prior to this, Somali's history was dominated by European colonial scholars. As Adan Makina, a Somali national, puts it, "Besides the few historical narrations mentioned in European texts, there remains a gargantuan task for the African historian and archeologist to unearth our vast buried historical treasures."[19] Such was the success of the educational program that within the first five years, 70 percent of Somalis achieved basic literacy.

The government also tackled the problem of health care for the Somalis. The health project concern was behind the government's decision to establish the first faculty of medicine at Somali University in 1970. The new program provided an opportunity for more Somalis to be trained at home and through this, extend efforts at modernizing hospital services. The government launched a massive immunization program to curb the tide of polio, whooping cough, and similar health issues. In realization of the crucial role livestock plays in the Somali economy, the government made a concerted effort to improve animal health care by establishing veterinary clinics to assist nomads. The clinics provided free vaccinations against animal diseases. With an increase in the inoculation of cattle, healthy animals were raised for both domestic consumption and overseas export.

In 1970, as part of the occasion to mark the first anniversary of the 1969 revolution, the government proclaimed the nationalization of all media houses like the radio, television, and newspapers. It also took over control of insurance companies, banks, the sugar refinery, and energy redistribution companies.[20] According to the *New Era*, "The Nationalization of the banking system unhooked monetary system from ultra-conservative restraints that starved the economy."[21] The regime created the first Somali National Bank in 1971 and centralized the budget system for the first time in Somali history. It may be recalled that after the merger of north and south in 1960, the respective regions continued to function like two independent nations, operating with separate annual budgets and using different currencies (lire for the ex-Italian Somaliland and the pound sterling for the ex-British Somaliland). Under Barre, this system was eventually abrogated.

The import and export business also became the government's monopoly as state-run companies were established to handle this sector of the economy. In a move reminiscent of the fascist economic policies in Somaliland in the 1920s and 1930s, the regime took control of the export of bananas, hides and skins, and imported cereals, fuel, medicine, and films. The intention was for the government to conserve its meager foreign earnings and put them to judicious use. These austere economic measures shored up the Somali economy.

A far-reaching strategy was also applied to the agricultural sector of the economy under the "Three-Year Plan" of development, with an aim to improve food production as well as export economy. The government created self-help schemes and crash programs ranging from group farms to tree-planting programs and sand dune stabilization. These programs required the contributions of every Somali. In a step dissimilar to Russia's treatment of the kulaks or serfs after the October revolution in 1917, the Somali government, in a courageous move it called "Crash Programme" or "Self-Help Programme," mobilized unemployed youths and organized them into agricultural teams.[22] The primary aim of the program was to "encourage the population to contribute funds for the country's socio-economic development. Much importance is also attached to volunteer work."[23] The program educated teams of youths in food production and afterwards compelled them to produce food. This was reminiscent of China's treatment of the peasants after Mao Zedong's rise to power (1949–1976). In the African context, it was akin to Julius Nyerere's *Ujamaa* program in Tanzania. Overall, the policy was conceived by the government as both the answer to unemployment and a way of curbing the increasing problem of urban crimes, especially in Mogadishu and Berbera.[24]

Barre further considered Somalia's role in international politics, particularly given the bipolar world order of the 1970s and 1980s. To this end, he realized that it would take a robust diplomacy along with modernized Somali armed forces to successfully play this role and gain respect in the community of nations. Under the administration, the cost of maintaining the Somali National Army (SNA) became the largest item in the national budget. Between 1961 and 1979, the size of the army was increased from 4,000 to 54,000; and by 1980, the annual expenditure on the military came up to $44.5 million. This amount might sound inconsequential in comparison with the military budget of any modest Western nation, but in fact it represented a big chunk of Somalia's revenue during this period.

Meanwhile, to secure some of its critical materials and fill its manpower needs, Barre's Somalia favored a closer relationship with the communist countries of Eastern Europe, from which it received considerable foreign aid and technical assistants. All branches of the armed forces—the army, navy, and the air force—were heavily supported by Soviet weapons and instructors, who provided training and logistics for the country's security. The implication was that Somalia could not realistically pursue an independent foreign policy without due consultations with the Soviet sponsors as well as USSR satellite countries like Cuba, to mention just one.

PROBLEMS AND CHALLENGES

Despite the initial achievements of the Somali socialist government, many problems and challenges dogged the country's development plans and consolidation of the newly rediscovered Pan-Somali consciousness. Some of these challenges and problems stem from Somalia's traditional social structures and inherited practices. Others were either created anew or simply reinforced by Barre's own interests and manner of leadership. Top among the challenges was the resilience of tribalism, nepotism, and clannish politics. Barre was from the south of Somalia and in a polity that was operated with a client-patron reward system; the Marehan people of Barre's Darod family clan were more supportive of his dictatorship. Ironically, during his 1969 radio address to the armed forces, Barre had seriously condemned tribalism as incompatible with national aspirations, saying, "Government progress, sophistication, national interest, raising of educational and level of production of the economy are incompatible with the groupings of tribal lines."[25]

Despite his condemnation of tribalism in all its ramifications, Barre was consolidating his position in power with the familiar divide-and-rule colonial strategy, which often exacerbated group differences and inculcated a pattern of perception in which certain groups felt disadvantaged and alienated in their own country. Within the Supreme Ruling Council, for instance, Barre built an inner circle comprised of his most trusted friends, political jingoists, and loyalists from his Marehan clan. This practice split the SRC in two—with the inner circle comprising those who shared common clan roots with the president versus the outer group, those who are not affiliated with his family clan. In the rank and file of the armed forces by which the dictatorship maintained its power, any officer rightly or wrongly perceived as having a divided loyalty was either dismissed, or retired, or killed. It got to a point where all successful applicants for admission into the military (cadet) academy were specifically from Barre's MOD, an alliance of three clans: the Marehan (the president's paternal clan), the Ogaden (his maternal clan), and the Dhulbahante (his son-in-law's clan)—all subclans of his Darod family clan.

A weary and annoyed public that watched public ceremonies where effigies of tribalism were set ablaze and buried were confounded by Barre's double standard. The Somalis soon came up with a national joke that goes that after the effigy of tribalism was buried by the government, Barre sneaked out in the middle of the night to exhume the remains and store them away in his personal closet.[26] Such an ironic mockery and betrayal of sacred trust of leadership represented the general debauchery of the dictatorship and its notorious practice of double standards. It is essential to underscore that the recourse of the "New Era" politics to the familiar pitfalls of parochialism cannot be blamed on Siad Barre alone. It was a stubborn sociopolitical ill that was mightier than Barre and his SRC.

The traditional clan politics had endured partly because the European colonists abused the traditional structures of power. In the ex-Italian territories, the colonial officials completely ignored the Somali clan elders and their authority in society. Particularly during the notorious regime of Benito Mussolini (r. 1922–1943), the Italians persecuted and humiliated Somali clan elders in the south. Such practices of alienation often tended to reinforce clan loyalties on the one hand and on the other, stifled the formation of national identity. In the north (British Somaliland Protectorate), the situation was not all that different, but new dynamics were introduced. The northern region's traditional clan elders were reconditioned by the British indirect rule system, which everywhere it was applied in the colonies tended to strengthen local leaders with new forms of authority that were often dictatorial in nature. As a result, while political alienation of the indigenous elders generally caused ordinary people to hold strongly to the security provided by membership in a clan—particularly as witnessed in the ex-Italian colony—what emerged in the north were more peaceful, democratic practices even though the indirect rule system permitted some arbitrary use of powers.

At independence, the emergent elite spent little or no time reconsidering the complex social structures of power bequeathed by colonial rule. When the constitution was suspended by Barre and his SRC in 1969, the underpinnings of opposition were laid among the northern decentralized groups such as the Isaaq clan, which constitutes about 70 percent of the entire population in the north.[27] In this context, a substantial segment of the Somali people started to question the whole idea of a nation and notions of sovereignty. It was in this sociopolitical milieu of transition and adjustments that the new political dispensation was trapped in a volatile dance of destiny. From this point, inter-clan relations began to accumulate the strains and strictures that would explode into bloody conflicts from the 1980s. Barre continued to instigate rural clan conflicts in hopes of distracting attention from his follies and preventing a common front against his dictatorship.[28]

As Somalia was caught up in a vortex of repression from the mid-1970s onward, the victims began to wonder how they ended up with Barre's nightmare. The common question became how did a presumed likeable compromise candidate for a nation whose politics were adrift in the 1960s turn out to be an endless terror? While this and similar questions agitated the minds of average Somalis, those who knew Barre from his early life and his career as a police officer under the Italian colonists were not altogether surprised. Barre was a human serpent: subtle in approach, cruel and vicious in attack. Somali historian Abdullahi states authoritatively that Barre "was not a normal person; he was a psychopath whose mercurial spirit vacillated between raving hatred in one moment and words of praise and reconciliation the next moment."[29] Indeed, most people raised under colonialism could easily fit this description, especially if they found themselves in a position of power where they are accountable to no one. If Barre was not normal, it was because most leaders of his generation who came up under colonialism were not—including Idi Amin Dada of Uganda, Jean-Bédel Bokassa of Central African Republic, Mobutu Sese Séku of the Congo, and others. The crucial angle missing from Abdullahi's evaluation of Barre is that he did not properly situate the analysis in the colonial situation.

Siad Barre represents a quintessential result of the crowd of notorious generation of African subjects created by colonialism—physically, spiritually, and psychologically. Perhaps Barre could not have acted differently given his family experience and career training as a policeman under the colonial setting. The making of this human tragedy commenced right from the onset of colonial conquests and the wars of resistance championed by Sheikh Muhammad Abdille Hassan from 1899 to 1920. According to his biographers, at the tender age of 10, young Muhammad first witnessed the murder of his own father in the Shilaabo area of Eastern Ethiopia where he was born. Subsequent to this, Barre became an orphan after his mother was also killed when the Mullah battled with the Europeans across the length and breadth of the Somali Peninsula. The shock and impact of this life experience and the difficult circumstances of life as an orphan put a very deep scar in his psyche. It is from this difficult childhood that Barre developed a complex sense of cunning, sadism, insecurity, and vengeance. These behavioral traits were exacerbated and solidified under the Italian fascist colonial rule. The fascist police trained Barre in the art of interrogation, cruelty, and intelligence gathering under the "special branch police" that carried out the dirty jobs for his imperial fascist Benito Mussolini.

As a commander of a colonial police station, Barre was notorious for his practice of corruption, torture, and guile. He often used intimidation and dismissal to punish junior officers who would not accept bribery in fear that such officers might one day cause him problems by witnessing against him in court. Considering all these factors, those who knew Barre from his early years were not therefore surprised about his leadership style. In his Mogadishu memoir, Hassan M. Abukar recalls that Barre was indeed "a master manipulator who was well adept in consolidating power incrementally."[30]

It is also important to add that Gen. Sani Abacha's dictatorship in Nigeria has revealed that no dictator can solely hold a nation for ransom without the active contribution of some of his countrymen and women.[31] There has not been a single report of an incident in which someone witnessed Barre personally shoot dead his victims; rather, Somalis carried out his dirty wars against fellow Somalis. Barre was urged on by a band of sycophants who had a stake in his government. For instance, in an editorial that appeared in the *New Era* Newspaper of October 1972, the editor among other things poured encomiums on the achievements of the "savior" Mr. Barre, and the Revolutionary Council: "Without the wise policies that emanate from the revolutionary theory that was been evolved by the savior and the great teacher, *Jaalle* President Siyad, Somalia would not have become able to achieve such a prestigious position among the nations of the entire world."[32]

At best, the circle of opportunists Barre put together to run the country acted like a mafia organization, and at worst members of his security forces acted like the dreaded German Gestapo under Adolf Hitler. Prompted by the expatriate security personnel from the Soviet Bloc, including a substantial number from Romania and East Germany, the SRC established the terrible National Security Service (NSS). The agency operated on Somalis a near inhuman administration of terror and torture. As a young man, Hassan Abukar observed and recorded what it looks like to have a date with the NSS in the 1970s: "In the early 1970s, 'Geedka' or the 'pole' [or tree] became popular because that's where criminals and some of Siad Barre's opponents were executed. . . . One constant tactic to use for both the civilian and the military Government's [opponents] was the use of torture to illicit confession. Suspects were normally slapped, shoved, beaten, and at times even taken to the ocean to be subjected to something similar to 'water boarding.' "[33]

The NSS worked closely with a popular militia group called the *Guulwadayaal*—which simply means "Pioneers of the Revolution." The officers of the *Guulwadayaal*, which operated in green camouflage uniforms, were mostly recruited from among common criminals, street urchins, and the illiterate urban youths of Mogadishu. Empowered by the state, the *Guulwadayaal* freely exercised criminal behaviors, with the primary assignment to spy on every household and ordinary people. The activities of the *Guulwadayaal* placed the NSS at liberty to focus their interest on the educated and political elites of the country who were considered treacherous by the junta. Operatives of both bodies used their power to plunder and settle personal scores with their enemies, including extrajudicial murders, some of which were never permitted by the regime. A huge part of the chaos that transpired after the exit of Barre were attempts by individuals and groups alike to avenge the extrajudicial murders of family relations and friends by state officials.

EXTERNAL FACTORS

Explanations of preconditions for democracy and political stability have gone beyond internal factors in a state to argue that external factors could determine the survival or collapse of a democratic institution. Eminent political scientist and theorist Robert Dahl argues that democratic institutions are less likely to develop in a country subject to intervention by another country. But this is not peculiar to democracies. As the recent history of Hosni Mubarak of Egypt, Muammar Gaddafi of Libya, and others has shown around the world, external factors could make or break other regime types. For example, Dahl contends that without the intervention of the Soviet Union after World War II, Czechoslovakia would probably be counted today among the older democracies. Additionally, Soviet intervention in Poland and Hungary apparently mired the development of democratic institutions in these Eastern European countries until the collapse of the USSR in 1990. Similarly, the United States until the last decade of the twentieth century continuously intervened in Latin America against popular governments considered injurious to U.S. interests.[34]

In connection with Somalia, it might not be difficult to figure out the impact of external influences on the outcome of Somali politics when this is analyzed in the context of the Cold War era and the politics of East-West ideological struggles. From 1969 to 1977, Somalia was heavily dependent on aid from the Soviet Union, which included financial subventions, material imports, technical advisors, and instructors. In fact, there are good reasons to believe that Soviet Union instructors played a crucial role in the coup of 1969.[35]

With the Cold War, the politics of fear, distrust, secrecy, alliance-making, political assassination, proxy wars, and political brinksmanship became common currents of international politics. The emergent postcolonial African leaders mastered the politics of the Cold War era and exploited the climate of fear and alliance-making to extract uncommon favors from the more developed Western countries, while entrenching cruel forms of leadership within their own countries. In Somalia, Barre declared his support for the Soviets and played on their fears to acquire Russian-made weapons, technology, food, in addition to bilateral exchanges in the areas of education and culture. With the weapons at his disposal, Barre, from 1974, began to antagonize and cause conflicts with his African neighbors. Although his quest was to attempt a unification of all Somalis in the neighboring countries of Djibouti, Ethiopia, and Kenya, the conflict was also a ploy to whip up popular support as his prestige diminished among his countrymen and women. This strategy led to periodic clashes with its East African neighbors. The regional tension continued on and off, escalating to a dangerous level in 1977 with the outbreak of the Ogaden war with Ethiopia.

While the Ogaden debacle was a conscious choice made by Barre to defray the pressures of his political failures, the war resonated what had transpired back in the sixteenth century when a total crushing of Ethiopia was averted by the intervention of a Portuguese army made up of 400 musketeers under the command of Christopher Da Gama, the son of the renowned navigator Vasco Da Gama. Back then, after initial setbacks in the war, Portuguese and Ethiopian forces had gained victory over the Somali Muslims at the battle of Wayna Daga in 1543.

The Ogaden war further rekindled the more recent colonial injustices that saw Britain relinquish the western parts of the Somali lands to its Abyssinian Christian ally.[36] Historically, uniting all Somali-speaking groups in the Horn of Africa has always been a popular sentiment among the Somalis. For a regime suffering from a widespread crisis of legitimacy, aggravating a popular war with Ethiopia was an irresistible opportunity to regain acclaim among the people. So in 1977, Barre began to openly send more Somali troops to aid an ongoing guerrilla struggle against Ethiopia's national army in the Ogaden region. At first, the move appeared successful as Somali forces pushed back Ethiopian forces into Ethiopia's territory. The early gains shored up Barre's popularity overnight.

But in reality, Barre chose an inauspicious time to stake his gamble. Three years back in 1974, Col. Mengistu Haile Mariam (r. 1974–1987), a young army officer and another adventurous traveler on the socialist road, had sacked an enduring Emperor Haile Selassie in Ethiopia, declaring Ethiopia a Marxist state. In the midst of the pandemonium that followed Emperor Sellasie's ouster, Barre had secretly begun to support various pro–Somali liberation groups in the Ogaden. Among these groups was the Western Somali Liberation Front (WSLF), which proved to be a tear in the flesh of Ethiopian security forces through its effective guerrilla operations. By 1977, Somalia, despite the government's denials, had secretly committed several thousands of its national army to aid the guerrilla movements in the contentious region.

Therefore, the 1977 escalation of violence was just an open move on the part of Barre to stop all denials and allow the war to assume a more conventional nature. By the middle of 1977, the Somali forces had achieved victories in several encounters as well as sustained some damages. It must be understood that when Somali forces explicitly attacked the interests of the government in Ethiopia in 1977, Barre acted against the wishes of his Soviet Union friends who from all indications had begun to express distrust over Barre's intentions and commitment to socialism. For the Soviets at this point, the situation demanded they make a choice between Somalia and Ethiopia, and the better choice was Ethiopia for obvious reasons. Among other things, Ethiopia was a bigger country, and the simple fact that it was being snatched from the West made it an even more interesting choice. Now Siad Barre would understand one crucial lesson in international relations: there are no permanent friends and enemies.

Having withdrawn all support from Somalia, the Soviets quickly started deploying into Ethiopia a huge arsenal of weapons and personnel drawn from Cuba and Yemen. The advanced logistics the communists provided Ethiopia proved too much for Somalia to overcome. In 1978, Somalia hurriedly signed a truce with Ethiopia, thus pulling out of the Ogaden a substantial number of its regular army in the border areas. Barre wanted to concentrate on quelling the internal unrest that had become very serious in his country. As a *Washington Report* claimed in 1983, "Somalia's President, fearing the attack might be a beginning of a wider offensive, appealed to the U.S. for help. The U.S. responded to Somalia's appeal with an emergency airlift of small arms, ammunition, air defense equipment, transport, and communication, supplies."[37]

Accordingly, in the 1980s, Somalia became part of the U.S.-led war of containment against the spread of communism around the world. In the Arab world, the Cold War struggle was getting more intense. With Russia's presence in Afghanistan and with the political developments in Iran brought about by the ouster of the Shah by radicals in that country, the U.S. government was everywhere scrambling for supporters to help combat the fast spread of communism, as it threatened the supply of oil from Iran in particular and the Middle East in general. It was in this context that the United States found Barre an august ally who offered the strategic Somali seaports (most importantly the northern Berbera ports, which had harbored Soviet naval and air personnel) and airports for movement and stationing of the American soldiers. The reward for Barre was the promise of American weapons and other crucial aids.[38]

With the new lifeline coming from the United States, Barre resolved not to heed the calls of his people to lighten their burden. Rather, he ratcheted up his program of crushing the opposition. One of the most brazen acts came in 1982 when he surprisingly jailed seven members of his regime. The victims included Omar Arteh (the well-known former foreign minister) and Ismail Ali Abokar (his vice president). Barre also ordered the arrest of two members of the regime who were from his Marehan clan. This move was a deliberate ploy to cause a distraction from his main motive, which was to crush the mounting opposition from the Isaaq clan. The Isaaqs had begun in 1981 to set up a guerrilla movement against Barre from across the border with Ethiopia to the West.

COUNTDOWN TO THE END: 1981–1991

An Igbo proverb goes that a cranky child who would not allow his parents some rest will also not rest. This proverb captures the events that would be witnessed in Somalia in the 1980s. The year 1981 marked the beginning of a long-sought end to Barre's dictatorship. It was the year that saw the launching of the Somali National Movement (SNM) by concerned citizens of the Isaaq clan. For clarity, the SNM was not the first Somali people's movement against Barre's absolutism. The first of these groups was the Somali Salvation Front (SSF), some of whose members were behind an aborted military coup against Barre in 1978 in which several hundreds were killed.[39] It was the SSF that later metamorphosed into the Democratic Front for the Salvation of Somalia (DFSS) in 1981 and that was again subsequently renamed the Somali Salvation Democratic Front (SSDF). The major actors in the SSDF remained political activists from the northeastern Majerteens, a subclan of the Darod.[40] Back then after the 1978 coup, Barre had employed a mixture of subterfuge, violence, and diplomacy to persuade the other Darod subgroups against the Majerteens, and at a point even managed to break up the cohesion within the SSDF, luring their fighters back into Somalia. Then with the appropriate doses of rewards, Barre attempted to set Majerteen militia up against the Isaaq-led rebellion in the northwest.

Subterfuge and repression were the paths Barre chose to tread in addressing the legitimate complaints of the Isaaqs, which included political and economic alienation. The fact that the northerners produced the mass of livestock that provided Somalia the bulk of its foreign earnings made their anger and complaints more legitimate. The Isaaqs as a family clan were not completely different from the Hawiye family clan (the most important clan in the south) or the Darod (Barre's family clan dominant in the western part of the country). It might be recalled that the Isaaqs, as the dominant group in the northwest, had championed the historical merger of the north and south after independence in 1960. Although the north had entertained fears over southern political domination in the first years of the union, it was the Isaaqs that quickly tried to integrate with the south economically and politically. Similar to the role of the Igbos in forging interethnic mixing in the immediate postcolonial Nigerian nation, the northern-based Isaaq group had arguably made more sacrifices in an attempt to keep the country one. The Isaaq, therefore, deserved a better treatment than Barre was prepared to offer.

Throughout the early 1980s, Barre's forces launched a program of systematic destruction of the Isaaqs, periodically practicing genocidal attacks against unarmed Isaaq villages. One such attack was in 1982 after the SNM and the DFSS (with substantial military help from Ethiopia) invaded and captured the central border areas of Somalia, taking complete control of two small towns. In response, and with arms from the United States and Italy, Barre's forces unleashed a vicious onslaught that included airpower in an attempt to repel the insurgents. When this proved difficult, the entire Majerteen clan, instead of the militia involved in the insurgency, became fair targets for Barre forces.[41] The Isaaq have cited these attacks, more than anything else, as a justification for the northern separatist group's agitation for an independent statehood. As the civil conflict expanded throughout the country, millions of refugees were settled in camps in different parts of the country. This allowed the SNM to secretly work closely with the Somali people against the Barre junta.

The Ethiopian military support for the insurgents was drastically slowed only after a January 1986 meeting between the leaders of Somalia and Ethiopia. The struggle with the insurgents made Barre realize that he needed to put his house in order first before fighting for a territory that had been outside Somalia's control for over a century and a half. In April 1988, after a decade of waste of human and material resources, Barre signed a peace deal with Colonel Mengistu of Ethiopia. This enabled Somalia to completely pull out of the Ogaden region the remnants of its army regulars. With a broken treasury, and floods of refugee movements comprising Somalis and Oromos (an Ethiopian secessionist group who were afraid of reprisals from the Ethiopian army) bringing additional pressures, the Somalis no doubt had had enough of Barre. Yet the dictator would attempt for the next three years to maintain his hold on power by raising his brutal campaign against the Isaaqs. After the insurgent forces attacked and occupied Burao and parts of Hargeisa in the northwest. In a bloody counteroffensive that lasted for two months, government forces led by the son-in-law of the president, Gen. Mohamed Siad Hersi, recaptured the towns.[42] By the end of 1988, the north as a whole faced the danger of total annihilation. One estimate of the number of deaths within a month totaled about 50,000, with about half a million refugees scattered across Somalia.

The magnitude of the devastation and deaths the government forces left in their wake made the SNM change its goal from a struggle to bring about a change in government to an unwavering fight to liberate the Isaaqs from a genocidal campaign of destruction. Although the SNM had lost its crucial supporter in Ethiopia, it nonetheless pressed on with the insurgency. Indeed, the ruthless manner in which government forces executed the counterattack served to increase support for the SNM within the Isaaq and other northern clans.

Between 1988 and 1989, Barre's menace could have fizzled out fast but for the aid supplied by the U.S. government. The year 1989 was when the intellectuals and disgruntled army officers of Hawiye clan in the south, on whose territory the capital city Mogadishu is located, openly joined the movement to remove Barre from power by establishing the United Somali Congress (USC). The USC was launched with a massive antigovernment demonstration in the Mogadishu area in July 1988. In an attempt to dampen the spirit behind the demonstration, government forces shot dead about 400 participants.[43] The new opposition force was actually made up of a weak coalition of about 15 political factions, and the basis for their coming together was to a large degree founded on affiliation with the Hawiye family clan, comprising all the subclans of Hawadle, Waadan, Habr Gedir, Abgal, Murosade, and Gaalgale. The USC set up operations headquarters just outside of Mogadishu with a firm determination to push Barre and his forces out of the state capital.

Another blow to Barre's power came in the form of a defection by some of his commanders. Prominent among them was Col. Omar Jess, a member of the Darod clan who would later form his own separatist group, the Somali Patriotic Movement (SPM). Colonel Jess's decision caused a split in the heart of Barre's MOD (Marehan-Ogaden-Dhulbahante) support triangle. From all angles, rebellion and war approached Barre and his henchmen even as they continued to take supplies of arms and materials from the United States, Italy, and Saudi Arabia. Most of the clashes between government troops and the various insurgents were contained within Mogadishu, Berbera, and parts of Hargeisa. Having lost the crucial support of the Ogaden clan, Barre, "offered to relinquish power and allow multi-party elections in August 1998."[44]

The offer came too late to deserve any possible consideration, for everywhere insurgent groups crept out against Barre. For instance, in addition to the SNM, the Somali Democratic Alliance (SDA) launched by the Gadabursi, a subclan of the Dir family clan in the northwest, had joined the face-up to Barre. In a last-ditch effort, Barre dismissed his government in January 1990, offering posts to opposition leaders, who all scorned his offers. By the beginning of 1990, the outcry of the Somali people had begun to receive sympathetic ears in the outside world. No doubt, this sudden change of things had to do with collapse of the Berlin Wall that year and the thaw in the Cold War. At this time, Ogaden deserters (from the Somali national army) had come together to launch an additional pressure group called the Somali Patriotic Movement (SPM).

In August 1990, the various factions—the SNM, USC, and SPM—came to a historic agreement to coordinate their separate military campaigns against Barre's government. Afterwards, it did not take too long to make Barre flee from Mogadishu. In November 1990, the southern region of Kismayo was captured by the SPM, and two months later, the USC's forces commanded by Gen. Farah Aideed had taken control of much of Mogadishu. The USC assumed power in Mogadishu, the SNM took control of the northwest, and the SSDF the northeast.[45]

Finally, Siad's 22-year regime collapsed on January 17, 1991 when he fled Mogadishu to the southwestern region of Gedo. Here, Barre established a new base. His abdication also marked the end of central authority in Somalia and the beginning of contested sovereignties. On May 17, 1991, about four months after the fall of Barre's regime, the northern region formally announced its voluntary secession from Somalia with the proclamation of the Somaliland Republic. After unsuccessful attempts to regain power from his Gedo base, Siad Barre eventually embraced reality and boarded a flight in early 1992 that first took him to Kenya. From there, Barre moved onward to his exile in Nigeria. From the West African country, Barre watched the unfolding consequences of his misrule until his death on January 2, 1995.[46]

NOTES

1. The Ministry of Information and National Guidance Mogadishu (hereafter MINGM), "A Note from the Publishers," *New Era: A Quarterly Journal* (Mogadishu), Aug. 1970, 1.

2. *The Times*, Editorial: "Coup in Somalia," (London), Oct. 22, 1969, 11.

3. Fareed Zakaria, "The Failed State Conundrum," *Washington Post*, July 19, 2010; David Blair, "Somalia: Analysis of a Failed State," *Daily Telegraph* (London), Mon., Nov. 18, 2008.

4. MINGM, "The List of Members of Government," *New Era: A Quarterly Journal* (Mogadishu), Nov. 1, 1969, 7.

5. Siad Barre, Speech of the President of the Supreme Revolutionary Council, Major-General Mohammed Siad Barre at the Officer's Club (Mogadishu), Oct. 31, 1969.

6. *New Era*, Editorial: "Scientific Socialism in Action" (Mogadishu), Mar. 1972, 2.

7. *New Era*, "The Only Way for Somalia . . . Scientific Socialism," (Mogadishu), Mar. 1972, 4–40.

8. Siad Barre, "Freedom with Hunger Is Better Than Humiliation, a Message to the Nation by General Siad" (Mogadishu), Oct. 26, 1969.

9. Julius Nyerere, "Ujamaa: The Basis of African Socialism," (1962) in Julius Nyerere, *Africa's Freedom* (Dar es Salaam: Oxford University Press, 1968), 67–77.

10. National Archives Kew (hereafter NAK), Dominions Office (DO) 195/6, and DO 195/7, Deterioration of relations with UK following Mr. Nkrumah's visit to Eastern Europe and China, 1961–1962; and NAK, DO 195/222, Reaction to Nkrumah book, *Neo-Colonialism: The Last Stage of Imperialism*, 1965.

11. Abukar, Mogadishu Memoir (Part VIII): "Crimes and Concoctions," July 15, 2010.

12. Maj.-Gen. Mohamed Siad Barre, Address to the Armed Forces over Radio Mogadishu, Nov. 9, 1969.

13. Ibid.

14. Mohamed Diriye Abdulahi, *Culture and Customs of Somalia* (Westport, CT: Greenwood Press, 2001), 30.

15. *New Era*, "Revolution: 1st Announcement SRC act on Behalf of the People" (Mogadishu), Oct. 1969, 3.

16. *New Era*, "Revolution: 1st Announcement SRC," 3.

17. Major-General Barre, Address to the Armed Forces.

18. *New Era*, "Revolution: 1st Announcement SRC," 3.

19. Adan Makina, email communication, May 1, 2011.

20. *The Times*, "Somalia: Takeover of Banks and Oil Groups (Banking and Finance" (London), May 8, 1970, 23.

21. *New Era*, "Implementing Somalia's Three-Year Plan" (Mogadishu), Oct. 1972, 27–32.

22. Ibid.

23. Gennady Kazakov, "New Times Comment on Somalia on the Upgrade," *New Era* (Mogadishu), Oct. 1972, 32.

24. Abukar, Mogadishu Memoir (Part VIII): "Crimes and Concoctions," July 15, 2010.

25. Major-General Barre, Address to the Armed Forces.

26. Abdullahi, *Culture and Customs of Somalia*, 31.

27. Hussein Mohamed Adam, *From Tyranny to Anarchy* (Trenton, NJ: Red Sea Press, 2007), 191.

28. Adam, *From Tyranny to Anarchy*, 191.

29. Abdullahi, *Culture and Customs of Somalia*, 33.

30. Abukar, Mogadishu Memoir (Part VIII): "Crimes and Concoctions," July 15, 2010.

31. Raphael Chijioke Njoku, "Deconstructing Abacha: Demilitarization and Democratic Consolidation in Nigeria after Abacha Era." *Government and Opposition: An International Journal* 36, no. 1 (Winter, January 2001): 71–96.

32. *New Era*, Editorial: "Three Candles" (Mogadishu), Oct. 1972, 6.

33. Abukar, Mogadishu Memoir (Part VIII): "Crimes and Concoctions," July 15, 2010.

34. Robert Dahl, *On Democracy* (New Haven, CT: Yale University Press, 1998), 147–48.

35. Payton, Gary D., "The Somali Coup of 1969: The Case for Soviet Complicity." *Journal of Modern African Studies* 18, no. 3 (Sept. 1980): 493–508.

36. For details see NAK, CAB/129/12, British Somaliland: Proposals by Ethiopian Government for an Exchange of Territory (marked "Top Secret C.P. 46 319"), dated August 6, 1946.

37. Washington Report, "Whatever Happened to . . . 'The Ogaden War,'" *The Washington Report on Middle East Affairs (1982–1989)* 1 no. 18 (Feb. 7, 1983): 3.

38. Charles Harrison, "American Arms for Somalia," *The Times* (London), July 26, 1982, 4.

39. NAK, HO 421/2 1986–2000, 5.

40. Charles Harrison, "Rebel Army Advances in Somalia," *The Times* (London), July 19, 1982, 4; and NAK, HO 421/2 1986–2000, 5.

41. NAK, HO 421/2 1986–2000, 5.

42. Ibid.

43. Ibid.

44. Ibid.

45. Ibid.

46. Anonymous, "Somalia's Former Dictator Dies in Nigeria," *Africa Report* 40, no. 2 (Mar. 1995): 10.

7

Dad-Cunkil (Cannibalism), Secessionism, and Operation Restore Hope

Following the end of Siad Barre's regime in January 1991, conditions in Somalia took a turn for the worse with famine, looting, indiscriminate shootings, and continuing civil war among different political factions and militia groups built around clans and subclans. The absence of a central government running the affairs of a war-ravaged and traumatized nation made the escalation of violence and anarchy in Mogadishu (the nation's capital city) look like a plot in a Hollywood movie. Across the country, the environmental degradation brought about by incessant warring compounded a severe drought and famine of that year. Consequently there were acute food shortages and a pervasive problem of starvation and deaths. The grim situation was exacerbated by combatants in the struggle who hoarded food supplies from international donors, and used starvation to punish rival groups in order to gain political supremacy.[1]

One of the prominent factions involved in the fight for the leadership of Somalia was the United Somali Congress (USC). Shortly before Barre was dislodged from Mogadishu in January 1991, a rift developed within the 14 different political/clan factions and interest groups that collaborated with the USC against Barre. Among the groups, two were most influential: the "USC-Mahdi," or USC-SSA, headed by Ali Mahdi Mohamed of the Abgal subclan (a branch of the Hawiye family clan), who unilaterally declared himself the interim president of Somalia in January 1991. The other faction, "USC-Aideed," or USC-SNA, was led by Gen. Mohamed Farah Aideed of the Habr-Gedir subclan (also a branch of the Hawiye family). In other words, the rift was an interclan rivalry for ultimate control of political power and influence. Prior to the quarrel between the two warlords, Aideed held the chairmanship of the United Somali Congress, and was also former ambassador to India. It may be recalled that Aideed was jailed in 1969 by Barre for initially declining his diplomatic posting. Having taken his revenge on Barre, Aideed was now determined to claim nothing less than the top spot in Somali politics.[2] Such a sense of entitlement has remained endemic in contemporary politics.

In November 1991, the continuing violence that had engulfed the nation's capital expanded as heavily armed opposition factions engaged in a desperate battle to establish their separate sovereignties across different parts of the country. The latest rounds of fighting primarily engulfed the central-south region of Somalia, which was the primary source of grains. This heavily populated region was still suffering from a drought that began in 1989.[3] The conflict created nearly one million refugees and forced farmers and other civilians out of their lands and as such, disrupted food production. Without food, shelter, and health care, the Somalis counted their deaths in large numbers. The victims died as a result of injuries, starvation, and illnesses related to malnutrition.[4]

International nongovernmental humanitarian organizations that arrived to assist the civilian population were unable to operate in midst of the crisis, and as their lives were continually exposed to danger, they began to leave the country. Left with only one aid agency, the Kinderdorf, an Austrian children's rights group, Somalia appeared poised for complete self-destruction. In the midst of this upheaval, the United Nations began to search for a way to halt the fratricidal warfare.[5]

Much has been written about the United Nations' humanitarian intervention in Somalia with regard to the initial goals of the mission and all that transpired in its expanded nation-building role. Some scholars have mercilessly attacked the role played by the United States in the mission.[6] Others, including some Somalis, acknowledge with appreciation the achievements of the UN peacekeepers, particularly the American soldiers that offered their lives for a cause they derived no special benefits from. Whatever view one might hold, it is appropriate to carefully consider the circumstances in which the international community acted as to whether their actions helped or complicated the crisis in Somalia. The crucial questions that are difficult to resolve are whether Somalia could have been salvaged after the exit of Barre and whether the various groups now locked in an uncompromising competition for separatist sovereignties should be recognized by the international community.

To this end, it is vital to first briefly reinstate the conditions in which unity within the Somali state unraveled. The immediate cause of the predicament was, of course, Siad Barre's dictatorship. But a critical look beyond Barre's rule reveals some serious structural problems that made violence and separatism rife in the land. Some of these problems were endemic in society; some were created by colonial rule and compounded by neocolonial tendencies of the Western world, particularly in the context of the Cold War era. The tendency for Western powers to meddle in the affairs of the African postcolonial state was a major factor in the quandary. In Somalia after 1960, this manifested either by way of arms supplies or the praxis of East-West ideological competition.

EXPLAINING THE ANARCHY IN POST-BARRE SOMALIA

Scholars have approached the question of war and causation from a variety of disciplinary perspectives.[7] These ideas have emerged in an attempt to understand the increasing and unending prevalence of civil war. Some of the emergent theories, such as Paul Collier and Anke Hoeffler's "greed and grievance" paradigm, were developed to explain specifically the African phenomenon.[8] Others were fashioned more generally in response to a common trend that has troubled mankind across the globe. A good example of this remains Mansoob Murshed's assertion that ethnicity plays a far larger role in civil wars because of its strong uniting force.[9] Other explanations state that wars result mainly from territorial disputes, religious schism, reactions to oppression, deteriorating economies, and control of mineral resources. The resilient legacies of colonialism, neocolonialism, and postcolonial "revolutionary" youth culture have also been blamed.[10]

The governing elite's practice of unfair redistribution of national wealth to the larger society is the deliberate deprivation of basic needs. Johan Galtung, a Norwegian sociologist, has alluded to such practices as "structural violence."[11] Underscoring the dialectics of economics and politics, Galtung argues that it is violence embodied by a structure and "characterized politically as repression and economically by exploitation."[12] This view corroborates Collier and Hoeffler's model of "greed and grievance" as factors linked to conflicts in Africa. The authors define grievance as based on "ethnic and religious hatred, economic inequality, lack of political rights, or economic incompetence on the part of governments."[13] Greed is related to the desire by political groups and individual leaders to continuously control national power, which also comes with control of national resources in most developing nations. Collier and Hoeffler suggest that there is minute evidence that grievance contributes directly to the outbreak of civil war, but the authors quickly assert that when civil war breaks out, greed-motivated factors and agendas seem more vital for sustaining and prolonging ongoing violent crisis than causing them.[14] A succinct digest of the applicability of these theories to Somalia is relevant in order to better grasp the turn of events from January 1991.

In the post-Barre era, Somalia sank into a gyration of bloody struggle and banditry because 30 years of postcolonial nationhood had entrenched a culture of political repressions, violence, and nepotism. Operating in an economic milieu where the basic needs of life were grossly lacking, this political culture gave birth to a new species of patron-client networks, warlordism, militarism, the erosion of traditional systems of social control, and revolutionary youth culture. In this order of things, the personal agendas of politicians and clan leaders in the conflict—that is, individuals like General Aideed and Ali Mahdi—engendered a system breakdown and the ensuing anarchy that rendered the country completely ungovernable.[15]

SECESSIONS AND COLLAPSE OF CENTRAL GOVERNMENT

One common rationale often cited for the collapse of central government in the post-Barre era has been the efforts of clan governments. Ismail Ahmed and Reginald Green, scholars of development studies, have closely looked at the structure of clans and lineage relationships and argued that "understanding state collapse in Somalia requires looking beyond clanism and ongoing factional intrigue, which is a symptom of state collapse rather than its cause."[16] The authors supported their view with the argument that institutional structures that incorporated concepts entirely alien to the existing indigenous institutions were imposed under colonial rule. As a result,

Armed Somali guerrillas. Since the early 1990s, battling clan factions have kept Somalia in a state of civil war. (Corel)

a discrepancy emerged between the inherited culture of highly decentralized pastoral political structures and the highly centralized postcolonial state bequeathed by Italian and British imperial regimes.[17] In other words, the crisis in Somalia was a manifestation of the struggle between the precolonial and Western systems.

On January 29, 1991, when Ali Mahdi Mohamed, of the Abgal (Hawiye) clan, unilaterally declared himself the interim president of Somalia, he drew the fury of both the USC-Aideed's faction as well as the Somali Patriotic Movement (SPM), commanded by Aden Abdullahi "Nur" Gabyow. Their expressions of bitterness were primarily because Ali Mahdi and his group acted contrarily to the previous pledge not to attempt governing without input of the other groups that had collaborated in the fight against Barre.[18] Therefore, Mahdi's decision to go it alone was shortsighted and criminally insensitive to the legitimate fears of the other factions. The path that was not followed in the process of Mahdi's self-proclamation was a consociational approach that should have guided the formation of an interim national government. This turned the country into a land of endless secessionism.

First, in the northwest region of the country, the Isaaq-dominated Somali National Movement (SNM) quickly convened a series of meetings of clan elders in the former British Somaliland, and the result of those summits gave rise to the decision to establish an administration and a legislature and the proclamation of the region's secession from the rest of the country on May 16, 1991. The council declared the SNM's chairman, Abdurrahman Ahmed Ali (aka "Tur"), president of the "Republic of Somaliland."[19] With this, the former British protectorate—the colony that "rejected freedom" in 1960—completed a turnaround induced by the painful pangs of nation building in a postcolonial state that was brought into existence with so many disabilities.

Second, Mogadishu, the national capital, was split between four main Hawiye clan-based governments. The leaders of the various factions included Ali Mahdi's USC-SSA, based in the northern area of Mogadishu and parts of the Bermuda district of southern Mogadishu; Farah Aideed's USC-SNA, based in southern Mogadishu; and Osman Hasan Ali Ato's breakaway faction of the USC-SNA, located in a small part of southern Mogadishu. Ato was former henchman, financier, and clansman of General Aideed. He separated from Aideed in 1995 and realigned with Ali Mahdi. The fourth group was led by Musa Sude, deputy chairman of the USC-SSA (Somali Salvation Alliance), in the Medina district of Mogadishu.[20]

Meanwhile, the political situation in central and southern regions of Somalia remained fragmented after Barre's exit. In this region are found large numbers of militia groups, some of whose sovereignties are no more than the size of a village. The Kismayo area has been under contestation between rival clans such as Marehan-SNF (Somali National Front), and the Ogaden-SPM (Somali Patriotic Movement). The Majerteen-SSDF (Southern Somali Democratic Front), dominant in northeastern Somalia (seceded in 1994), had stakes to territorial claims in Kismayo. Rival factions of the SPM—one allied with Hussein Aideed's (who succeeded his father General Aideed) USC-SNA, the other with the SNF and Ali Mahdi's USC-SSA—took control of different parts of Kismayo.[21]

The Middle Shebelle district is also owned by the Abgal (Hawiye) and is politically under Mahdi's USC-SSA. Similarly, the Hiram region is dominated by the Hawadle strand of the Hawiye family clan. However, the local administration in the area today was established by UNOSOM. It includes local and clan councils of elders. It also has a volunteer police force established by UNOSOM.[22]

The Gedo region bordering Kenya and Ethiopia is under the sovereignty of the Marehan-SNF (Somali National Front). Many Marehan (Siad Barre's people) had fled to this region to escape retributions following the fall of Barre in January 1991. Here in the early 1990s, they established an effective administration with a police force and a sharia court for the region.[23] This was the series of events that led concerned Somalis and international actors to begin the daunting search for peace in hopes that unity will return to the beleaguered nation.

ELUSIVE HOPE FOR PEACE UNDER THE UN MANDATE

The primary reason the United Nations decided to take action in Somalia was to bring to an end a humanitarian crisis engendered by competing sovereignties and the deadly struggle for control of national power. There are four major interrelated reasons why peace eluded Somalia in the 1990s and may continue to do so for a long time to come. One of these is the country's agro-based primary economy, and the dominant nomadic mode of production. Unlike cash crops, food crops as a mainstay of a developing economy are difficult to control, especially in expanding tax revenue. This could explain why Mogadishu and other southern parts of Somalia notable for a striving food production have been insecure. In contrast, the northern region of Somalia has been more stable because the economy is based mainly on livestock production. Nonetheless, one may dispute this hypothesis in the sense that the economy of the north is not all that easily adapted to government control, given that nomadic mode of production goes with constant movements, and this might pose serious difficulties for tax revenue administration.

Second, the personal and selfish interests of the major stakeholders in the crisis were perhaps the biggest hindrance to peace. These leaders reaped quick profits from the state of war and lawlessness through the black market, selling illicit drugs, weapons, controlling the ports and airports (therefore the exports and the bribes), and by stealing food shipments sent by the United nations.[24] The capacity to control the flow of food helped the warlords maintain power and terrorize ordinary people. Some businesses also made brisk profits from the trade and aid contracts sponsored with monies from international donor agencies. Some of the monies were frequently diverted and used for the acquisition of more arms and ammunition that further sustained the war.

Third, with the collapse of the central government, clan identity became more attractive for individual and group survival. Individuals have used the clan as a political unit to mobilize military force and recruited other clans/subclans to gain more power and access to wealth.[25] There were also independent neighborhood militias that had sprouted up to protect their neighborhoods. These *mooryan*, or "bandit groups," provided fighters for hire. As rewards for their services, the warlords gave them generous quantities of rice or *khat* (a mild amphetamine). This is reminiscent of the use of rice to reward the Japanese samurai (military nobility) prior to the Meiji Restoration that restored imperial rule in Japan in 1868. While many of the bandit groups were loosely tied to clans, they also reserved the initiative to act independently to raid other militias' territories.

Fourth, as the conflict continued, personal and clan interests superseded national interests. The fighting between the clans was heaviest in the city of Mogadishu. There was also heavy fighting in the port city of Kismayo (located about 326 miles to the southwest of Mogadishu) and in the northwest, where local secessionist leaders launched a sovereign Somaliland.[26] The civil war created a humanitarian crisis of immense proportions. Refugees fleeing the fighting with no way to earn a living resorted to looting and scavenging. The ruinous combination of a civil war in a period of drought and famine left a significant part of the country's population in danger of starvation. The United Nations estimated that 300,000 people died during this time, another 2 million were displaced, and all governmental and infrastructural developments destroyed.[27] The United Nations desired to establish a command structure and distribution line that would enable its aid workers to effectively deliver food to millions of starving people without the food being hijacked by militia groups.

THE UN-U.S. INTERVENTION

Moved by increasing gruesome accounts of widespread sufferings and deaths, the United Nations campaigned for and won popular approval to send a humanitarian mission to Somalia. The unintended outcome of events proved undoubtedly that the United Nations' initial assessment of the Somali situation and execution of the peacekeeping mission was poor and inconclusive. On January 23, 1992, after a protracted deliberation on a letter initiated by the chargé d'affaires of Permanent Mission of Somalia to the United Nations, and addressed to the Security Council, the members adopted Resolution 733, and in accord with Resolution 746 (1992), a strict arms embargo was imposed on all deliveries to Somalia.[28]

On January 31, 1992, a joint meeting of the Organization of African Unity (OAU) now simply known as the African Union (AU), the League of Arab States (LAS), and the Organization of the Islamic Conference (OIC) convened in Addis Ababa to discuss the immediate end of hostilities in Mogadishu. The signing of the "Agreement on Implementation of a Ceasefire" took place on March 3, 1992, after four days of intensive negotiations between Ali Mahdi and General Aideed. The multiparty discussion also considered staging of a national reconciliation conference to which all Somali factions would be invited.[29]

Later that month, the rival groups agreed to a cease-fire and to allow the United Nations' team of observers to monitor it. The peacekeeping units were charged primarily to protect and assist the aid workers distributing foods and supplies. They were also directed to enforce any peace accords formally approved among the warring factions. Their third mission was to become actively involved in the settlement of political disputes among the warring factions. The preceding period of delay prior to formal signing of the agreement was due to the fact that General Aideed, one of the principal actors in the conflict, distrusted the motives behind the actions of Boutros Boutros-Gahli, the UN secretary-general. Boutros-Gahli, an Egyptian, was suspected of having sympathy for the Darods, the family clan of the ousted dictator Siad Barre. Rightly or wrongly, Aideed believed that Boutros-Gahli was now using the United Nations to hunt him down.[30]

In March also, the United Nations passed a resolution to continue delivering humanitarian goods to a destitute and needy population. The task was difficult to execute because of the continuing menace of rival militias and bandits. This led the United Nations to approve deployment of security personnel to be added in the March 3, 1992, agreements. The request was considered necessary in order to provide military escorts to deter attacks by Somali militias on aid shipments. The secretary-general of the United Nations devised a three-month plan that immediately provided food for 1½ million people as well as other sundry provisions like tools, food, basic health care, and water to an additional 3½ million Somalis.[31]

This humanitarian mission code-named UNOSOM I was formally passed on April 24, 1992, by the UN Security Council's Resolution 751.[32] The mission included 50 unarmed observers. A proposal for the deployment of a security force to back up the UNOSOM I team was also made, and on approval, the team was led by a Pakistani officer, Gen. Imatiaz Shaheen. The observers were sent from Austria, Bangladesh, Czechoslovakia, Egypt, Finland, Indonesia, Jordan, Morocco, and Zimbabwe.[33] Efforts were also made by the UN secretary-general's representatives in cooperation with the Organization of African Unity (OAU) to support the process of bringing about an end to violence and initiate national reconciliation.[34]

On July 27, 1992, the proposal was secured to establish four operations zones for safe aid distribution—Berbera, Bossasso, Mogadishu,

A refugee woman and child in an emergency shelter during
the floods in Somalia. (World Food Programme)

and Kismayo. Boutros-Gahli believed that "the desperate and complex situation in Somalia required energetic and sustained efforts on
the part of the international community to break the cycle of violence
and hunger."[35] Between August and September 1992, the Security
Council boosted the number of security forces to 4,219 troops in addition to the original 50 observers. The first UN troops eventually
arrived in Mogadishu on September 14, 1992. The contingent were
charged with the task of helping secure the implementation of the
action plan's eight main objectives: (1) massive infusion of food; (2)
aggressive expansion of feeding program; (3) provision of basic

medical care and immunization for measles; (4) provide emergency sanitation, hygiene, and clean water; (5) provide shelter materials, clothing, and blankets; (6) simultaneously deliver seeds, tools, and animal vaccines; (7) prevent further refugee outflow and promote repatriation; (8) institution building and rehabilitation of civil society.[36]

Even after signing the agreement allowing deployment of the peacekeepers, unrelenting differences and violence persisted among the competing factions in Somalia which made the smooth execution of the proposed plans very difficult. On October 28, 1992, Aideed declared that he would no longer tolerate the presence of the Pakistani-led UN battalions. Aideed backed up his words with action when he expelled the peacekeepers, along with UNOSOM I's coordinator of humanitarian assistance. Aideed's forces also began attacking the UNOSOM I forces in apparent demonstration of his resentment. UNOSOM I troops were poorly prepared to return fire on Aideed's forces at this time. Also Mahdi's troops shot at UN supply ships in order to force UNOSOM I to take full control of the port. Overall, international relief organizations experienced an increase in hijackings of vehicles, looting of supply shipments and warehouses, and kidnapping of their civilian workers.

The question arises as to why the two enemies, the Aideed and Ali Mahdi factions, opposed the UN mission. The simple explanation is

Somalis throw stones at a passing U.S. military forklift truck in Mogadishu on February 24, 1993. Crowds took to the streets in protest of the military presence in their city. (AP Photo)

that these leaders and their militias reaped quick profits from the state of disorder through the black market, selling illicit drugs, weapons, and controlling the ports and airports which enabled them to divert aid shipments.[37] These undue privileges faced elimination if the warlords were to accept the UN presence. The complex explanation is that the decades of dictatorship and war had created a militarized society where Somali citizens had learned how to get what they wanted through the barrel of the gun. It was a society where the average order of business operated with the dictum "survival of the fittest," with intimidation and bloodshed as a way of life.

As many as 3,000 Somalis were estimated to have died daily from starvation during this time while armed gangs disrupted the humanitarian efforts and intimidated the UN workers. The plight of both the aid workers and the Somalis portrayed through televised footage evoked a more active interest in Somalia's affairs by the international community, sparking fervent public and political pressure in the United States and Europe for stronger action to be taken by the UN Security Council in Somalia.[38]

UNITAF/Operation Restore Hope

Criticized for demonstrating reluctance to be involved, in December 1992, the U.S. president, George H. W. Bush (1988–1992), announced the U.S. mission to Somalia. Under the broader context of the UN's United Task Force (UNITAF), the U.S. contingent was named Operation Restore Hope.[39] This would be the last major decision of the president in an election year in the United States. The forces were deployed under the strict stipulation that the United States would assume total command of the UNITAF. The mission would remain only until UN peacekeepers were able to resume their duties safely and efficiently.[40]

The joint UNITAF-U.S. forces began to deploy to Mogadishu on December 9, 1992, and were empowered under Chapter VII of the UN Charter to use force (only when necessary) to create a stable and secure environment for deliveries of humanitarian supplies. They were also assigned the risky task of disarming those factions breaching the cease-fire agreement. UNITAF-U.S. was essentially conceived of not as a traditional peacekeeping force like those already in place in Somalia, but as a force that was comparable to the U.S.-led coalition forces in Korea (1950–1953) and to Operation Desert Storm (a mission to free Kuwaiti from Saddam Hussein's Iraq) (1990–1991). UNITAF-U.S.'s 45,000 troops (comprising 28,000 U.S. officers and 17,000 others from

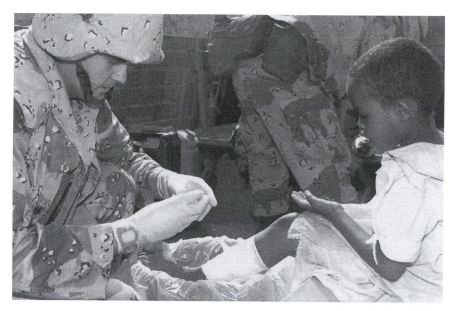

A young Somali boy (right) receives medical treatment to his left leg from a U.S. Army medic as part of Operation Restore Hope. (Department of Defense)

24 countries) were deployed to southern and central regions—a territory that covers about 40 percent of the country's landmass. Because their basic mission was part of the broader UN peacekeeping mission, UNITAF-U.S. members were also referred to as peacekeepers. For clarity, UNOSOM I remained fully responsible for all political and humanitarian assistance in Somalia, while UNITAF-U.S. troops played the role of an armed sheriff.

The first contingent of UNITAF-U.S. troops landed unimpeded on the beaches of Mogadishu, and shortly afterwards, the troops gained control of the southern airfields at Baledogle and Baidoa. This was in accordance with a four-phase program to secure major air and sea ports, key installations, and food distribution points; provide secure routes to transport humanitarian aid; and provide security for aid convoys. The United Nations was also actively trying to promote national reconciliation, with a modicum of success as discord persisted between the Somali factions and the foreign peacekeepers. Cedric Piralla, head of the Red Cross delegation to Somalia, aptly summed it up with the observation that by the end of December 1992, "The Somali no longer have any point of reference with their system. They are lost. They no longer have any structure to rely on. Their sphere of influence is limited to the end of their Kalashnikov [in reference to the Russian-made assault rifle aka AK47]."[41]

To a reasonable extent, the UNITAF-U.S. mission was perceived as a success in that the security they provided allowed food to reach the needy in sufficient quantities as to effectively halt the spread of famine. An estimated 200,000 Somali lives were saved during UNITAF-U.S.'s operation.[42] However, disarming the factions proved to be a much more difficult task, and incidents of violence continued to undermine UNITAF-U.S.'s efforts. There was neither a government to head the country nor organized civilian police/disciplined national army to maintain civil order. The security risks posed to both UN civilian workers and the UNITAF-U.S. troops continued to interrupt the overall peacekeeping efforts.[43]

In January 1993, newly elected U.S. president Bill Clinton assumed office. Clinton had criticized his predecessor, George H. W. Bush, in his campaign speeches for not acting more closely with the United Nations to resolve global conflicts. The new president therefore promised to bring in a new policy with regard to the nature of the U.S. forces not only in Somalia but also in other countries with which the United States had become involved. It was in this context that President Clinton and the secretary-general of the United Nations, Boutros Boutros-Ghali, decided to make a deeper commitment by including nation building as a step forward in Somalia.

On March 3, 1993, the UN secretary-general submitted a proposal to transition from UNITAF-U.S. to UNOSOM II. Although the presence of the Task Force's 37,000 troops over southern and central regions of Somalia had helped improve the security situation there and the delivery of aid, most parts of Somalia remained insecure, and violence continued unabated. Additionally, UNOSOM I and UNITAF-U.S. needed to establish some presence in the northern parts of the country as well as in the Kenyan-Somali border (also known as the Frontiers region), where security remained a "matter of grave concern."[44] In light of this, the United Nations and Washington concluded that a shift to a more robust engagement would expedite actions in restoring peace and stability to the entire country and provide the Somalis an opportunity for a national reconciliation program that would lead to a new democratic Somali state.[45]

UNOSOM II and the Collapse of Relations

UNOSOM II was formerly announced on March 26, 1993, under the UN Security Council Resolution 814. This was about four months after UNITAF-U.S. had begun operations in Somalia. The primary goals of the new mission were articulated as monitoring the cease-fire;

preventing violence; seizing unauthorized small arms; disarming militias, criminals, and plain terrorists who had thus far obstructed the activities of the relief workers; maintaining security at all ports of entry; safeguarding the lines of communication vital to the delivery of humanitarian aid; clearing mines; and assisting the people with the rebuilding of institutions necessary for democratic government.[46]

The task of overseeing the ground operations was assigned to U.S. admiral Jonathan Howe, called "Animal Howe" by General Aideed's propagandists. After his initial arrival in February 1993, Howe had expressed profound shock at the poor state of the country. As an outsider, he could not comprehend why Somalis subjected their country to this manner of destruction and thus felt nothing but contempt for the headstrong warlord gangs led by Mahdi and General Aideed. It was also clear to Howe that power sharing was not an option for both the Mahdi-led USC/SSA and Aideed's USC/SNA. Each of the two groups felt entitled to the throne.

Regrettably, the Security Council did very little planning before deploying UNOSOM II, and U.S. proposals were not effectively integrated before the start of the operation. The United States had advised the United Nations that for a successful transition between UNITAF-U.S. and UNOSOM II, a planning team should be sent ahead to the troubled country. This idea was ignored until the UNOSOM II forces had arrived in Somalia. As a result, the transition was bungled as the UNOSOM II commanders were neither properly informed about the number, capability, and concept of their use of force, nor about the rules of engagement. Yet neither the military commanders nor civilian workers received the help they needed from the overworked UN Secretariat staff. For instance, the military advisor to the secretary-general had a staff comprised of two officers, whereas two years later in the United Nations' operation in Haiti (UNMIH), over 100 experienced civilian officers were provided for the same type of mission.[47]

Thus, it is not altogether surprising that UNOSOM II ran into several problems, which vindicated the opinion of some Washington insiders that the mission was not a good idea. One vocal opponent of the mission was U.S. ambassador to Kenya Smith Hempstone. Upon learning of President Clinton's intentions to send U.S. troops, he admonished the State Department that Washington should seriously reflect on the decision before becoming entangled in Somalia's affairs. He described the Somali people as "natural-born guerillas" that "will inflict—and take—casualties." Then in a reference to the disastrous 1983 U.S. operation in Lebanon where over 260 Marines were killed, Smith concluded gravely, "If you liked Beirut, you'll love Mogadishu."[48]

Another notable antagonist to Operation Restore Hope was Ambassador Robert Oakley. Besides being the U.S. ambassador to Somalia in the 1980s, Oakley garnered a wealth of experience as a diplomat both in Vietnam during the 1955–1975 conflict and in Lebanon during the country's civil war (1975–1990). In his own words, "I felt very strongly that the United States should not become the Godfather of Somalia."[49]

Further compounding the mission was UNOSOM II's lack of proper understanding of the prevalent Somali political culture and society and how this was going to interact with the more intrusive mandate of Resolution 814. The ordinary Somali had also come to see the sudden departure of UNITAF-U.S. forces from Mogadishu in 1993 as a sign of weakness on the part of the international peacekeepers; this was at least in the minds of General Aideed and his group. UNOSOM II failed to present itself as possessing both the concern and authoritative leadership skills that the warlords and citizens alike could rely on. It was in this shortcoming that major confrontations with armed Somali factions became imminent.

UNITAF-U.S. had carried on with its mission with much more knowledge of the combustible nature of the Somali clan leaders, and they were especially wary of the political factions headed by General Aideed and his formidable foe Ali Mahdi Mohamed. To their credit, UNITAF-U.S. avoided taking sides in the clan wars and political struggles. Through these precautions, the peacekeepers resisted taking sides in the conflict and thus won the respect of the Somalis.[50]

This was the circumstance in which the UNITAF-U.S. command departed from southern Mogadishu on May 4, 1993. A smaller, poorly trained and poorly equipped contingent of 4,000 Pakistanis were brought to replace the reassigned UNITAF-U.S. forces. The Pakistani troops discontinued the nightly rounds and other aggressive strategies used by U.S. Marines to effectively maintain a position of control in the area. They also ceased to carry on the daily peace summits with General Aideed and his commanders, which helped in fostering cooperation and reduction in tensions in the Mogadishu region.

General Aideed perceived the withdrawal of UNITAF-U.S. as a sign of weakness on the side of the United Nations to police his movements. Also, the emphasis placed on disarmament prompted Aideed to take a more combative and hostile attitude toward the peacekeepers. He challenged the authority of UNOSOM II by dispatching his armed militia, whose acts of violence in the streets of Mogadishu targeted the UNOSOM II staff as well as the humanitarian workers. UNOSOM II countered this threat by attempting to further marginalize Aideed's political power. UNOSOM II officials held regular meetings with other clan leaders than Aideed. They further incited more anger through conducting short-notice inspections of Aideed's weapons depots and radio station.[51]

On June 5, 1993, Aideed's troops gunned down 24 Pakistani UN troops (some of whom were disemboweled and skinned) while they were inspecting a Somali weapons depot in Mogadishu. Another 10 UN soldiers were reported missing, and 54 more men were wounded in a series of ambushes by the Somali militia. In defense of their action, the Somalis claimed they were under the impression that the UN soldiers were trying to shut down Aideed's radio station, which was located next door to the weapons depot. In his report to the secretary-general, Admiral Howe stated that the UN soldiers were "murdered as they sought to serve the neediest people in the city." The report prompted the United Nations to take immediate action to rectify this "new and difficult situation."[52]

The secretary-general condemned Aideed's "unprovoked attacks," and under the Security Council's Resolution 814 gained authorization to "take all necessary measures against those responsible for the armed attacks and for publicly inciting them, including their arrest and detention for prosecution, trial and punishment."[53] Without further delay, the United Nations declared Aideed's USC-SNA a fugitive group and started targeting him for punishment. A few weeks later, Aideed's operational base was raided, forcing him underground. One of the casualties of that raid was Radio Mogadishu, which was located close to Aideed's command headquarters. Despite the danger that hunted him, Aideed proved resilient, maintaining his propaganda broadcast by using mobile and difficult-to-discover antennas. Now and then, his fighters shelled the UN bases with mortars and grenades. Also the USC-SNA militia continued to hunt down and execute Somali UN employees they considered traitors. As attempts to apprehend Aideed proved fruitless, his status continued to rise among his Hawiye people of the Mogadishu area.

On July 12, 1993, a frustrated Admiral Howe, commander of UNOSOM II, authorized an attack on a meeting of the USC-SNA's top leaders. The ambush killed or injured many, tarnishing the humanitarian image of the United Nations in the international community, and drove many moderates in Somalia to support Aideed. Throughout June, UN forces led by U.S. helicopters carried out attacks on illegal weapons depots. Aideed's forces responded with retaliatory strikes at U.S., Pakistani, French, and Italian troops. They also continued targeting Somali civilians working for the United Nations. Then on July 12, the State Department issued a warning that the U.S. Central Intelligence Agency (CIA) had received a secret memo regarding a large-scale plan to attack UN officials in Mogadishu by Aideed's faction, the USC-SNA. In a move that has all the marks of a preemptive doctrine, the United States responded to this information by launching a missile attack that resulted in 70 Somali deaths. On that afternoon, any remaining prospects for peace were destroyed. Shortly afterwards, it was disclosed that the CIA had reported in error; in fact, Aideed's followers had assembled not to discuss more war strategies, but to consider the latest peace proposal put forth by Howe.

Now realizing that the nation-building mission was in peril, Howe requested the use of the U.S. elite Delta Force to assist in catching and destroying Aideed and his group. Washington initially ignored his request until August 1993, when four American soldiers were killed by remote-controlled landmines. A few weeks later, seven other U.S. servicemen were targeted and injured in a similar attack. President Clinton then authorized the deployment of a 420-man Task Force Ranger, under the command of Maj.-Gen. William F. Garrison. The team arrived in Somalia on August 23, 1993.

Although the Pentagon repeatedly denied the fact, the mission of the Rangers was to get the operation up and running, capture Aideed, and target his command structure. As soon as they arrived in Mogadishu, the Americans began capturing and imprisoning Aideed's top advisors and supporters. Under unrelenting pressure, in late August, Aideed appealed to former president Jimmy Carter to help set up a new round of peace negotiations. The first of these series of meetings was scheduled for November. In the meantime, Task Force Ranger would maintain their mission objectives. Five weeks into the mission, the Rangers had flown six successful "snatch and grab" by sending the elite Delta Force soldiers deep into the city to arrest key targets.

Meanwhile, little did Howe and Garrison realize the weight of anger and hate that had risen against the U.S. presence. Not only did the Special Forces raids cause deaths and injuries to ordinary bystanders, they also caused property damage to roofs, trees, and disturbed the peace of whole neighborhoods. On some occasions, some onlookers claimed, it stripped infants out of their arms. Somalis who had at first welcomed the arrival of the United Nations now felt "brutalized and harassed."[54] Cashing in on the new public mood, Islamic fighters from the Sudan, some of them veterans of the war between the USSR and Islamists in Afghanistan (1979–1988), began to sneak into the country to instruct Aideed's men in the use of rocket-propelled grenades (RPGs) to take down helicopters.

THE *MAALINTI* RANGER ("THE DAY OF THE RANGER")

On October 3, 1993, U.S. commanders received key intelligence that two of Aideed's officers—Omar Salad-Aideed, a top political advisor, and Mohamed Hassan Alawe, chief spokesman—were meeting in the Bakara market area of Mogadishu, which was the center of Aideed's territory. Eager not to let pass what appeared like a rare opportunity to apprehend these two men, the Task Force Ranger quickly assembled a total of 19 aircraft, 12 fighting vehicles, and 160 soldiers. Although the Delta Force troops completed their assault and captured their targets, the operation ran into an unforeseen situation when Somalis began rushing to the area as soon as the attack had started. The crowd blocked the roads, and armed men fired automatic weapons and RPGs at the U.S. forces, bringing down a Black Hawk (UH-60) helicopter.

Shortly after, the shooters brought down another Black Hawk UH-60 helicopter piloted by Michael Durant. The Rangers were now confronted with the very difficult task of rescuing their soldiers from the masses of armed fighters streaming toward the crash sites. The ensuing disorder was partly engineered with the very familiar propaganda that the Americans were in Somalia to destroy their Islamic religion. The angry mob began hacking apart the bodies of the dead soldiers and dragging them through the streets. Eventually, Durant was saved from the mob by a local militia leader, Yousef Dahir Mo'alim, who planned on using him as a ransom for the release of imprisoned clan members. But soon after his rescue, the local militias took Durant to Aideed.[55]

The entire charade of bringing down the two UH-60s, hacking the bodies of dead U.S. soldiers, and dragging them along the streets was repeatedly aired on televisions around the world. The effect was that it provoked a widespread outcry in the United States and Europe. As a result, the decision was quickly made on October 5, 1993, to pull the U.S. forces out of Somalia. Michael Durant was released on October 15, 1993, in a deal that later freed all of Aideed's men held by U.S. forces. Despite the fact that the episode was in theory a victory, considering the fact that the American soldiers were not overrun, the *Maalinti Ranger*, or "Day of the Ranger" as the Somalis referred to it, was considered a failed mission. A total of 18 U.S. soldiers died on the Day of the Ranger, and dozens more were injured. Somali casualties were conservatively estimated at 500 dead and 1,000 injured.[56]

This outcome forced the United Nations to modify the mandate of UNOSOM II's mission to exclude the use of coercive measures. By 1995, all UN forces had left Somalia. Mohammed Farah Aideed died of an apparent heart attack in August 1996 after being shot in Mogadishu. His son, Hussein Mohamed Aideed, was chosen by the USC-SNA as successor.[57]

Momentarily, the overall behavior of the Somalis sowed the belief in certain Western minds that it is the people, not necessarily their leaders, that turn terrible countries into a mess. One U.S. official claimed that "Somalia was the experience that taught us that people in those places bear much of the responsibility for things being the way they are. The hatred and the killings continued because they want it to. Or because they don't want peace enough to stop it."[58] A year later, this unfortunate perception held by some U.S. lawmakers influenced American policy toward other areas of conflicts in Africa. A good example was the Clinton administration's refusal to stop acts of genocide in Rwanda (1994), Zaire (1997), and Darfur (2006).

It is now time to try to address the two most crucial questions. The first is whether Somalia could have been salvaged after the exit of Barre in 1991, and the second is whether the sovereignties of various separatist regions that have already established viable institutions for self-governments should be recognized by the international community. Both questions are not only interrelated and reinforcing; they hold answers as to the future of Somalia. For organizing purposes, the second question will be addressed in the next chapter.

First, the optimism that informed the efforts of the international community in sponsoring a peacekeeping mission to Somalia attests to the common notion held by non-Somalis that the East African country could be saved after the Barre dictatorship's collapse. The problem, however, is that both the United Nations and the United States grossly underestimated the formidable power of clan consciousness, particularly in the post-Barre Somalia. In a reflective comment on clan loyalty in Somalia following the 1993 battle in Mogadishu, Gen. Colin Powell pointed out that it was farfetched to think that 450 soldiers, no matter their efficiency, could "uproot it [i.e., clan divisions] violently, clearing the way for an outbreak of Jeffersonian democracy."[59] Nothing could be closer to the truth than this.

What the postcolonial order taught Somalis, just as their ancestors had demonstrated in the centuries past, was that Jeffersonian forms of big government and big business will not and may never work for the people, their environment, and their temperament. Thus, when critics berate President Clinton's decision to pull out U.S. soldiers after the 1993 disaster that ensued, they fail to realize that the militarization of society struck a sensitive cord in the indigenous culture of confrontation and warfare, which have for centuries marked the life of nomardism and of manhood attainment in Somalia. This also touched base with the dominant Islamic belief system and willingness to die a glorious death under the jihad doctrine. Together, acute shortage of the basic needs of life, cultural trends, religion, and widespread distrust formed a highly combustible mixture that was extremely difficult to defuse in the Somali society of the 1990s.

Perhaps the only remedy to such a situation would have been to infuse a significant amount of wealth and material comfort in the country in hopes that it would make the people quickly forget their recent harsh experiences. It is telling that as many as 6,000 Somalis lost their lives in the violence following the arrival of UN forces in Mogadishu in December 1991. To have continued the mission as usual would have amounted to what a critic described as propagating the "warrior mentality—to win the war." After the *maalinti*, the humanitarian operation was drastically scaled down, but it remained for an additional two years while UN envoys unsuccessfully tried to bring reconciliation between the Somali warring factions. Talking about anarchy and resistance to America, a disquieted Abdirzak A. Hassan, former chief of staff for Somali's Transition Government, was apt in his statement that "Even if we turned Mogadishu into Houston, there would still be people resisting us. I am talking about the guys bringing in expired medicine, selling arms, and harboring terrorists."[60]

On a broader note, the efforts at peace failed perhaps because those who offered help did not do quite enough. For instance, Canada estimated sending 900 troops, France 1,700, Italy 1,500, and Belgium 800. Tokyo offered to send money but would not send any troops. The most conspicuous absentees remained the African countries whose lack of a more diligent effort was surprising in that the Somali conflict falls within the type of regional problem that the continental body was made to handle.[61] All these shortfalls explain why the U.S. soldiers bore the brunt of the mission and the resultant backlashes.

Today, Somalia is still without a national government, as peace efforts are continuing. Since 1997, Amnesty International has consistently reported that "hundreds of deliberate and arbitrary killings, scores of politically motivated detentions, hostage-taking, torture, including rape, and ill-treatment" have continued to obstruct peace and national reconciliation.[62] This order of things shows the relevance of the question of whether the various secessionist groups should be formally recognized by the international community. As fully addressed in the next chapter, the answer to this question is absolutely "yes."

NOTES

1. Mark Bowen, *Black Hawk Down: A Story of Modern War* (New York: Signet Press, 1999), 111; Caleb Carr, "The Consequences of Somalia," *World Policy Journal* 1, no. 4 (1994): 1–4.

2. Ambassador Robert B. Oakley and David Tucker, *Two Perspectives on Interventions and Humanitarian Operations* (Carlisle Barracks, PA: Strategic Studies Institute U.S. Army War College, July 1, 1997), 10–16.

3. United Nations Security Council (hereafter UNSC), "United Nations Operation in Somalia II (hereafter UNOPII)," Report to the Secretary General of the UNSC, Nov. 30, 1994.

4. Ibid., 1.

5. Kristin Spivey, "The United Nations' Humanitarian Intervention in Somalia and the Just War Theory," MA Thesis Submitted in Fulfillment for the Award of Degree in Political Science, Vrije University, Brussels, Belgium, June 2008, 5.

6. For instance, see Eric Schmidt's "U.S. Mission in Somalia: Seeking a Clear Rationale," *New York Times*, Aug. 23, 1993; and Robert D. Warrington, "The Helmets May Be Blue, but the Blood's Still Red: The Dilemma of the U.S. Participation in UN Peace Operations," *Comparative Strategy* 14, no. 1 (Jan–Mar. 1995): 25.

7. See Toyin Falola and Raphael Chijioke Njoku, eds., *War and Peace in Africa* (Durham, NC: Carolina Academic Press, 2010), esp. 3–18; 19–34.

8. Paul Collier and Anke Hoeffler, "Greed and Grievance in Civil War," *Oxford Economic Papers New Series* 56 no. 4 (2004): 564 [563–95]; and Paul Collier and Anke Hoeffler, "On the Incidence of Civil War in Africa," *Journal of Conflict Resolution* 13 (Feb. 2002): 13–28.

9. S. Mansoob Murshed, "Conflict, Civil War, and Underdevelopment: An Introduction," *Journal of Peace Research* (July 2002): 387–93.

10. See Ogechi Anyanwu and Raphael Chijioke Njoku, "The Causes of Wars and Conflicts in Africa," in Falola and Njoku, eds., *War and Peace in Africa*, 19–34.

11. Johan Galtung, *Peace by Peaceful Means: Peace and Conflict Development and Civilization* (London: SAGE Publications, 1996), 197.

12. Ibid., 93.

13. Collier and Hoeffler, "Greed and Grievance," 564. See also Christian Webersik, "Wars over Resources? Evidence from Somalia," *Environment* 46, no. 58 (May/June 2008): 49 [46–58].

14. Collier and Hoeffler, "Greed and Grievance," 564–69.

15. UN, *United Nations Report on UNOSOM I*, updated March 21, 1997.

16. Ismael Ahmed and Reginald Herbold Green, "The Heritage of War and State Collapse in Somaliland: Local Level Effects, External Interventions and Reconstructions," *Third World Quarterly* 20, no. 1 (1999): 115.

17. Ahmed and Green, "Heritage of War and State Collapse," 115.

18. NAK, HO 421/2 1986–2000, 6.

19. Ibid., 6.

20. Ibid., 18–19.

21. Ibid., 19–20.

22. Ibid., 20.

23. Ibid., 21.

24. Mathew Eck, *The Farther Shore* (Minneapolis, MN: Milkweed Press, 2007), 6.

25. Webersik, "Wars over Resources?" 51.

26. UN, *United Nations Report on UNOSOM I*, updated March 21, 1997.

27. Ibid.

28. Letter dated 20 January 1992 from the *chargé d'affaires* of the Permanent Mission of Somalia to the United Nations addressed to the president of the Security Council (S/23445).

29. UN, *United Nations Report on UNOSOM I*, updated March 21, 1997, 1–2.

30. Bowen, *Black Hawk Down*, 84.

31. UN, *United Nations Report on UNOSOM I*, updated March 21, 1997.

32. See United Nations Security Council, *Security Council Resolution S/RES/873 (1993) Resolution 873 (1993) Adopted by the Security Council at its 3291st meeting, on 13 October 1993*, Oct. 13, 1993, S/RES/873.

33. UN, *United Nations Report on UNOSOM I*, updated March 21, 1997.

34. Brian Urquhart, "Security after the Cold War," in Adam Roberts and Benedict Kingsbury, eds. *United Nations, Divided World: The UN's Roles in International Relations* (New York: Oxford University Press, 1993), 90.

35. UN, *United Nations Report on UNOSOM I*, updated March 21, 1997.

36. Ibid.

37. Eck, *The Farther Shore*, 6.

38. Oakley and Tucker, "Two Perspectives," 16.

39. Department of Public Information (hereafter DPI), *United Nations Somalia—UNOSOM II* (New York: Department of Public Information Printing Office, March 21, 1997), 93.

40. Ted Galen Carpenter, "Setting A Dangerous Precedent In Somalia," CATO Foreign Policy Briefing No. 20, Dec. 18, 1992, 3.

41. Cedric Piralla, cited by Donatella Lorch, "Shooting in Somalia Reflect Rising Tension for U.S. Troops," *New York Times*, Dec. 30, 1992.

42. Oakley and Tucker, "Two Perspectives," 15–16.

43. DPI, *United Nations Somali—UNOSOM II*, 1.

44. Ibid., updated March 21, 1997.

45. David Bentley and Robert Oakley, "Peace Operations: A Comparison of Somalia and Haiti," National Defense University's Strategic Forum transcript (Institute for National Strategic Studies), no. 30, (May 1995), 1.

46. DPI, *United Nations Somalia—UNOSOM II*, 1; and UN, *United Nations Report on UNOSOM II*, updated August 31, 1996.

47. For the Haiti operation, see UN Security Council, *Security Council Resolution S/RES/873 (1993) Resolution 873 (1993) Adopted by the Security Council at its 3291st meeting, on 13 October 1993*, Oct. 13, 1993, S/RES/873; and United Nations Department of Public Information, The United Nations and the Situation in Haiti: United Nations Department of Public Information, 1995.

48. See Alex de Wall, "U.S. War Crimes in Somalia," *New Left Review* 30 (1998): 131–44; Carpenter, "Setting a Dangerous," 3.

49. See Spivey, "United Nation's Humanitarian Intervention in Somalia," 10. Cable News Network International (hereafter CNNI) "Black Hawk Down: The U.S. mission in Somalia, Perspectives," June 5, 1998.

50. Bentley and Oakley, "Peace Operations: A Comparison of Somalia and Haiti," 2; and Oakley and Tucker, "Two Perspectives," 30.

51. Oakley and Tucker, "Two Perspectives," 15.

52. United Nations Operation in Somalia II (hereafter UNOSOM II), *Report to the Secretary General of the UNSC*, Nov. 30, 1994, 7.

53. Ibid., 7.

54. Bowen, *Black Hawk Down*, 87.

55. Ibid., 312–15.

56. Ibid., 408.

57. Amnesty International, AI Report 1997: Somalia (Amnesty International Publications 1997), 1–2.

58. Bowen, *Black Hawk Down*, 410.

59. Ibid., 418, 429.

60. Abdirzak A. Hassan, Interview with Jeffrey Gettleman, "Profiteers, too, Fight Government in Somalia," *New York Times*, Apr. 24, 2007.

61. Carpenter, "Setting a Dangerous," 3.

62. Amnesty International, AI Report 1997: Somalia, 2.

8

Back to the Future: Disunity, Disorder, and the Consociational Imperative

The consociational (or power-sharing) model is a system of government that recognizes the existence of diverse ethnic, religious, and minority groups in a polity and thus uses principles of elite cooperation and accommodation in the decision-making process for system stability. Considering the high level of interest scholars, politicians, diplomats, arbitrators, and others have recently demonstrated in Somali studies, it is auspicious to end a book of this nature with exploratory thoughts on how best to effectively moderate violent and conflictual politics, and thus move the troubled country forward. It must be promptly stated that there is no solitary pathway to peacemaking in highly divided societies, especially those whose politics are marked by deadly ethnic conflicts; often a combination of diverse strategies has been found more efficacious. Since every case is special, the permutations scholars bring to theoretical musing vis-à-vis the issues that are considered on the political negotiation table must be germane to that country's unique situation.

Taking into account all that has transpired in the past decades, the Somali political landscape is evidently evolving into a commonwealth of independent states, and this needs to be supported. This might also be arranged in the form of a highly decentralized/ autonomous self-governing confederate structure aligned to the existing clan system. The most critical starting point, and indeed a decisive element for future progress, remains a system that allows each of the secessionist regions to maintain their much-desired autonomy or sovereignty while delegating certain duties like foreign affairs and military co-operation, to mention but two, to a loosely reconfigured central care-taker (government) committee. This center must be constituted on the principle of a consociation or power-sharing arrangement with every clan proportionally represented in the national government. The proposed center should exercise a very limited power and ensure a proviso for ethnic and ideological minorities such as the Bantus to veto any decision that will directly affect their lives. This approach holds the best prospects for political peace and system stability on the Somali Peninsula. The expected stability will not come automati-cally. It will require some time to kick in once the enabling structures, as proposed here, have been put in place.

In the wake of Siad Barre's fall, several regions of Somalia seceded from the central government and went about organizing their own in-dependent governments: Somaliland was the first to cede the territory to the northwest in 1991. Then in 1994, the Puntland military, tradi-tional, and political elites proclaimed their rule over the northeastern parts of Somalia. In 1998, a band of bitterly aggrieved militias announced its sovereignty over Jubaland, the territory in the southwest. While the secessionists in Jubaland have continued to contest their rights to secede amid enduring opposition from Mogadishu, today, both Somaliland and Puntland are in fact independent states. Neither the African Union (AU) nor the United Nations (UN) have so far for-mally granted the crucial recognition desperately sought by each of the secessionist enclaves. The main problem is that the majority of member nations at both the AU and UN (including veto-holding China, one of the few remaining land empires) are stoutly indifferent to the idea of secession for fear that similar political demands could material-ize and affect politics within their own borders.[1]

Despite the international opposition, ironically Somaliland has earned a good repute among its local and international observers as being under a more effective government than the other regions of the country, including the decimated and hapless Transitional Government based in Mogadishu. This is regardless of Somaliland's extreme condition of poverty.[2] An AU mission that visited the separatist northern territory in 2006 raised the hope of recognition of Somaliland, but the favorable report of that mission was not followed through on by the AU's governing Heads of States. The AU "refused to recognize Somaliland's independence, citing the maxim that there would be chaos if colonial boundaries were not observed."[3] Puntland is also ably managed internally today, although its incremental achievements in the sociopolitical and economic fronts are mired in the disorder and global outcry emanating from the Indian Ocean piracy.

Unlike Puntland and Somaliland, the stability of Jubaland's self-determining administration is still in question. Seven years subsequent to Siad Barre's exit from power, one of the factional groups in Jubaland led by Mohamed Siad Hersi Morgan (Majerteen from the Abdirahim lineage)—the son-in-law of General Barre and former defense minister under the former dictator—declared Jubaland's independence in 1998. Morgan and his comrades in the Somali National Front (SNF) autonomously ran the territory with the center at Gedo until 1999 when they lost control of the region to a rainbow coalition of opposition forces that came together under the name Allied Somali Force (ASF). In 2001, the ASF was renamed Juba Valley Alliance (JVA), and its administration came under the headship of Col. Barre Hiiraale. The JVA threw its support for the Transition National Government (TFG) or *Dowladda federaalka kumeelgaarka* that was launched in November 2004 through the efforts of neighboring Horn of Africa countries led by Djibouti in an attempt to bring about political peace in the region.[4]

However, things took a dangerous dimension in the Southern region in 2006 when the radical Islamists group known as al-Shabaab began military operations against the TFG. The al-Shabaab tried to justify their cause with what they perceived as the TFG's alliance with Ethiopia and some AU/UN countries they consider to be enemies of Somali peace and therefore disliked. As the insurgency expanded, the al-Shabaab started to create sharia laws in areas under its control. When Ethiopia sent its forces to battle the al-Shabaab militants, the popularity of the Islamists improved fast because most Somalis are united in their resentment of Ethiopia's meddlesomeness in Somalia's local politics. While neither the TFG nor the al-Shabaab is presently in total control of the entire southern and central regions, the latter has continued to exert influence in isolated areas.

After the Ethiopian forces withdrew from the south in 2009, an initiative supported by Kenya enabled the residents of Jubaland to establish a new secular administration modeled after the "Elders Council" of Somaliland, which also mirrors the Puntland initiatives.[5] In other words, Jubaland is now a self-governing region to a degree. Although this region could be predictably brought back under the TFG's authority centered in Mogadishu, it remains doubtful whether there is adequate political prudence to meet the demands of the Jubaland people in general and the al-Shabaab in particular.

The ongoing search for unity and cooperation among the competing secessionists will remain wishful thinking unless each of the groups in conflict first moves aside as a form of therapy for the political and psychological traumas brought about by Barre's misrule and anarchy. In other words, chances for cooperation among the competing sovereignties reside in recognizing the legitimacy of their contested claims instead of attempts to deny them. More damaging to the society today are the futile efforts led by the international community to reconstitute the defunct nation. This idea has done more harm than good to the search for harmony and political cooperation. The reality is that the notion of a Somali nation now exists merely as an expression of nostalgic sentiment and imagination. By first recognizing the rights of the different regions to self-determination, the opportunity would be created for negotiated terms of a new association. Only through a conscious process of consensus, negotiation, and a constitutional provision—that will include the right to secession for each group—would a more enduring peace and national unity emerge.

To fully address this pathway to peace, it is important to reexamine the recent efforts at peacemaking and underline why they have not been quite successful. This will be scrutinized through the prism of the three major fragmented polities that have emerged out of the rubbles of war and conflicts. These are Somaliland (Northwest Somalia), Puntland (Northeast Somalia), and Southern Somalia (including Mogadishu and Jubaland). The three typologies of geopolitical realignments as identified here present options that are already in operation in Somalia and that have produced varied results. Among these options are: (1) the reorganization of the country along a federalist system consisting of self-governing constituencies as exemplified in the Puntland idea; (2) the reinvention of Somalia with free governing states like secessionist Somaliland Republic; and (3) the attempt at reconfiguring the country after the defunct postcolonial republic.[6] The imperative is to carefully and realistically look at which of these alternatives offers the best chances of bringing stability to the region.

FEDERAL AUTONOMY ALTERNATIVE: NORTHEAST (PUNTLAND)

Although the intention to secede was first expressed in 1994 under the instrumentality of the Somali Salvation Democratic Front (SSDF) dominated by the Majerteen of the Darod family clan, the Puntland state was formally proclaimed an independent territory in July 1998. As His Excellency, Abdirahman Mohamed Mohamud, the incumbent leader of Puntland, explained in a recent speech delivered in London, "Puntland opted for a federal government structure in 1998, followed by the 2004 signing of the Transitional Federal Charter, where Somalia officially adopted federalism as a national government system."[7]

Soon after the proclamation of the new state, the territory was enveloped in a cloud of protracted leadership struggle within the SSDF hierarchy. At the center of the struggle were two top officers from the Majerteen group: Gen. Mohamed Abshir Musa, who was the former police commissioner, and his opponent, Col. Abdullahi Yusuf, first president of Puntland state. The leadership tussle negatively impacted the reputation of these two elite figures as well as the ability of the SSDF to effectively run Puntland. Not even the innovative move to stabilize the political order through the *Isimo* (or titled clan and sub-clan heads, and lineage leaders) system was allowed the potential benefits for political building. After Yusuf joined the TFG and effectively resigned his position in the Puntland government, an election was held in 2009 that saw to the election of the current leader, Abdirahman Mohamed Mohamud (Farole). Although the problem of crisis within the Puntland hierarchy has since been arrested, it was in the midst of this initial crisis of leadership and corruption that Puntland gradually degenerated into a haven for high sea piracy. The scourge of high sea piracy is principally intense in Puntland as a result of its central position between the coasts of the Indian Ocean and the Gulf of Aden. This very important channel hosts global sea trade involving about 20,000 vessels per annum.

Commenting on the problem of piracy off Somali coastal waters, President Mohamud observes that the piracy was a by-product of several years of civil war. The activities of Somali pirates caused socio-political uncertainty as well as economic suffering by way of capital flight and zero foreign direct investment (FDI) in this region. As the president further observed, pirates not only harass vessels owned by overseas investors, they also affect merchant ships leaving the Puntland's Bossasso Port. The pirates' menace constitutes serious threats to "Puntland's lifeline trade link to the outside world. The policy of the Government of Puntland is strictly not to pay ransom money to pirates, because ransom payments help fuel future pirate attacks and attract new recruits."[8]

Additionally, the problem of piracy has robbed Puntland of its record of progress as a legitimate and effective self-governing territory. First, it must be acknowledged that the government has made huge strides in regard to social reintegration, by overcoming much intra- and interclan adversity and animosity created by fanatical sects comprising local youths early in the 1990s. It took serious efforts and elite disposition to cooperation and accommodation as evident in the coming together of the intelligentsia, traditional rulers, politicians, and religious leaders, to forge a program of reconciliation built on grassroots level to moderate the conflict and bring about a peaceful resolution. The key to the accomplishment was the inclusion of all the interest groups and the pervading sense of a common good that eventually transcended the vested good of few elite figures that were reaping profits from persistent upheaval.

In summation, President Mohamud claims that "Puntland is a role model state for a future Federal Republic of Somalia." The Puntland's system of politics today is a hybrid of indigenous systems with Islamic practices and modern principles of popularly elected government. All this according to Mohamud is to guarantee the proper protection of both individual and group rights. The president reiterates that the separatist province will likely support the ongoing proposal for reconstitution of the country as a federal state and that this desire is exemplified with its participation in the various peace summits since 1991. Nonetheless, Mohamud emphatically asserts that "Puntland is not willing to compromise its hard-won stability and progress for any political system short of federalism. Puntland is committed to federalism as the only viable solution to the Somali civil war."[9]

Implicit in the brand of federalism advocated by the Puntland leader is clearly a structure that would guarantee self-rule for each region that desires it. This is particularly important for the regions that have already ceded. It is therefore crucial to recognize and respect the various secessionists' determination to maintain "hard-won stability and progress" in order to avoid frustration with the envisaged federal system. In other words, what President Mohamud has in mind is not the same federalist constitution operated by the United States or any Western country's for that matter. As will be further elaborated on, the call here is for a confederation or what has been labeled here as a Commonwealth of Independent Somali States (CISS) with a loosely organized center.

INDEPENDENT STATES ALTERNATIVE: NORTHWEST (SOMALILAND)

Somaliland refers to the breakaway northwest territory that was proclaimed an independent republic on May 8, 1991, by the Isaaq-dominated Somali National Movement (SNM). Its chairman, Abdurrahman Ali "Tur," served as the region's first executive president with the approval of the clan elders. In an attempt to justify secession, a good percentage of Somaliland elite figures have advanced the argument that secession was simply a decision to recover the independence secured from imperial Britain on June 26, 1960, and sooner than they sought and accepted unification with southern Somalia to form the defunct Somali Republic on July 1, 1960. Relative to the rest of the country, Somaliland has made substantial progress in institutional stability from the programs of "internal" reconciliation through the clan elders' initiative.

As also witnessed in Puntland after secession, the first few years subsequent to the declaration of independence were a marked period of uneasiness as civil conflicts, petty robberies, and criminal extortions proliferated. These problems challenged the capacity of the secessionist leaders and the new administration they created to manage a self-proclaimed sovereign territory. Additionally, the period also witnessed some clan tensions and schism within the SNM. For instance, clan fighting broke out in places like Burao and Berbera in early 1992 among the Habr Awal and Habr Yunis—both of which are Isaaq subclans. Peace negotiations brought the conflict to an end later in 1992, although Berbera remained outside government control as a result of continuing tensions.[10] The situation was worsened by fighting between the tripartite interest groups—namely, the Somali National Movement (SNM), elements of the Darod family clan, and militia of the Habr Yunis (a subclan of the Isaaq). The competing militias eventually handed in their weapons in December 1996 in order to make way for peace and system stability.

The truce with the Habr Yunis opposition allowed the SNM to cross the threshold into a transition phase that recognized the role of the elders in conflict reconciliation and political stability. The historic Guurti Congress of the Elders first held in Hargeisa toward the end of April in 1991 had involved not only the elders of a democratically elected House of Representatives but also all the elders of the other minority clans as well as the rank and file of SNM leadership. As a priority, the new administration took the responsibility to accommodate non-Isaaq interest groups in the new dispensation. The executive committee of the SNM served as the first legislature of the newly independent Somaliland. It also chose to start the process of constitution building as well as to conduct a national election.

Meanwhile, the defining event for stability in Somaliland came between January and May 1993 in the form of the *shir beeleed* in Borama city of Awdai region where the national *Guurti*, or council of elders, supervised a nonviolent handover of authority from the Abdulrahman ("Tur")-led SNM rule to a civilian administration under elder statesman Mohamed Egal, a Habr Awal clansman, and ex-prime minister of the Republic of Somalia before the Barre coup of 1969. Before the conference ended in May 1993, the Borama delegates approved a Cabinet of Ministers and a bicameral Parliament, comprising the *Guurti* and the House of Representatives, each with 75 members.[11] The summit also "produced an Interim Peace Charter and Transitional National Charter that reestablished the basis for law and order by setting out a code of conduct (or *xeer*—i.e., unwritten contracts, laws, agreements, or social codes between clans) for the people of Somaliland in accordance with their traditions and the principle of Islam."[12] This return to precolonial tradition of politics and alliance-making has created an original model for grassroots politics that has the potential, if fine-tuned, to bring about a more peaceful political order for all African societies. The Borama charter envisaged a three-year period of transition that would lead to adoption of a formal constitution and a general election in 2000. The election, however, was delayed until 2002 to enable the various candidates, particularly the opposition groups, enough time to prepare for the voting.

Although this is hardly pointed out in the historiography, the overall most significant accomplishment of the Borama summit was the various programs of demilitarization, which is crucial for peace in a postwar society. This was revealed in the fact that after the summit, the Somaliland independence experiment progressed much faster, although internal bickering continued but in ways that saw a drastic reduction in violence. Moved by his nationalist consciousness, President Egal implied in a speech at the beginning of 1999 that he was not entirely against the idea of returning all Somalis under a single union. This evident about-face to his previous stand on Somaliland's independence infuriated many opinion leaders in both the government and ordinary citizens. The outrage expressed by his comrades explains why Egal did not try to push the reunification idea too hard. Nonetheless, Egal is best remembered today as an example of a generation of Somalis who were strongly opposed to any form of ethnic politics based on clan or religious sentiments. Egal clearly demonstrated his loyalty to the Somali nation and dislike for parochialism in May 2001 when he endorsed a decision permitting the freedom of other parties to campaign and compete for elected positions in the region with a provision requiring that "any new parties are not based on religion or clans."[13]

Another expression of Egal's desire for one Somalia nation was revealed in the May 2001 referendum on a new constitution, which mandated that "every citizen shall cast his vote for or against the Constitution."[14] The president allowed that referendum because he wanted to gauge the pulse of the ordinary people on secession, hoping that the popular opinion would turn to his side. It is noteworthy that the outcome of that referendum was apparently not anything he had expected. Although there was no voters' register, the officials claimed that 97 percent of the 1.3 million voters supported the Somaliland independence constitution.[15] In fact, international observers from Britain, the United States, and Switzerland corroborated that the referendum was conducted in a free and fair atmosphere. The foremost principle of the new bill *inter alia* affirmed Somaliland's sovereignty:

> The country which gained its independence from the United Kingdom of Great Britain and Northern Ireland on 26th June 1960 and was known as the Somaliland Protectorate and which joined Somalia on 1st July 1960 so as to form the Somali Republic and then regained its independence by the Declaration of the Conference of the Somaliland communities held in Burao between 27th April 1991 and 15th May 1991 shall hereby and in accordance with this Constitution become a sovereign and independent country known as "The Republic of Somaliland."[16]

Other parts of the constitution made new provisions for establishing political parties and elections. In line with this proviso, President Egal, in June 2001, declared the launching of his Allied People's Democratic Party (UDUB)—a political party, connoting "pillar." The new party was announced in readiness for the presidential and parliamentary elections slated for 2002. Egal went ahead to support the selection of one of his executive members as secretary-general of UDUB. The opposition immediately began to question the legality of Egal's new party and launched a motion accusing the president of misuse of public funds to further his political ends. After a number of deliberations, the motion was rejected in August 2001 because no offense was found.

Soon after the fight over Egal's party launch was resolved, the peace of Somaliland was once again troubled when an attempt was made by government forces to stop a group of elderly traditional and religious leaders on their way to summit in Burao. The trouble with the planned gathering was that it did not seek approval by the government. In an ensuing brawl between the sultans' private guards and state security forces, five people were killed and all the traditional elders involved in the altercation were arrested and thrown in jail. Through its action, first the government of President Egal wanted to make sure that there are no illegal seats of power. Second, the steps taken by the government to stop the use of private militias was in tune with the overall effort to demilitarize the society. Before the culprits were freed after a month of incarceration, they signed a pledge that they would henceforth respect the laws of the land as enshrined in the Constitution.

In October 2001, certificates of registration were issued to seven political parties, including UDUB. To create an atmosphere of freedom and understanding, President Egal convened a summit of all the parties legally approved by the government. Prior to this, the opposition parties had been expressing serious concerns that the president's party would cash in on advantages of the incumbent to declare victory in the polls scheduled for 2002. Egal and the opposing party leaders agreed to hold further meetings in order to allay the fears of the opposition candidates.

Despite the loud voices of opposition and challenges he faced, President Egal's tenure was extended for a year by the elder's council in January 2002. This was considered expedient in order to give the opposition time to get ready for the elections. The elections were still in plan when the president suddenly took ill and subsequently died in early May 2002. Without much rancor, Dahir Riyale Kahin, Egal's second-in-command, was approved to succeed the president in agreement with the constitutional stipulations.

Eventually, the planned election was held in 2003 by the National Election Commission (NEC). The three candidates who vied for the presidential race were the incumbent, President Dahir Rayale Kahin of the United Democratic People's Party representing the Uruka, Dimuqraadiya, Umada, and Bahawday (or UDUB); Faisal Ali Warabe of the Ucid (or Justice and Welfare) party; and Ahmed Mohamed Mohamoud (Silanyo) representing his Kulmiye (or United) party. The hotly contested election was won by the ruling party by merely 80 votes.

The next round of elections came in 2010, and the three major candidates were the same three who competed in the 2003 presidential race. Like in the previous elections, the incumbent, President Dahir Rayale

Abdullahi Yusuf Ahmed, a former guerrilla leader, was elected president of Somalia in October 2004. (Simon Maina/AFP/Getty Images)

Kahin, represented the UDUB party, and his main competitor in the 2003 elections, Ahmed Mohamed Mohamoud (Silanyo), vied under the banner of the Kulmiye or United party. The third candidate representing the Ucid party was the same as Faisal Ali Warabe. Against ordinary expectations, Ahmed Mohamed (Silanyo) of the Kulmiye garnered 50 percent of the 538,000 valid votes on the road to victory. He is now the current president of Somaliland. The UDUB received 33 percent of the votes cast, and the Ucid received 17 percent. The new president was officially sworn in on June 26, 2010.[17]

A quick appraisal of events in Somaliland reveals that the secessionist region has put in place adequate institutional and logistic structures to carry on as an independent and self-governing territory. By no means suggesting that all internal schisms have ceased, the truth is that Somaliland has demonstrated enough maturity to deserve international recognition. This view is supported by Mark Bradbury, who devoted a chapter in his book *Becoming Somaliland* to analyzing whether Somaliland deserves international recognition and the economic and political benefits this implies. Bradbury argues that Somaliland has earned due recognition even more than the TFG, which has very limited capacity to govern. As he concluded, Somaliland is a state "rooted in popular consciousness and embedded in society."[18] Apparently there is no reason to think that Somalilanders will willingly abandon their hard-won independence. As such, all efforts should be made to accommodate this very model, which is simple and closely allied to the Commonwealth of Independent Somaliland States (CISS) as proposed here.

CENTRALIZED STATE ALTERNATIVE: SOUTHERN/CENTRAL SOMALIA

The United States and some other foreign actors have in the past strongly favored the centralized option while also suggesting it incorporate structures allowing for decentralization in form of federalism. The preference for restoration of a central power by the international community is best attested to by the various UN missions to restore order in Mogadishu since the 1991 political rupture. This is further revealed in the role the various African, Western, and Arab governments played in the founding of the Transition National Government (TNG) in 2004.

Credit for the realization of TNG is rightly attributed to Ismail Omar Guelleh, the president of Djibouti who hosted the historic May 2000 Arta summit, as agreed to by the various Somali actors and countries involved in the Intergovernmental Authority on Development (IGAD).[19] After a protracted period of negotiation, an agreement was reached among the nearly 2,000 delegates representing various factional governments, clan and subclan leaders, warlords, religious leaders, NGOs, businessmen, intellectuals, and other power brokers. These delegates were drawn from a coalition of both smaller and major Somali clans, including Darod, Digil-Mirifile, Dir, and Hawiye. The group favored Abdiqasm Salad Hassan as a candidate for the post of President of the Federal National Government.[20]

While notable stakeholders in the fight for Somalia such as Ali Mahdi attended the summit, their counterparts from secessionist Puntland and Somaliland did not attend. Also absent were such powerful faction leaders as Hussein Aideed and Musa Sude. Prior to the Arta summit, all efforts at forming a national government of unity were abandoned at least 13 times. The delegates at the peace conference had as one of its primary objectives to outline a power-sharing formula and a constitution that was calculated to guide the order of government through a three-year period of transition. The major accomplishments of the delegates to the August 2000 meeting included the selection of a

Transitional National Assembly (TNA) comprising 245 members and a quasi Constitution. Subsequent summits followed the Arta conference as renewed schism and conflict continued. In 2001, the NCRPS (or National Commission for Reconciliation and Property Settlement) was established to help consolidate the incremental achievements made in the previous year. Unfortunately, the SRRC (Somali Reconciliation and Restoration Council) led by Hussein Aideed mounted a campaign against the TNG.

One of the major successes in the peace process came with the IGAD-sponsored conference for reconciliation held in Eldoret, Kenya, in October 2002. Some of the major actors at the meeting were Hassan Abshir Farah (the TNG Prime Minister), Abdullahi Yusuf (the leader of Puntland), and Hussein Farah Aideed (leader of the SRRC), who had until then scorned similar efforts. Other prominent figures at the summit were Osman Ali Ato (a business tycoon and financier), Umar Finnish, Muse Sude Yalahow, and other representatives of the SRRC.[21] The summit eventually led to the signing of the TFG agreement in 2004, and the sitting president of the TNG, Hassan, was dropped by the participants, who instead selected Abdullahi Yusuf Mohamed as president of the TFG.

It is not quite clear why Adbullahi Yusuf Mohamed, the first president of independent Puntland and who was serving out a second term in office, abandoned his secessionist goals in 2004 for the TFG position. Being a power-hungry politician and warlord, Yusuf could not have ignored any deal that served his personal agenda. Nonetheless, the various parties behind the peace process shared the common hope that the TFG would help bring peace after 16 years of anarchy and complete collapse of a central government. This aspiration has proved nearly impossible to attain because of the fear and reluctance of the various competing parties to give up their separatist claims for what appears a bogus idea of reconstituting a Grand Somali nation that has long ceased to be real and appealing.

After its establishment, it took the TFG's leader Yusuf and his executive as long as January 8, 2007, to set foot on Mogadishu soil for the first time because of increasing security concerns. Also, TFG parliament was not able to come together anywhere inside the country until 2006, when it eventually sought a safe shelter inside a storehouse in Baidoa. While it started operating its business from the southern cities of Jowhar and Baidoa, the TFG was bogged down with the Jubaland separatist movement. With the help of U.S. arms and logistic support, Ethiopia sent troops to attack the Islamic Courts Union's (ICU) fighters that had rendered the oppressions of the TFG ineffective by taking control of authority in the southern towns of Kismayo and Gedo. The Ethiopian military intervention helped to momentarily empower the TFG, but at the same time worsened the plight of ordinary people trapped in the battles between Ethiopian troops and the ICU fighters. This climate of insecurity remains several years after the Ethiopian troops were pulled out of the region. As result, there was the need to bring in a neutral peacekeeping force sponsored by the African Union (AU). The majority of the international peace-keepers drawn from Uganda are now providing crucial support for the TFG.[22]

It was with the AU backing that the TFG parliament and president were able to finally enter Mogadishu in 2007. The landing of the officers in Mogadishu was so significant that it was celebrated as a remarkable victory over the radical Islamists who had since 1991 independently administered sections of the southern parts of the country as a separate state, using the sharia courts to run the areas under their control. As soon as the TFG began to exercise power over Mogadishu and some parts of the southern region, it was viewed by the masses with suspicion and considered incompetent. Matters were made worse when petty bickering and internal divisions engrossed the official hierarchy. Once this conflict was made public, the Islamists were emboldened to launch a strong comeback and successfully regained control of sections of the southern regions.

In July 2007, the TFG convened a national reconciliation conference in an attempt to gain legitimacy and thus consolidate its little political gains. Efforts were made to invite all the key parties to the negotiation table, but the radical Islamists chose not to participate. Consequently, the good intentions of the conference were defeated even before the negotiations kicked off. Most political watchers, then, considered the conference a failure. Unrelenting allegations of corrupt practices continued to erode both the legitimacy and credibility of the TFG.

Also, the TFG's capacity to run the country has been adversely limited by clan-warlord dynamics. More complex is the fact that the Somali family clans and subclans are now tightly held in the palm of warlords who have constructed their power around militias, and have continuously played the ethnic card with the bogus claim that they are fighting for the survival of their clan members. It is no secret that the warlords are motivated more by personal greed than the group interests they pretend to represent.

More grievous is the fact that President Yusuf was unable to transcend the problems of ethnic politics and nepotism the TFG was intended to resolve. For instance, a 2007 study by the International

Crisis Group (ICG) reported that the president constituted his government with only those individuals that were friendly to Ethiopia. The problem with such practice of nepotism then was that individuals could be chosen for positions they were not well qualified for except on the grounds that they share similar views with the president of the TFG. A striking example remains the choice of Ali Mohamed Gedi—a professor who is widely seen by his own clan, the Hawiye, as a political affront that marginalizes rather than unites the people.[23] The Hawiye have been at the forefront of opposition against the continuing meddling of the Ethiopian government in the internal affairs of Somalia. Understandably, those moderates who present Ethiopia-Somalia relations as a positive thing do so to the anger of the Hawiye. This explains why Professor Gedi was forced to resign his appointment in October 2007, with persistent pressures from within and from without.

Another report indicted the top echelon of TFG officials for corruption, which involves not only the problem of legitimacy, but also the conflict between national interests and personal greed. As discovered by the *Power and Interests News Report* (PINR), at the center of the quarrel between Gedi and Yusuf was access for control of oil exploration deals. During the fight, each competitor played the ethnic card to mobilize clan support within the TFG parliament. The effect was a TFG governing body torn apart by ethnic animosity, client-patron dynamics, and political intrigues. Such tendencies have made the ordinary Somali feel more disenchanted with the TFG as the divisions deepened. A report of 2008 shows that there were three major divisions within the TFG: respectively, the groups represent the president, the prime minister, and the commanders of the armed forces. Whereas the armed forces (i.e., the paramilitaries) wear the TFG barge and are supposed to be answerable to the president, they are only loyal to their commanders, over whom the president of the TFG has no control.

One of the bold moves that was expected to bring some legitimacy to the TFG was the 2009 elections, which became necessary after the resignation of President Yusuf on December 28, 2008. It was believed that the election would provide the Somali electorate with the opportunity to choose a leader and thereby bring some measure of legitimacy to a poorly regarded transition administration. Unfortunately, the election became a joke as the only voters were members of the parliament. The election was actually conducted in Djibouti on February 2, 2009, due to security concerns. Prior to the election, the parliament was enlarged by 275 seats in order to accommodate the demands of the Islamist opposition, who were assigned 200 seats, and the citizens groups and diaspora Somalis, who received 75 seats.

Originally, those who founded the TFG had thoughtfully considered inclusion of each of the Somalis' family clans under the so-called 4.5 formula, a quota system of power sharing that saw the four main family clans—Digil-Mirifle, Dir, Darod, and Hawiye—occupying a total of 61 seats in the TFG's legislative body.[24] By solely considering only the family clans in the power-sharing equation, the 4.5 formula tended to alienate certain sections of the competing factions in the allocation of seats in the legislative body. As a result, the aggrieved groups withheld their full cooperation from the Transition Government. It is fair to state that it is a serious challenge to accommodate all parochial demands in a polity of this nature, but all the important stakeholders (no matter their sizes) deserve consideration for system stability.

With this in mind, the TFG voted to increase the parliamentary seats in order to make peace with the Islamists, other visible and important groups, and certain individuals who could not be ignored. Altogether there were 550 voters—who were also members of the TFG parliament—in the 2009 elections. Amidst the usual rancor and horse trading that characterize all politics, Sharif Ahmed emerged victorious among the 14 candidates that vied for the presidency and has remained in power for three years.

OLD WINES IN NEW SKIN: THE RESILIENCE OF THE OLD SIADISTS

At this juncture, there is a need to briefly consider why peace has continued to elude the TNG or TFG in Somalia. One explanation for the continuing disunity and political bickering is that most of the major actors engaged in the rhetoric of reconciliation and reunification have been the remnants of the old brigade that started off with either the first civilian government in 1960 or the Siad Barre regime of 1969–1991. This view has been corroborated by scholar I. M. Lewis, who cited the comments of Robert B. Oakley, an ex-U.S. Special Envoy to Somalia. During his brief stop in Djibouti while the 2000 Arta meeting was in session, Oakley was piqued by the huge presence of the former Siadists. So he jokingly but sarcastically asked a group of the delegates, "Where is Siad?" As Lewis summed up, "Siad's ghost certainly hovered over the gathering at Arta."[25]

Among the Siad-era politicians were Abdullahi Yusuf Ahmed, who through his brand of politics revealed himself as a source of concern for "many Somalis and international observers."[26] While serving as president of Puntland (for nearly two terms), "he eliminated much of his political opposition while playing up to Ethiopia interests, which has been unpopular with Somalis."[27] There have been reports also that Yusuf has an ambiguous connection with Sheikh Hassan Dahir Aweys, a senior officer of al-Itihaad al-Islaami, an Islamist group strongly claimed to have ties with al-Qaeda. In connection with peace and reconciliations, Yusuf was a disaster; his ruthless clashes with opponents earned him staunch hatred from the Isaaqs, the Ogaden, the Marehan subclans of the Darod family clan, and Hawiyes. Lewis authoritatively concluded that Yusuf's role in the peace process was nothing more than a ploy to present himself as a presidential candidate for the federal constitution he proposed.[28] It is therefore fair to conclude that individuals like Ahmed have served as a bad influence in the peace process in Somalia.

Nur Adde Hussein is another individual in this category. He had previously served as chief of police and attorney-general under the TFG. On November 22, 2008, Abdullahi Yusuf Ahmed, the TFG's president tapped him to succeed Ali Mohamed Gedi. Hussein is a Hawiye family clansman from the Abgal subclan that has continued to dominate the politics and society of Mogadishu since independence. Hussein is also the head of a humanitarian organization named the Somalia Red Crescent Society. Despite his credentials, Hussein's critics say that he lacks the political base to be an effective politician and leader. He has also been accused of profligacy. For instance, after his cabinet was constituted in 2008, it comprised 73 officers. For a country mired in abject poverty, critics rightly considered that number too large and therefore expensive to maintain. Consequently, the cabinet was pruned down to 20 (comprising 15 ministers and 5 assistant ministers).[29] This shows the problem of big governments constituted in postcolonial Africa after the Western systems, which the Africans lack the means and resources to operate. Hussein, who was appointed ambassador to Italy in 2009, fell out of favor with President Ahmed as a result of personal and administrative disputes. Despite popular support from the parliamentarians, Ahmed removed Hussein from his post in December 2008. It is worth noting that during his time in office, Hussein showed that he is ready to take criticism in a positive manner. For instance, he has expressed his readiness to negotiate with Islamists, but he lacked both the financial and military power that could have enabled him to infuse some level of discipline and order.

That brings us to one of the individuals who is in the TFG and yet pursues his personal agenda—an act that mitigates the process of national unity and reconciliation. This man is the mayor of Mogadishu since May 2007, Mohamed Omar Habeb Dheere. He was sacked as mayor by ex-Prime Minister Hussein for his alleged corrupt practices including embezzlement of public money, abuse of power, and insubordination.[30] Dheere was the Mogadishu Jawhar area's militant commander from 2001 to 2006. An opportunist and a clever politician, Dheere (best known as Mohamed D.) in 2006 joined a CIA-sponsored group of militia commanders known as the Alliance for Peace and Counterterrorism (ARPCT), The Mogadishu-area warlords were united by their common opposition to the spread of the fundamentalist ideology and regime of terror imposed with their own interpretation of the sharia corpus. Being a native of the Mogadishu area, Dheere was considered to be better placed to bring his influence to bear on the peace and reconciliation initiatives.

Figures like Mohamed Dheere and other power brokers have displayed sometimes very ambiguous and disturbing positions quite unfavorable to the ongoing peace programs. There is persistent doubt whether this treacherous dynamic will change in the near future, especially as the Hawiye group continues to hold a sense of entitlement to the government of Mogadishu. Such ideas will hardly create room for national peace and unity. The privileges accruing to the power brokers from the current situation mean that they could perpetuate war in order to keep themselves relevant rather than risk everything in a unity that would mean shrinking of divisions and positions in the separate governments that exist now. Even on occasions where the leaders have tried to act in the larger interest of the nation, their cronies have acted in ways not helpful to the cause of national unity.

Worse still, an investigation by the Amnesty International and Human Rights Watch has alleged that TFG forces have raped women and children, killed civilians without due process of the law, and also engaged in theft and looting.[31] Closely connected with these allegations is the revelation that the TFG forces are not regularly paid their salaries. Furthermore, they sometimes engage in interclan wars or try to take matters into their own hands by attempting to annihilate the Islamists and their sympathizers drawn mainly from the powerful Habir Gedir Ayr subclan of the Hawiye family clan. All these combined corroborate the opinion that among the three major competing regions (Puntland, Somaliland, and Southern Somalia), the Mogadishu-based TFG appears the least qualified to claim political legitimacy.

Also, the diverse interests of foreign actors like Kenya, Ethiopia, Djibouti, and Eritrea, to mention but four, have together constituted a big part of the Somali crisis. For instance, Kenya has tended to support the activities of the Islamic courts in the south because it believes that favors its security, while Ethiopia considers the same group as detrimental to its own national security. It was to eliminate the Islamists that Ethiopia sent its forces to Somalia in 2006, to the displeasure of Kenya's government. At the behest of the AU, Ethiopia, however, withdrew its forces in early 2009. A sizeable group of armed mediators drawn from the African Union countries were left to support the TFG.

The al-Shabaab is an Islamic faction composed of Islamic militias derived but separate from the Islamic Courts Union. Today, the al-Shabaab threatens to dominate not only the southern and central parts of Somalia, but the entire the country. Periodic fighting provoked by the al-Shabaab has disturbed the peace of the population of Mogadishu, bringing with it refugee movements and serious concerns for the safety of aid workers and humanitarian organizations helping inhabitants of the capital city. There are talks that neighboring Eritrea is the sponsor of the al-Shabaab militants with the goal to frustrate and weaken Ethiopia's internal security and by implication its overall influence in the Horn region.[32] There is no mistaking the fact that Eritrea is using the Somalia battleground for a proxy with its enemy, Ethiopia.[33] It is in this context that the Somali historian Mohamed Abdullahi has said that for a lasting peace and stability to return to the troubled region, "what the Somalis need from others the most is to be left to themselves."[34]

A related issue mitigating the stabilization of Somalia is the international community's genuine fear that the country may become a terrorist safe haven. This idea is fueled by al-Shabaab's self-proclaimed links with international terror groups like al-Qaeda.[35] The truth is that terrorism goes hand-in-hand with piracy and other forms of organized crime including drug trafficking. No one can say for sure the nature of al-Shabaab's relationship with al-Qaeda despite its dubious claims. Several years of anarchy brought about a spike in the activities of pirates in the Indian Ocean. Perhaps the high point of the pirates' operations was the 2008 hijack and extraction of heavy ransoms from Saudi and Ukrainian tankers carrying heavy military weapons. To curb the activities of the pirates, U.S. security forces stationed in neighboring Kenya and Ethiopia have launched air attacks on individuals in Somalia suspected of having affiliations with al-Qaeda.[36]

With the killing of Osama bin Laden on May 1, 2011, by the U.S. Special Forces in Pakistan, one hopes that the use of al-Qaeda as a cover to foment troubles around the world would be curtailed. Unfortunately, peace might be far from coming in view of al-Shabaab's reaction to the death of bin Laden. Speaking at a press conference on May 6, 2011, Sheikh Ali Mohamed Raghe vowed that the group will avenge the death of their "hero." "The killing of our brother Osama bin Laden is not going to affect us. We are going to take revenge for him. We shared the jihadist philosophy with him."[37] If al-Shabaab's militias live up to their threats, the crisis in Somalia might take a new turn for the worse.

Altogether, Somali politics since the fall of Barre reveals a polity crying for understanding. All indications are that the old Republic of Somalia founded by the Somali nationalists in 1960 and destroyed by the dictatorship of Siad Barre (1969–1991) is dead for now. All the ongoing peace initiatives aimed at resuscitating the old order could be likened to attempts at making a corpse walk. One would therefore reiterate that one of the possible ways to salvage any semblance of association between the fragmented groups is to embrace a consociational arrangement through a commonwealth of associations that allows for self-rule for every clan or subclan that desires to independently manage its internal affairs. As the maverick Puntland leader summed it up recently, "Since Somalis are a decentralized society, self-rule is a key factor in the restoration of the nation-state in a new political paradigm. The clan-based society with its unique chiefs and customs cannot all be placed together under a single order imposed from above. Such a formula is a recipe for failure and will ultimately lead to disaster. The new political paradigm must show respect for the distinctive qualities of Somali socio-political culture. As such, centralism cannot work."[38]

A COMMONWEALTH OF NATIONS WITH A CONSOCIATIONAL IMPERATIVE

Politicians and political watchers are unanimous in the belief that political reconciliation is necessary in order to stabilize Somalia. What is not commonly agreed upon remains the most potent pathway to peace and political stability. While it has been generally and wisely suggested that the TFG needs to include those individuals and groups considered tangential in the political process for peace to come, the contention here is that rather than seeking a reunification of all Somali territories, a Somalia national polity reconstituted in form of a Commonwealth of Independent Somali States (CISS)—with provisions for secession at any time while observing due procedure—holds the best prospects for system stability. It might be recalled that when a similar problem of secessionism threatened the Ethiopians in the 1990s after the fall of Col. Mengistu's Marxist regime, a new federalist constitution that took into consideration the fears of all the aggrieved groups was adopted. Among other provisions, however, the most important part of Ethiopia's federalist constitution remains article 39, which states that "every Nation, Nationality and People in Ethiopia has an unconditional right to self-determination, including the right to secession."[39] Guaranteeing a similar charter in the proposed CISS will help bring about the trust crucial for future cooperation among the fragmented Somali clans.

The potential benefits of such a political arrangement are many. First, autonomy guaranteed in the form of a decentralized confederate arrangement could create room for all interest groups—the type only self-government could provide. Second, as evident with the separatist regions, autonomy guaranteed in the form of self-government as proposed here has been found helpful in dispersing both elite and inter-ethnic conflicts from the center in societies troubled by deadly conflicts. This is efficacious because political autonomy creates multiple centers of political power for the strategic elites of the competing groups. This strategy will remain ineffectual until the United States and other foreign actors also modify some of their positions toward the opposition groups, particularly the Islamists.

The CISS option will create a forum for national elites of the commonwealth to operate in a consociational, power-sharing framework. Strategic elites in some countries troubled by ethnic conflicts have used cosociational and federalist models of power sharing to moderate explosive political affairs into a more cordial arrangement. Similarly, this approach holds great potential for Somalia. As witnessed in places like Nigeria, Lebanon, Belgium (before the 1970s), and the Netherlands (prior to the 1960s), the willingness of the Somali political elites to implement power sharing as a model of government would be highly effective. The structural scope and peace-enhancing power of this system are examined in brief in order to underscore its possible adaptation in Somalia given that the polity is deeply fragmented and political authority is synonymous with violence, exclusion, and control of available resources.

A track of cases have proved that the power-sharing approach is more efficacious in solving problems of ethnic conflicts than the other responses that include population transfer, genocide, partition, ethnic cleansing, and unilateral imposition of power as solutions. In their appraisal of its nonviolent principles, Rudolph Jr. and Thompson emphasized that the benefits of political accommodation far outweigh the costs of violence and divisions.[40] This corroborates the view of Arend Lijphart, the godfather of consociationalism, whose multiple studies of 21 countries around the globe have proved beyond all reasonable doubt that there is no better model than this power-sharing model for polities troubled by sectarianism.[41]

For conceptual clarity, autonomy guaranteed in the form of the proposed Commonwealth of Independent Somali States and consociationalism is offered here as complementarities in light of Somalia's historical trajectories. The practice will require decentralized administrative structures and power sharing at the national, regional, clan, and subclan levels.

NOTES

1. Besides China, the other remaining land empire that has so far weathered the problem of ethnonationalism and secession is the United States. These two members of the Security Council are often unaccommodating to secessionist movements around the world.

2. See, for instance, Michael Walls, "The Emergence of a Somali State: Building Peace from Civil War in Somaliland," *African Affairs* 108, no. 432 (July 2009): 371–89.

3. Jean-Jacques Cornish, "African Union Supports Somali Split," *Mail and Guardian* (London), Feb. 10, 2006.

4. The only internationally recognized government in both the UN and AU is the TFG of Somalia. The TFG has embassies in 19 countries.

5. Bar Kulan, "Al-shabaab's Spokesman Asks Jubaland Residents Not to Support New Administration," *Sunatimes* (Mogadishu), Nov. 10, 2010.

6. M. Igbal D. Jhazbhay, "Somaliland: Post-War Nation Building and International Relations, 1991–2006," a thesis submitted in fulfillment of the requirement for the degree of Doctor of Philosophy in International Relations, in the Faculty of Humanities, Social Sciences and Education, of the University of Witwatersrand, Johannesburg, South Africa, Feb. 2007.

7. Abdirahman Mohamed Mohamud (Farole), "Puntland Is a Reconciliation Model for a New Somalia," Keynote Speech delivered by His Excellency Mohamed Mohamud (Farole), Chatham House Royal Institute of International Affairs, London.

8. Mohamud, "Puntland," 2–3.

9. Ibid.

10. HO 421/2, Oct. 2002, 16.

11. National Archives Kew (hereafter NAK), Home Office (HO) Somalia: Country Assessments Report, Oct. 2002.

12. Jhazbhay, "Somaliland: Post-War Nation Building," 68. See also Samiira Jama Elmi, "Somaliland," *Women's World* 36 (June 30, 2002): 1.

13. NAK, HO 421/2, Oct. 2002.

14. The Parliament of the Republic of Somaliland, the Law of the Referendum on the Constitution of the Republic of Somaliland, Hargeisa, May 2011, article 1.

15. NAK HO 421/2, Oct. 2002, 17.

16. The Constitution of the Federal Republic of Somaliland, Hargeisa, 2001, Article 1.

17. Steve Kibble and Michael Walls, "Hope and Caution in Somaliland: Three Months after the Presidential Elections, Where Are We?" *The Somaliland Times* (Hargeisa), Dec. 11–17, 2010.

18. Mark Bradbury, *Becoming Somaliland* (Bloomington: Indiana University Press, 2008), 242.

19. The Inter-Governmental Agency for Development (IGAD) is a regional organization comprising the seven states in the Horn of Africa—Sudan, Eritrea,

Ethiopia, Djibouti, Somalia, Kenya, and Uganda. See I. M. Lewis, "Recycling Somalia from the Scrap Merchants of Mogadishu," *Northeast African Studies* 10, no. 3 (2003): 213–24.

20. Alessandro Shimabukuro, "ODUMUNC 2010: Issue Brief for the United Nations Security Council–the Situation in Somalia," 2.

21. NAK HO 421/2, Oct. 2002, 14–15.

22. Shimabukuro, "ODUMUNC 2010: Issue Brief," 2.

23. World Bank, "Conflict in Somalia: Drivers and Dynamics," Policy Working Paper, 2005, 14.

24. The "4.5 formula" was developed during the peace talks held in Kenya in 2002.

25. Lewis, "Recycling Somalia," 216.

26. See Natalia Rigol, "Clash of Clans," *Harvard International Review* 27, no. 1 (Summer 2005): 6, 7–13.

27. Rigol, "Clash of Clans," 6.

28. Lewis, "Recycling Somalia," 218–20.

29. See *Al Jazeera*, "Somali Interim PM Names New Cabinet," Jan. 4, 2007.

30. *People's Daily*, "Heavy Fighting Resumes in Somalia," (Beijing) June 19, 2002.

31. Amnesty International, "No End in Sight: The Ongoing Suffering of Somali Civilians," Doc. AFR 52/003/2010 of March 25, 2010, 2–9.

32. Shimabukuro, "ODUMUNC 2010: Issue Brief," 2–3.

33. Eritrea seceded from Ethiopia in the 1990s after years of bloody conflict. The animosity still exists between the two countries.

34. Mohamed Diriye Abdullahi, *Culture and Customs of Somalia* (Westport, CT: Greenwood Press, 2001), 48.

35. See Kenneth J. Menkhaus, "The Somali Catastrophe: Bigger Than the Horn—and Not Over Yet," *Current History: A Journal of Contemporary World Affairs* 106, no. 700 (May 2007): 195–201.

36. Shimabukuro, "ODUMUNC 2010: Issue Brief," 2–3.

37. Abdulkadir Khali, "Al-Shabaab Threatens to Revenge Osama's Killing," *Africa Review* (Nairobi, Kenya), May 8, 2011.

38. Mohamud, "Puntland," 2.

39. The Constitution of the Federal Republic of Ethiopia, Addis Ababa, 1994, 18.

40. J. R. Rudolph Jr., and R. J. Thompson, *Ethnoterritorial Politics, Policy and the Western World* (London: Lynne Rienner Publishers, 1989), 224.

41. Arend Lijphart, "Non-Majoritarian Democracy: A Comparison of Federal and Consociational Theories," *Publius: The Journal of Federalism* 15, no. 2 (1985): 3–15; "Constitutional Design for Divided Societies," *Journal of Democracy* 15, no. 2 (2004): 96–109.

Notable People in the History of Somalia

Abdullahi Yusuf Ahmed (1934–Mar. 23, 2012) was one of the founding members of the Somali Salvation Democratic Front (SSDF) and served as the co-leader of the National Security Council (NSC). Abdullahi was imprisoned by Siad Barre for declining participation in the October 1969 coup. After his release in 1975, Abdullahi plotted and executed a failed revanchist coup against Barre in 1978. To evade capture, he fled to Kenya, from where he launched a guerrilla-style insurgency against Barre's government with the backing of Ethiopia. In 1985, Abdullahi was jailed in Addis Ababa following a conflict of interest between him and Colonel Mengistu over the Ogaden question. The anarchy of the 1990s enabled Abdullahi to return to his native Puntland province of Somalia in 1991 to claim a center stage in the region's politics of secession. A shrewd politician who was determined to remain relevant amidst the rubble of Somali politics, Abdullahi was the first President of the self-proclaimed independent Puntland. While serving out his second tenure, Abdullahi vacated his seat in 2004 amidst a heated power struggle with his prime minister, Nur Hassan Hussein. Alienated by the parliament at Baidoa, Abdullahi returned to a Pan-Somali project under the Transitional National Government. He played a pivotal role in the inauguration of the Transition Federal Government (TFG) and was appointed TFG's president of Somalia from 2004 to 2008.

Shire Jama Ahmed (1935–?) was a former member of the Somali Youth League (SYL), the inaugural head of the Somali National Academy of Culture (SNAC), and a distinguished linguist. He is revered by his people as the father of the Somali national script. This Marehan clansman who, like most Somalis of his generation, first attended Quranic school in Somalia, also received his education in Egypt (1951–1954) and spent a year in Russia in 1967 studying. The search for a Somali script goes back to the colonial period, but the national project that led to this invention was launched soon after independence in 1960 as part of the effort to promote Somali culture and national unity. It was not until 12 years later in 1972 that the Somali Language Committee (SLC) endorsed Shire's creative orthography adapted from the Latin script. On the committee's recommendation, the Somali tongue was declared the sole official language in 1972. Soon after, the entire country became a virtual classroom of the local language in an effort by the Barre regime to build a national consciousness. A cultural nationalist icon, Shire was also the founder of the *Iftiinka Aqoonta* (*The Light of Knowledge and Education*), the first national magazine published in Somali language. The first six issues he produced addressed themes on Somali grammar, history, proverbs, and folklore. On the request of the Somali Education and Legal Assistance Peace Corps at the Teacher's College, Columbia University, Shire worked along with Charles Kozoll to produce a grammar book for non-Somali speakers and tourists entitled *An Elementary Somali Drill Book* that was published in 1966.

Hussein Mohamed Farah Aideed (1962–?) is a Hawiye clansman and the son of Gen. Farah Aideed. He was a former U.S. marine who served the U.S. army as a translator during the extraordinary UN-Somali mission code-named Operation Restore Hope. In 1996 when his father died, Hussein was tapped by his father's comrades in the USC/SNA to succeed General Aideed. Initially opposed to the Transitional Federal Government (TFG) efforts aimed at restoring national unity, Hussein helped in establishing the Somali Reconciliation and Reconstruction Council (SRRC) in 2001 and served as the first chairman. Later in 2003, Hussein joined forces with the TFG in an attempt to rout the Islamic Court Union (ICU) out of Mogadishu in December 2006. However, one of the controversial ideas attributed to him was the suggestion that Somalia and Ethiopia could share a common passport. Such ideas that seek cooperation with Ethiopia have been very vexing for the average Somali. During the 2007 cabinet reshuffle by Prime Minister Ali Mohamed Gedi, Hussein was moved from his Agriculture Portfolio in February to the position of deputy prime minister. Two months later, Hussein was sacked from the new post.

Mohamed Farah Aideed (1934–1996) was the father of Hussein and arguably one of the most outstanding personalities besides Barre whose career left a significant impact on Somalia today. He was the military commander of United Somali Congress (USC), which was one of the major factions that helped force Barre out of power. When internal rivalry within the USC led to a split in the movement in 1991, Aideed became the head of the USC-SNA faction. Aideed was a big torn in the side of the UN-Somali mission peacekeepers as his militia consistently created conditions that made the task of the peacekeepers rough and frustrating. In 1995, Aideed proclaimed himself Somalia's president after years of a resilient factional war against his rivals, particularly Ali Mahdi, leader of the other faction of USC. His iron march across the sands of Somali politics took a sharp twist in 1969 when he was jailed for six years by Siad Barre on suspicion of planning a coup and for declining his diplomatic posting when it was meant to avert his assumed threat to the regime. After his release in 1975, Aideed joined forces with other anti-Barre elements in an effort to exact his revenge. After Barre's overthrow in 1991, Aideed emerged as a powerful figure and was determined to claim the ultimate control of Somali politics at all costs. He died in 1996 of gun injuries sustained during a fierce battle with his opposition in Mogadishu.

Abdurrahman Ahmed Ali (aka "Tur") (1931–2003) was the leader of the Somali National Movement (SNM). His role in the struggle that in the end dislodged Barre from power made him a popular figure among his northern Isaaq people. Therefore it was easy for the SNM officers and the clan leaders to approve Abdurrahman as the first executive president of the secessionist Republic of Somaliland. He held this position between 1991 and 1993 when the *Guurti*, or council of elders, supervised a peaceful transfer of power from the government of SNM under Abdurrahman to a civilian administration headed by Mohamed Haji Ibrahim Egal, a Habr Awal clansman and one of the greatest Somali nationalist leaders.

Osman Hassan Ali (aka "Ato") (1945–?) is a Hawiye clan multimillionaire businessman and ex-financier and aide of General Aideed. He was one of the five cochairmen of the National Somali Congress

(NSC). A shrewd capitalist, Osman reaped bountiful profit from his heavy investments in real estate, especially in the Mogadishu metropolis. His rise to success began at the age of 14 when he was a truck driver for local companies representing the United States oil company Conoco. Osman later started his own private trucking business that would bring him enormous profits. His company operates from a strategically situated headquarters at Eldoret in the northwestern part of Kenya, distributing petrol to several landlocked eastern and central African countries including Uganda, Burundi, and Rwanda. During the UN mission in Somalia, Osman professed support for the mission and executed several contracts for the peacekeepers. However, he had his troubles with the UN officers and was imprisoned for four months during the 1993 debacle. When he split with Aideed, Osman waged wars against his rivals in an attempt to take control of Mogadishu and possibly become the president of Somalia. Although he is yet to be officially charged, Osman has been linked with several shady deals involving arms and drug trade by both the UN Security Council and the United States.

Hassan Dahir Aweys (Sheikh) (1935–?), was a colonel in the Somali National Army (SNA) under Barre's government. The army decorated him with medals for bravery in the 1977 border war against Ethiopia. He is the leader of al-Ittihad al-Islamiya militant sect. He once headed the 90-member shura council of the Islamic Court Union (ICU) fighting to institute sharia laws across the country. Hassan personally led the fighters that momentarily seized control of the Somali capital of Mogadishu in June 2006. After the September 11, 2001, terrorist attack on the World Trade Center in New York, Hassan and the ICU came under closer scrutiny by the United States because of his strong Islamist standpoint. He resigned from the ICU on December 28, 2006 after the militants were forced out of Mogadishu by the TFG aided by Ethiopia's army.

Mohamed Siad Barre (1919–1995), is unarguably the most influential personality in the modern history of Somalia. A Marehan (Darod) clansman, Siad ruled as a military revolutionary figure from 1969 to 1990 when he was driven from power by his opponents. While his authority lasted, Siad was as ruthless as Louis XIV of France. He spared nothing, including the use of political intrigue, mass killings, and ethnic politicking to accomplish his goals and to maintain his hold on power. However, it is important to add that despite his failings, most Somalis still consider him an effective leader and stabilizer of the country. Perhaps one of Barre's major problems was the pretense that he was interested in any involvement by the West in Somali political matters. Many politicians claim that his downfall lay in his decision to declare war against Ethiopia over the Ogaden region. Barre died in 1995 while living in exile in Nigeria.

Aden Abdullah Osman Daar (1908–2007) is highly revered as one of the founding fathers of modern Somalia. He was a nationalist pillar who played a key role in the establishment of the Somali Youth League (SYL) in 1944. Aden first served the SYL as secretary and soon after rose in the ranks to become the chairman of the party. At independence in 1960, Aden became the first president of his country until 1967. He was one of the few voices of sanity in the early 1990s when the civil conflict in his country took on a frightening dimension. His exasperation and expression of displeasure for the way the government was managing the affairs of his country caused his arrest and imprisonment by Barre. After the fall of Barre, Aden was released from jail, and he quietly retired to his farm in Janale, southern Somalia. The news of his demise was announced on June 8, 2007. In his honor as a true patriot, the people of Somalia observed a 21-day period of national mourning.

Mohamed Haji Ibrahim Egal (1928–2002) was an advocate of one Somalia and the first prime minister of British Somaliland at its independence in 1960. He personally led the movement for the historic amalgamation of the ex-British Somaliland and ex-Italian Somaliland in 1960. Egal served his country variously as defense minister (1960–1962) and education minister (1963–1964), before emerging in 1967 as prime minister of the Somali Republic. He was in office in 1969 when Siad Barre seized power in a military coup. Egal was jailed twice by Barre, but upon his release, the government appointed him an envoy to India (1976–1978). Although his heart was for Somali unity, Egal later sacrificed his Pan-Somali ideals for a separate Somaliland state. Egal served as the new territory's president from May 1993 until his death in office in May 2002. During his administration, Somaliland accomplished a lot in terms of stability, including the adoption of the constitution of Somaliland.

Nuruddin Farah (1945–?) is perhaps Somalia's most celebrated novelist and one of the greatest contemporary writers in the world. He started his career with short stories in his native Somali language. While a student in India, Nuruddin began to publish in English in order to reach a global audience. His foremost novel, *From a Crooked Rib* (1970), which was an instant success, focuses on a nomad girl who absconded from home in order to escape a prearranged wedding to a much older man who could have been her father. Nuruddin crossed paths with Barre's government because of the uncomplimentary political tone of his 1976 work entitled *A Naked Needle*. His self-imposed exile took Nuruddin to distant lands, among them Nigeria, the United States, Italy, Germany, Sudan, and India, while consolidating his career as a writer. His beautiful prose and knack for storytelling have earned Nuruddin many awards and accolades including the prestigious German Neustadt International Prize for Literature, which he received in 1998. On several occasions, Nuruddin has come close to winning the most celebrated prize, the Nobel Laureate in literature, following his multiple nominations for the award.

Hirsi Magan Isse (1935–2008), a major actor in the Somali political crisis of the 1980s and 1990s, is best known for his leadership role in the Somali Salvation Democratic Front (SSDF). The movement was one of the earliest and most powerful factions in the Somali civil war. Hirsi was an ally of former president of Somalia Abdullahi Yusuf Ahmed, who came to power after the assassination of President Abdirashid Ali Shermarke in 1969. He was jailed by Barre in 1972 on suspicion of treason. Hirsi escaped prison in 1975 and sought refuge in Saudi Arabia. From his exile, Hirsi joined other anti-Barre elements that served as forerunners of the SSDF. With supplies from the Ethiopian government, the SSDF provoked the second armed conflict between Somalia and Ethiopia in 1982 after they executed several guerrilla attacks in Somalia from across the border. In 1988, Hirsi and his comrades expanded their goal to drive Barre out of power. After Barre was ousted, Hirsi led the SSDF to declare Puntland a sovereign state.

Jama Ali Jama (date of birth unknown) was elected president of Puntland by the traditional elders in 2001, and he was in office until May 2002. Jama's appointment was seriously resisted by Abdullahi Yusuf Ahmed, who would later succeed him in office in 2002. Jama was a former officer in the Somali national army and was imprisoned for 11 years during the reign of Barre on suspicions of treason endangered by his dislike for Barre. He is presently a parliamentarian in the Transitional Federal Government.

Fatima Jibrell (1947–?) is a popular environmentalist, perhaps best identified as the cofounder and executive director of both the Horn of Africa Relief and Development Organization ("Horn Relief"), and the Sun Fire Cooking (SFC). She also played a pivotal role in the creation of the Women's Coalition for Peace with a primary aim to empower

Somali women through contribution in politics and other socioeconomic issues that directly affect their lives. Her SFC represents a forum for promoting solar cookers as an environmentally friendly and substitute source of energy. The main goal of this innovation is to help conserve the environment by reducing the popular dependence on charcoal as a fuel. To encourage her pet environmental project, Fatima wrote and coproduced a short film with the title *Charcoal Traffic*. The film employs a fictional storyline to create popular awareness about the consequences of sole reliance on charcoal. Fatima initiated a local campaign to rescue the region's acacia trees (otherwise called the "black gold"), fast disappearing because they were being cut down to make charcoals. In recognition of her grassroots environmental activism, Fatima was awarded the Goldman Environmental Prize in 2002. She was also honored with the National Geographic Society/Buffett Foundation Award in 2008.

Dahir Riyale Kahin (1952–?) succeeded former Somaliland president Mohamed Haji Ibrahim Egal as president in May 2002 following the latter's death in office. Prior to his succession, Dahir was serving as incumbent vice president. He would proceed to win a hotly contested election in 2003 under the banner of the United Democratic People's Party, or *Ururka Dimuqraadiga Umada Bahawday* (UDUB), by a very narrow margin. In 2008, the council of elders (*Guurti*) extended his tenure for one year amidst logistical hitches encountered in holding a national election. However, he remained in power until 2010, when he was finally voted out of power by the Somalilanders. A shrewd politician, his career reminds us about Barre's notorious National Security Service, which served as the most senior office in the 1980s in the Berbera region. Dahir was also an envoy to Djibouti and briefly served as governor of the Awdal province.

Ali Mahdi Mohamed (aka "Ali Mahdi") (1940–?) is a native of the Abgal Hawiye clan and the leader of one of the United Somali Congress factions better known as the USC-Mahdi. The self-declared interim president of Somalia in 1991 fought ruthlessly to keep his title and privileges to the detriment of peace and unity. Like his peers, Mahdi began his public career in the 1960s as a civil servant in the ministry for health and rose to become the head of the malaria division. He was later elected deputy governor of the Jowhar Benadir region until 1969, when he was demoted by Barre. Mahdi, who ironically was an ex-UNICEF director in Somali, was one the strongest opponents of the UN-Somali mission. His intransigence and belligerent attitude toward the peacekeepers cost the lives of thousands of Somalis.

Halima Khaliif Omar (aka Magool) (1948–2004), popularly known as *Hoyadii Fanka*, or "Mother of Artistry," was a controversial singer of substance who could not shy away from airing her feelings about the politics of depredation that destroyed her country. In the 1970s during the Ogaden conflict with Ethiopia, for instance, Halima's voice reverberated across the country as a source of inspiration for many Somali patriots. At the same time, Magool used her lyrics to criticize the Barre dictatorship for not piloting the affairs of the country well. To avoid the wrath of Barre, she embarked on a self-imposed exile. Her exile ended in 1987 with a special concert held in Mogadishu. Never one to shy away from political confrontations, Magool also took an active part in the Somali civil war in the 1980s and 1990s. She was reportedly seen cruising around Mogadishu on a pickup truck with loud speakers calling out the Aideed militias to attack the opposition, particularly the Darods.

Said Sheikh Samatar (1943–?) is a world-class scholar and teacher who grew up in a humble family of Ogaden. Like most young people of his generation, Said spent his early years in a nomadic environment, which enriched his total experience as a writer and a poet. A prolific writer, Said has authored several books and published in prestigious academic journals. Among his most popular works are *Oral Poetry and Somali Nationalism: The Case of Sayyid Mahammad 'Abdille Hasan* (Cambridge University Press, 1982). Said was one of the managing editors of the highly respected *Horn of Africa* journal. Among other things, Said is also a prominent figure in the executive committee of the Somali Studies International Association (SSIA), as well as a consultant to both *The Somali Experience* project (a forum for connecting Somalis in the diaspora) and the Voice of America (VOA).

Abd ar-Rashid Ali Shirmarke (1919–1969), the father of the Omar Abdirashid Ali Shirmarke who became the TFG's Prime Minister in 2009, served as an elected member of the Legislative Council in 1959 and the next year became the second prime minister of Somali Republic from 1960 to 1964 under the government of President Aden Abdullah Osman Daar. In 1967, he was elected president of the Republic of Somalia. His assassination in 1969 set in motion sequences of events that brought Said Barre to power in October 1969. A true nationalist figure, Shirmarke was one of the founding members of the Somali Youth League (SYL) and served the British colonial civil service in the 1940s and 1950s.

Selected Bibliography

PRIMARY SOURCES

National Archives Kew (NAK) Great Britain

CAB 129/86. The Suez Canal of 1888 by Reginald E. Manningham-Butler, dated Mar.6, 1957.

CAB 129/80. The Horn of Africa: Memorandum by the Secretary for Foreign Affairs and the Secretary of State for the Colonies (marked "Secret C. P. 56 84"), dated Mar. 24, 1956.

CAB 129/85. Somaliland Protectorate and the Horn of Africa, July 25, 1956.

CAB/120/64. Somaliland Protectorate: Exchange of Territory with Ethiopia, Dec. 22, 1953.

CAB/129/101. Policy in the Somaliland Protectorate: Memorandum by the Minister of State for Colonial Affairs, dated Apr. 4, 1960.

CAB/129/85. Somaliland Protectorate and the Horn of Africa, dated Feb. 15, 1957.

CAB/129/93. Aden Protectorate: Memorandum by Secretary of State for the Colonies, dated June 24, 1958.

CAB 129/8. Policy towards Ethiopia: Future of the Somali Territory, Mar. 9, 1946.

CAB/129/12. British Somaliland: Proposals by Ethiopian Government for an Exchange of Territory (marked "'Top Secret' C.P. 46 319"), dated Aug. 6, 1946.

CAB/24/256. Italo-Ethiopian Dispute (file marked secret C.P. 161 [35]"), dated Aug. 16, 1935.

CAB/24/275. Anglo-Italian Conversations marked "Secret C.P. 50 (38)," dated Feb. 28, 1936, annex 2, 23.

CAB 129/86. Report, dated Mar. 6, 1957.

CAB/24/256. file marked "Secret C. P. 161 (35)."

CAB 24/3. Fourth Report of the Sub-Committee on Territorial Changes (marked "Secret G-11 8c"), dated July 17, 1917.

Correspondent Report. "Greater Somalia Demand Opposition to Return of Italians." *The Times* (London), Saturday Aug. 20, 1949, 3.

Dominions Office (DO) 195/6, and DO 195/7. Deterioration of relations with UK following Mr. Nkrumah's visit to Eastern Europe and China, 1961–1962.

DO 195/222. Reaction to Nkrumah book *Neo-Colonialism: The Last Stage of Imperialism*, 1965.

Foreign Office (F.O.) 84/1928, Memo, Kirk confidential, Sept. 24, 1888.

F.O. Confidential Print (East Africa), 5037.

Harrison, Charles. "Rebel Army Advances in Somalia," *The Times* (London), July 19, 1982, 4.

Harrison, Charles. "American Arms for Somalia." *The Times* (London), Monday July 26, 1982, 4.

Home Office (HO) 421/2. Records created or inherited by the Home Office, Ministry of Home Security, and Related Bodies, 1986– 2000.

Khedive Ishmail to Admiral MacKillop, Secret Letters from the Khedive of Egypt in Connection with the Occupation of the East Coast of Africa, dated Sept. 17, 1875.

Menelik II, Letter, 1891. See also NAK, CR 2017/C1217, Menelik II [emperor of Ethiopia] to Colonel [Sir John L.] Harrington [agent and consul-general at the court of Menelik II c. 1898– 1908], a letter written in characters.

Menelik II, The Emperor of Ethiopia, Letter to Great Britain, France, Germany, Italy, and Russia, 1891.

Rhodes House Oxford. Salisbury Papers, F.O. 84/1980. Portal to Salisbury, Sept. 23, 1889.

Rhodes House Oxford. Salisbury Papers A/179. Portal to Barrington, Sept. 24, 1889. Special Correspondent. "Somalia Planning

Army of 20,000 with Russian Aid." *The Times* (London), Nov. 11, 1963, 10.

The Times. "The Abyssinia Expedition against the Mad Mullah." (London), Oct. 19, 1901, 12.

The Times. "The Somaliland Expedition: Bombardment of Illig," (London), Oct. 26, 1903, 6.

The Times. "Capture of Illig. Stronghold Stormed by a British Force." (London), Apr. 28, 1904, 5.

The Times. "The Mad Mullah: His Death Confirmed." (London), Sept. 18, 1921, 7.

The Times. "The Mad Mullah: A Twenty Years Struggle." (London), May 8, 1923, 19.

The Times. "Abdi Rashid Shermarke: President of Somalia since 1967" (Obituary). (London), Oct. 16, 1969, 14.

The Times. Editorial: "Coup in Somalia," (London), Oct. 22, 1969, 11.

The Times. "Somalia: Takeover of Banks and Oil Groups (Banking and Finance." (London), May 8, 1970, 23.

Other Primary Sources

Amnesty International. "No End in Sight: The Ongoing Suffering of Somali Civilians." Doc. AFR 52/003/2010 of Mar. 25, 2010.

Amnesty International. *AI Report 1997: Somalia*. New York: Amnesty International Publications 1997.

Anant, Victor. "The Colony That Rejected Freedom." *The Herald* (London), June 29, 1960.

Archives of the Ministry of African Italian (ASMAI), pos. 65, f.1, Letter from Mancini to Prime Minister Depretis.

Barbosa, Duarte. *A Description of the Coasts of East Africa and Malabar in the Beginning of the Sixteenth Century*. Trans. Henry E. Stanley. 1540. Reprint. London: Hakluyt Society, 1866.

Barre, Major-General. "Address to the Armed Forces over Radio Mogadishu." Nov. 9, 1969.

Barre, Mohamed Siad. "Revolutionary Speech by Mohamed Siad Barre to the Nation." Oct. 24, 1969.

Barre, Siad. "Freedom with Hunger Is Better Than Humiliation, a Message to the Nation by Major-General Siad" (Mogadishu), Oct. 26, 1969.

Barre, Siad. Speech of the President of the Supreme Revolutionary Council, Major-General Mohammed Siad Barre at the Officer's Club (Mogadishu), Oct. 31, 1969.

Burton, Richard Francis. *First Footsteps in East Africa or An Exploration of Harar.* London: Longman, Brown, Green, and Longmans, 1856.

The Constitution of the Federal Republic of Ethiopia. Addis Ababa: 1994.

The Constitution of the Federal Republic of Somaliland. Hargeisa, 2001.

Drake-Brockman, Ralph E. *British Somaliland.* London: Hurst & Blackett Ltd, 1912.

Jardine, Douglas J. *The Mad Mullah of Somaliland.* London: Jenkins, 1923. Reprint. New York: Negro Universities Press, 1969.

Johnston, Charles. *Travels in Southern Abyssinia: Through the Country of Adal to the Kingdom of Shoa Vol. 1.* London: J. Madden and Co., 1844.

Kazakov, Gennady. "New Times Comment on Somalia on the Upgrade." *New Era* (Mogadishu), Oct. 1972, 32.

Legum, Colin, ed. *Africa Contemporary Record: Annual Survey and Documents.* (Annuals 1978–1979 through 1990–1991). New York: Africana, 1980–1992.

Legum, Colin, ed. *African Contemporary Record.* Annual Survey and Documents 1968–1969: Somali Republic. London: African Research Limited, 1969.

Letter dated Jan. 20, 1992, from the *chargé d'affaires* of the Permanent Mission of Somalia to the United Nations addressed to the President of the Security Council (S/23445).

MINGM. "A Note from the Publishers." *New Era: A Quarterly Journal.* Mogadishu: Aug. 1970, 1.

MINGM. "The List of Members of Government." *New Era: A Quarterly Journal.* Mogadishu: Nov. 1, 1969, 7.

The Ministry of Information and National Guidance Mogadishu. "A Note from the Publishers." *New Era: A Quarterly Journal* (Mogadishu), Aug. 1970, 1.

New Era. "Implementing Somalia's Three-Year Plan." (Mogadishu), Oct. 1972, 27–32.

New Era. "Revolution: 1st Announcement SRC Act on Behalf of the People" (Mogadishu), Oct. 1969, 3.

New Era. "The Only Way for Somalia ... Scientific Socialism." (Mogadishu), Mar., 1972, 4–40.

New Era. Editorial: "Scientific Socialism in Action." (Mogadishu), Mar., 1972, 2.

New Era. Editorial: "Three Candles" (Mogadishu), Oct. 1972, 6.

The Parliament of the Republic of Somaliland. The Law of the Referendum on the Constitution of the Republic of Somaliland. (Hargeisa), May 2011.

United Nations. *Statistics Pocket Book: Somalia*. New York: United Nations Statistics Division, May 2010.

United Nations. *United Nations Report on UNOSOM I*. Updated Mar. 21, 1997.

United Nations. *United Nations Report on UNOSOM II*. Updated Aug. 31, 1996.

UNDP (United Nations Development Program). *Human Development Report 2001 Somalia*. Nairobi: UNDP, 2001.

United Nations Operation in Somalia II. *Report to the Secretary General of the UNSC*, Nov. 30, 1994.

United Nations Security Council. *Security Council Resolution S/RES/873 (1993) Resolution 873 (1993) Adopted by the Security Council at its 3291st meeting, on 13 October 1993*, Oct. 13, 1993, S/RES/873, 1993.

United Nations Technical Assistance Program (UNTAP) Report. The *Trust Territory of Somaliland under Italian Administration*. New York: United Nations, 1952.

SECONDARY SOURCES AND RARE BOOKS

Abby, Mohamed Hussein. "The Land of Poun (Punt)." Working Paper, Center for Research and Development, University of Hargeisa, n.d. 1–28.

Abukar, Hassan M. "A Memoir about Growing Up in Mogadishu in the 1970s and 1980s." July 15, 2010.

Andrezjewski, Bogumil Witalis. "Notes on Inshā' Al-Mukātibat 'Asrīyna Fī Al-Lughah Al-Sūmāliya by Muhammad 'Abdi Makāhil (Somali in Arabic Script)." In Andrezjewski Mss., Manuscript Department, the Lilly Library, Indiana University, Bloomington.

Cassanelli, Lee Vincent. "The Benadir Past: Essays in Southern Somali History." PhD Dissertation, University of Wisconsin. Ann Arbor, MI: Xerox University Microfilms, 1973.

Cerulli, Enrico. *Somalia: Scritti vari editi ed inediti* (3 vols.). Rome: Istituto Poligrafico della Stato, 1957–1964.

Danish Immigration Service. "Report on Minority Groups in Somalia September 17–24, 2000." Copenhagen: Sept. 24, 2000.

Department of Public Information (DPI). *United Nations Somalia—UNOSOM II.* New York: Department of Public Information Printing Office, Mar. 21, 1997.

Hess, Robert L. "The 'Mad Mullah' and Northern Somalia," *Journal of African History* 5, no. 3 (1964): 415–433.

Kaplan, Irving, Margarita K. Dobert, James L. McLaughlin, Barbara Marvin, H. Mark Roth, and Donald P. Whitaker. *Area Handbook for Somalia*, 2nd ed. Washington, DC: U.S. Printing Central Office, 1977.

McNeill, Malcolm. *In Pursuit of the "Mad Mullah" (Mohamed Abdullah): Services and Sport in the Somali Protectorate . . . with a Chapter by Lieutenant A. C. H. Dixon* (with illustrations and a map). London: C. Arthur Pearson, 1902.

Samatar, Said S. *Oral Poetry and Somali Nationalism: The Case of Sayyid Mahammad Abdille Hasan.* Cambridge: Cambridge University Press, 1982.

Spivey, Kristin. "The United Nation's Humanitarian Intervention in Somalia and the Just War Theory." MA Thesis Submitted in Fulfillment for the Award of Degree in Political Science, Vrije University, Brussels, Belgium, June, 2008, 5.

World Bank. "Conflict in Somalia: Drivers and Dynamics." *Policy Working Paper*, 2005.

Index

About the Author

RAPHAEL CHIJIOKE NJOKU, PhD, is the chair/director of the International Studies Program, Department of Economics, and professor of African/World History at Idaho State University. He received his doctorate in African history from Dalhousie University, Halifax, Canada, in 2003. Dr. Njoku had earlier earned a doctorate in Political Science from Vrije University Belgium in 2001. He is the author of *Culture and Customs of Morocco* (2005), *African Cultural Values: Igbo Political Leadership in Colonial Nigeria, 1900–1966* (2006), and coeditor of four books: *Missions, States and European Expansions* (2007), *War and Peace in Africa* (2010), *Africa and the Wider World* (2010), and *African History* (2011). Dr. Njoku has also authored 30 scholarly articles and is the founding editor of *Notes and Records: The International Journal of African and African Diaspora Studies.*

Other Titles in the Greenwood Histories of the Modern Nations
Frank W. Thackeray and John E. Findling, Series Editors

DEC 0 2 2015